Gender and Work in the Third World

SEXUAL DIVISIONS IN BRAZILIAN INDUSTRY

John Humphrey

TAVISTOCK PUBLICATIONS
London and New York

First published in 1987 by
Tavistock Publications
11 New Fetter Lane, London EC4P 4EE

Published in the USA by
Tavistock Publications
in association with Methuen, Inc.
29 West 35th Street, New York NY 10001

Typeset by Scarborough Typesetting Services
and printed in Great Britain by
T J Press (Padstow) Ltd, Padstow, Cornwall

British Library Cataloguing in Publication Data

Humphrey, John, *1950–*
Gender and work in the Third World:
sexual divisions in Brazilian industry.
1. Sexual division of labor – Social
aspects – Brazil 2. Brazil – Industries
I. Title
305.9 HD6059.5.B6

ISBN 0-422-61900-0

Library of Congress Cataloging in Publication Data

Humphrey, John, 1950–
Gender and work in the Third World.
Bibliography: p.
Includes index.
1. Sexual division of labor – Brazil. I. Title.
HD6060.65.B6H86 1987 305.5′3′00981 87-12416

ISBN 0-422-61900-0 (cased)

To the memory of
Sally Henry (1950–84)

Contents

Acknowledgements

One might expect that writing a second book would be that much quicker than writing the first. One should after all learn something from experience. Unfortunately things are not so simple. This book has taken some time to emerge since my first interest in the sexual division of labour in Brazilian industry was stirred up during a research visit in 1980. In over six years a large number of debts of various sorts have been run up.

The largest of these, without doubt, is due to Helena Hirata, who happened to be in Brazil both in 1980, when I first began the project, and for part of 1982, when the main fieldwork for this book was undertaken. A central part of the 1982 fieldwork was a joint project, and our intellectual collaboration extends up until the present day. Her help has been invaluable. In 1982 I also enjoyed the opportunity of discussing ideas and putting them on paper with Leda Gitahy, Elizabeth Lobo, and Rosa Moyses. In England I have particularly appreciated the chance to discuss ideas with Diane Elson, Nigel Haworth, Susan Joekes, Ruth Pearson, and Alison Scott. The final project has certainly been improved by these discussions, even if at the cost of occasional bouts of intellectual anguish.

Getting to Brazil for fieldwork required support of a different type. I thank the Joint Council on Latin American Studies of the American Council of Learned Societies and the Social Science Research Council (New York) for support in 1980 and 1982, and the University of Liverpool for support in 1982 and 1983. In Brazil itself I was particularly fortunate to have institutional support from CEBRAP and CEDEC in São Paulo, and the co-operation of DIEESE and the Research Department of SENAI in São Paulo. In addition to this, I also received essential help from the various firms who allowed access to their plants and from a number of trade unions.

With the rush of new technology into the social sciences, I ought to be thanking various hardware and software manufacturers for the means of producing the final typescript. Unfortunately my plans did not come to fruition, and I required and received substantial assistance from Doris O'Connor, Dianne Murgatroyd, and Patricia McMillan at various times in the preparation of the text. They did an excellent job. Even so, no amount of hardware, software, secretarial help, or academic advice can eliminate all the errors and omissions in the text, and they remain my responsibility.

Introduction

This study of the sexual division of labour in Brazilian manufacturing industry arose out of earlier work on labour markets and management-labour relations among hourly-paid workers in the motor vehicle industry (Humphrey 1982). Originally a general study of labour processes and labour markets in the metal-working industries had been planned, but visits to a number of factories in 1980 quickly revealed that the sexual division of labour was a fundamental aspect of the organization of work and the structuring of labour markets. Women workers constituted an important part of the labour force in many firms, and women's share of manufacturing employment had increased significantly in the 1970s. However, this incorporation took a characteristic form. Women workers in manual jobs were overwhelmingly classified as unskilled, and they were concentrated to a large extent in exclusively female jobs at the bottom of the job hierarchy. Male workers, in contrast, were found in a broad range of skills and functions, and they had better chances of promotion and much higher rates of pay.

Findings such as these have provided the basis for many analyses of job segregation by sex. Dual labour market theories, in particular, have tried to explain the mechanisms which lead women to be concentrated in unskilled jobs, while skilled jobs are monopolized by men. However, it was evident that the differences in the experiences of work of female and male workers were much more extensive than this. Managements clearly viewed male and female workers in quite different terms. The sexes were segregated to a very large extent, and managements seemed to tailor their employment strategies to the sex of the workers, not the jobs they performed. Similarly the way workers were treated on the shop floor varied considerably according to sex. The kinds of work performed, the way orders were given, and the degree of control over time and space were by no means the same for the two sexes. The everyday experience of male and female workers seemed to be different, even to the extent of controls over going to the bathroom or having the right to wear a sweater. Gender, it soon became evident, permeated all aspects of factory life, going much deeper than merely the allocation of workers to certain types of jobs. The preliminary findings established that no analysis of labour processes and labour markets could proceed without an explicit analysis of the sexual division of labour and its causes.

Making sense of these differences required that a critical position be taken with respect to much of the economic theory which deals with sex discrimination and the sexual division of labour. This is because such theories have assumed that the economic sphere – the sphere of the market – operates in accordance with economic laws which are gender-blind. As a result, the origin of sex differentiation has to be located outside this sphere. As Walby has noted, even writers such as Barron and Norris, who explicitly address the issue of sex discrimination, analyse the operation of the market in non-gender specific terms:

> 'Sexual differentiation is seen as largely determined outside of the labour market in the sexual division of labour in the household.'
> (Walby 1983: 155)

However, criticism of the failure of economic theory to come to terms with the issue of gender is only the first step. It has to be followed up with the development of an alternative analysis which focuses on the construction of gender both in society as a whole and in the work-place. This makes possible a discussion of the way in which the identities of workers as male and female structure employment, labour markets, and the organization of work. Attempts to do this have involved the development of 'feminist economic theory' (Elson 1982) or 'feminist economics' (Phillips and Taylor 1980). In a more sociological mode Cockburn's (1983) analysis of print workers takes up the same challenge.

The task of creating a space in which gender theory could develop was made imperative by the prevalence of economic models which located the causes of women's disadvantage largely or exclusively outside the market sphere. Generally speaking economists have analysed capitalist economic processes in terms of laws of value – mechanisms of commensuration of distinct objects and activities – which render the diversity of use-values comparable through the common yardstick of money. Within such models of commensuration, gender has no place. An hour's work is an hour's work and, it would be argued, only a fool would value identical work differently were it to be performed by a woman or a man (or a black or a white person, and so on). More importantly the market is an excellent mechamism for eliminating fools and foolishness. Individuals and institutions applying arbitrary valuations on goods and services should be forced out of economic activity altogether by the inexorable laws of competition. Hence inequalities in the situation of different classes of labour, if persistent, must derive from outside the market sphere altogether.

In neo-classical formulations of the problem, for example, the position of men and women in the economy is explained by reference to household decisions about such matters as the allocation of labour to domestic tasks, investments in the earning capacities of household members, and the benefits of work and leisure. Accordingly women's position in the labour market can be explained by family decisions which affect the quantity and quality of female labour offered for sale. While the possibility of 'pure' discrimination, where employers actually have an irrational preference for employing particular categories of labour, is allowed for, the workings of the market should eliminate this, too, because it makes the individuals and institutions which practise it less efficient than those which do not. The persistence of discrimination depends, in fact, on certain assumptions about the inability of markets to overcome such prejudices when there are large costs involved in making the shift. But in the absence of such difficulties, discrimination remains inexplicable and irrational (Lloyd and Niemi 1979: 199).

Much the same kind of result is found in the classical Marxist view of the economy. Once again, it is suggested that capitalists employ labour power without direct reference to gender. This position is summed up in Humphries' analysis of the incorporation of women into the labour force:

> 'There may, of course, be sex discrimination on the part of employers and/or workers, and there may be reasons for collective

capital to seek to permanently crystallise the existing structure of employment along sex lines, but these forces are antithetical to the logic of capitalist development. For once women have been drawn into the labour force in large numbers, their relatively lower wages must force a substitution of the kind Marx envisaged. This is the prediction of the theory.'

(Humphries 1983: 16)

Market forces should oblige employers to abandon segregation and discrimination once women become a full part of the industrial labour force. The problems women face in the labour market at the present time must stem, therefore, from their inadequate incorporation into the market for labour power, and not the operation of the market itself.

Perhaps rather less obviously, dual and segmented labour market theories also absolve the market and employers from responsibility for discrimination. Such theories generally start from the assumption that male and female workers have different qualities of labour to offer employers as a result of their domestic responsibilities. Women workers may be less stable in their jobs, for example,[1] or they might be less trainable or have less experience, or they might be easier to fire (Barron and Norris 1976: 53–64). Certain types of recruitment, training, and promotion may increase these differences and reinforce initial disadvantages, but they do not cause them. The market itself does not discriminate on the basis of race or sex.[2] Once again, as Lloyd and Niemi (1979) have argued, the clinching argument is that discrimination is inefficient and those who practise it will either be eliminated because of it or be forced to change their ways. In these models the power of competition and the pursuit of profit are, in effect, held to offset the power of men.

One important critique of this perspective has come from Hartmann, who argues that while the theoretical tendency of capitalism might be the eradication of status differences between workers based on sex, in practice men (in particular male workers) limit the type and extent of women's participation in waged work (1979: 207). Above all, they exclude women from the better jobs in order to increase the benefits to their own sex. Men enforce job segregation in order to maintain male superiority – both in the factory, taking the best jobs, and in the home, where they are the key wage-earners. Men therefore enforce male superiority in opposition to the logic of capital. A different critique has emerged from the school of 'feminist economics', which suggests that gender subverts the categories of economics rather than opposing them. As Elson has expressed it:

> 'The core of the argument is that "economic" phenomena, such as skill classifications and wage levels, are not determined by purely economic factors. They are neither "objective" in the sense of deriving simply from the material requirements of the processes of production of goods and services, and reproduction of labour power, nor are they the result of purely personal preferences about type of work and hours of leisure. On the contrary, they are structured systematically by the hierarchy of gender, a hierarchy in which women as a gender are subordinate to men as a gender.'
>
> (1982: 488)

In this perspective, the explanation of 'economic' phenomena requires an understanding of gender relations within the wider society and the way in which such relations structure employment situations.

In modern western societies, as Rubin has argued (1975), there are two, and only two genders, and these genders are dichotomous categories. Individuals are forced into gender strait-jackets through the repression of 'unsuitable' traits, and the two categories are defined as opposites. The sex/gender system in modern society defines two contrasting types of life and behaviour for women and men and also defines the general tenor of relations between them. It assigns primary parenting functions to women, limiting their access to activities outside the home while allowing men much greater scope for such activities. Much more than just a division of tasks, the sex/gender system establishes male control and power within the home and gives male activities greater value than female ones. The sex/gender system creates sets of expectations, norms, and obligations for women and men concerning their behaviour and also their desires.

When women and men go to work in factories, they assume identities as workers. Such identities are partly established within the work-place, and they can vary according to time and place. Workers' identities will indicate to them the kind of work they are expected to perform, who is entitled to give them orders and in what manner, and the 'career' they can expect over their working life. A skilled craftsman (a man), for example, will have clear notions of the work he is supposed to do, the type of work he is entitled to refuse, and the manner in which his foreman (a man) will treat him. Unskilled production workers will also have clear notions of their future job prospects, the work management can and cannot ask them to do, and the way in which other workers and managers will relate to them. Such behaviour and expectations are learned by workers on-the-job, developed in conflict with management and established by custom and practice and the routine of everyday life in the factory. A worker's identity will establish how a worker expects to experience factory life.

When men and women go to work in factories, they acquire identities as workers, and this has been evident to classical industrial sociology for decades. What has been ignored, however, is the fact that workers do not shed the expectations and norms of their gender upon entering the factory. There are, in the words of Kergoat (1982), 'masculine and feminine ways of being workers'. From the moment they set foot in the factory, workers are classified and treated as either male or female, and on the basis of such classifications the workers themselves develop expectations about their own behaviour and prospects and those of other workers. Clearly the identities of male and female workers are related to the constructs of masculinity and femininity in the wider society, but they are by no means reducible to them. Within the general parameters of both the construction of gender itself – segregation, emphasis of difference, the suppression of traits defining the other gender, and so on – and the attributes of masculinity and femininity established in the wider society, specific work identities have to be constructed and maintained in terms of work categories such as skill, strength, competence, and discipline. Identities for men and women as workers are developed which indicate suitable work, aptitudes, authority relations, careers, and so on. These have to be both defined and maintained in the course of the everyday life of the factory.

The adoption of this perspective for the study of the sexual division of labour requires that a gender perspective be used for the analysis of male workers as well as female. The marginalization of women's work by traditional industrial sociology has led some writers to see studies of women workers as complementary to the study of men (Westwood 1984: 11). The specific characteristics of female labour are described, but the sexual division of labour and the relation of female and male workers are not discussed. Such studies have the value of recuperating women's employment from the obscurity to which it has been consigned intellectually and ideologically, and they provide a basis for women to consider such questions as the dynamic of women's struggles. However, as Wajcman has noted, this perspective runs the risk of using a class model to analyse male workers and a gender model to analyse female workers [1982: 144–45], leaving the traditional sociology of male workers untouched by the gender perspective. This allows the male model to remain the general model with which the specificity of female labour is to be compared (Delphy and Kergoat 1982: 3). One major attempt to avoid this problem has been Cockburn's analysis of print workers. The importance of Cockburn's work is precisely that it analyses a largely male labour force from both a gender and a class perspective. It not only challenges traditional, gender-less analyses of male workers, but also shows that gender identities, like class identities, are constructed mutually. Therefore women earning 'pin-money' makes sense only in relation to the male bread-winner. 'Women's work' has meaning only in relation to a notion of masculinity and male work. Both are equally gendered. Such an analysis stresses that capitalist economic relations themselves are not objective, and also that class and gender are themselves open to constant redefinition in the course of social practice (Phillips and Taylor 1980: 82). They have to be defended or attacked within the work-place, and within the context of decisions taken with reference to the requirement of the employer.

There are various ways of examining gender identities and their impact on the sexual division of labour. Cockburn (1983) examined the construction of gender identities in the context of the challenge posed by new technology to the 'masculine' world of the compositor. This study will examine the construction and impact of gender identities in factories employing both female and male workers. It will be possible to see how gender stereotypes provide patterns of behaviour to which all men and all women are expected to conform and how the mutually defined positions of strong men and frail women, or future housewives and future bread-winners, permeate the factory and provide conditions under which both workers (male and female) and managers construct everyday factory life.

An examination of these issues can be carried out most effectively at the level of the establishment. The processes of segregation, specification of tasks, recognition of skills, and so on, could hardly be studied at any other level, since many general sources of information about factories use precisely those categories which need to be questioned. However, this presents a number of problems. One common option is to take one establishment and study it in depth, and this approach characterizes the bulk of the studies of both the classical industrial sociology of male workers and also the more recent studies of women workers. Much rarer is the detailed survey of a large sector, such as Madeleine Guilbert's brilliant and pioneering analysis of women's work in the Parisian metal-working industry (1966). Few researchers have the stamina or resources for this kind of work. But single case studies present problems of their own. Their representativity must always be suspect. Each establishment is unique, not only in terms of tangible aspects such as size, sector of the economy, technology, and product, but also with regard to less obvious factors such as company style. There is little quite as chastening for a researcher as the second case study, when all the certainties nurtured by the first are found to be less than absolute.

To avoid this problem, the research leading to this study was extended to seven factories in the electrical, motor components, and pharmaceutical-toiletries branches of Brazilian industry. All conformed to certain criteria. First, they were chosen from the more modern sectors of industry. This maintained the focus of earlier research and also balanced previous studies of women workers carried out in Brazil, which almost without exception examined the textile and garment industries. The initial choice of the metal-working industries[3] was widened to include pharmaceuticals, toiletries, and plastics firms, even though it proved impossible to gain access to a plastics firm. Second, the firms clearly needed to have a mixed labour force in order that the study of the sexual division of labour be facilitated. In two of the factories the production labour force was overwhelmingly female (although the stores, transport, and maintenance departments were mainly male), while in the other five factories there were significant numbers of both female and male workers in production jobs. Third, it was essential that the firms studied should be sufficiently large and well organized to have explicit and well-developed personnel policies in order that these be examined and information about employees be readily available. Fourth, for reasons of convenience and compatibility, the study was confined to the industrial region of the centre-south of Brazil, where labour markets were well developed and many important firms concentrated. All but one of the establishments was located in the state of São Paulo, and those within the state were distributed across the industrial areas within the city and in the corridors of development to the north and east. Finally, and perhaps most importantly, the firms had to allow some access to at least the personnel department.

These criteria led to the selection of seven firms. All were large in relation to others in their respective sectors, and six of the seven were owned wholly or partly by multinational companies. Inevitably they are not a representative sample of Brazilian industry, but they do provide a broad view of the range of policies that might be adopted by large firms in the more modern industrial sectors. Throughout the book these establishments will be denoted by a combination of a letter and a number, in order to preserve confidentiality. The letters will denote the industry – A for automotive components, E for electrical, and F for pharmaceuticals and toiletries – while the numbers merely distinguish one factory from another. El refers to the first electrical factory, E2 to the second, and so on.

The decision to study more than one factory avoids some of the problems of the single case study, but it produces problems of a different kind. For purely technical reasons information which is readily available in one company can be impossible to obtain in another. More importantly there can be restraints on access to people and information. In all the factories studied, access was granted to personnel department records, and this gave a general idea of the nature of the labour force and the sexual division of labour in each plant. This information, in some cases quite extensive, was complemented by interviews with managers in personnel departments about company policies in order to gauge their perceptions and attitudes on the sexual division of labour. In six of the plants it was also possible to visit the production departments and at least see what was going on, and in five it was possible to talk with some production managers and supervisors.[4]

However, access to workers for interviews was a major problem. The research was undertaken in 1982, when the Brazilian economy was in deep recession, and a number of firms declined to co-operate with the research altogether, on the grounds that workers would be made uneasy by interviews at a time of job cuts. Only two of the firms studied allowed workers to be interviewed in the plant. In the second motor components firm a small number of interviews were carried out (largely to elucidate information on certain specific issues), while the main body of the research interviews with workers was undertaken in the third electrical factory. Here one hundred workers (sixty women and forty men) drawn from the quality control and production departments were interviewed. In both plants the interviewing was carried out together with Dr Helena Hirata of the Groupe d'Etudes sur la Division Sociale et Sexuelle du Travail of the Centre National de la Recherche Scientifique in Paris, who was researching subsidiaries and parent companies of French and Japanese multinationals with operations in Brazil. The study of a multinational company in the electrical industry was a point of contact between two broader research projects.[5] Clearly the variety of access and the limitations of time mean that the material available on the different firms is uneven. The intention was not to provide consistent, comprehensive analyses of all seven firms, but rather to obtain enough information across them to enable some control of the findings in one firm to be exercised through comparison with the findings in some of the others, thereby reducing the problems often associated with case studies.

Clearly the findings of this study cannot be taken as indicative of the situation in other countries in the First or Third Worlds. Brazil is by no means an 'average' or representative country with respect to either industrialization or the employment of women, but it can provide a fruitful ground for the exploration of many issues about the sexual division of labour which have been raised with respect to both the developed and underdeveloped worlds. While the choice of Brazil is just as arbitrary as the choice of any other country, it does provide a suitable site for research. Brazil's strategy of import substitution industrialization led to the development of a broad range of industries, including heavy and consumer durable sectors, and women have been incorporated into many of them. From the point of view of the sexual division of labour, Brazil offers a broad range of industries with many women working in large establishments where there are also plenty of male employees. At the same time, during the 1970s, increasing numbers of married women were incorporated into the industrial labour force, and by 1980 they formed a substantial minority of the female manufacturing labour force. Therefore there is scope to study management strategy with regard to women of differing marital and parental statuses, as well as the strategies of women workers with respect to paid employment and their domestic situation. Finally, Brazil offers an interesting contrast to European patterns of the sexual division of labour because historically the trade union movement there has been very weak in the area of plant bargaining. Therefore there is an opportunity to study the structuring of the sexual division of labour in a situation where the formal union movement has little control over management prerogatives – either to impose or to prevent discrimination against women workers.

The analysis will begin with an account of the growth of female employment in Brazilian industry in the recent period and the patterns of occupational segregation and hierarchy by sex found in the factories studied. This material, in Chapters 1 and 2, provides the background for the study as a whole and also highlights a series of issues (for example hierarchy, skill, segregation) which need to be addressed. Chapter 3 first examines the impact of workers' domestic situations upon their factory employment, considering performance of domestic labour by workers employed in the third electrical factory and the division of domestic responsibilities between workers and other household members. It further considers the impact of actual and expected family responsibilities and situations on the working patterns of the workers interviewed, examining not only workers' attitudes, intentions, and experiences but also how managements construct employment policies both around such patterns and also around their stereotypes of female and male workers and their situations. This will be followed in Chapter 4 by an examination of the way in which the sex/gender system in the factory establishes a gendered hierarchy of status, power, and reward. This system is controlled by men, both workers and managers. The findings of these two chapters are then used to account for the different patterns of work and employment seen for the two sexes in the factories studied. Chapter 5 discusses the question of definitions of work and forms of control seen in the daily life of the plants, while Chapter 6 examines the employment policies adopted by managements, looking at the patterns of wage levels, skill recognition, promotion, and training accorded to male and female workers. In the light of the findings of these chapters, consideration will be given in

Chapter 7 to the impact of the 1981 recession on male and female employment and the sexual division of labour. This chapter provides an opportunity to consider some of the general issues concerning the sexual division of labour and the construction of female and male worker identities, but full consideration of these issues is reserved for the concluding chapter, Chapter 8.

1
Industrial development and employment in Brazil

INTRODUCTION

At first sight, it might be thought that the study of the sexual division of labour and its impact on labour markets and labour processes should be studied at macro level, not through a micro-level study of several plants. Both of the dominant analyses which describe women's position as industrial workers in the Third World would seem to make micro-level research largely redundant. One analysis argues that women are being marginalized from industrial employment by the nature of dependent capitalist development in the Third World. This view has been particularly influential in Latin America, including Brazil, where it has been suggested that industrialization has created few jobs overall, and the jobs created have been largely taken by men. If this were an accurate description of employment trends, then there would be very little to study. The sexual division of labour would involve outright expulsion from industrial tasks rather than a division of industrial work between sexes. At the very least, it would confine women to a limited range of 'female' industries and jobs whose determinants could be analysed at the macro level. The second analysis has suggested that women workers are being employed in large numbers in the export-oriented and labour-intensive industries, seen initially in northern Mexico and south-east Asia, but now found in many countries in the Third World. In this case the sex-typing could be considered to be so evident that there would be little point in studying it at micro level. Women seem to be found in specific 'female' occupations in industries and labour processes which are sex-typed as female in many countries. The typical industries concerned would be garments and electronics. In such cases most of the manual workers would be female, and the lines of demarcation of male and female would be clearly and unambiguously established. A detailed study of particular plants might be expected to add only information concerning the types of women employed in such plants.

However, the industrial employment of women workers in the Third World is much more complex and variegated than either of these two analyses would indicate. In the case of Brazil, in particular, by the beginning of the 1980s (when the research leading to this study was carried out), women were neither marginalized, nor confined to work in a small range of largely female industries. Women in Brazil worked in numerous industries and the sexual division of labour at plant level could be complex. However, in spite of this widespread incorporation of women into industrial employment, women were still firmly tied to the bottom of job hierarchies, earning lower wages, on average, than male workers and working in largely single-sex jobs. Segregation of women and men was very evident. In other words, the question of gender and its role in structuring labour processes and labour markets is as relevant in Brazilian industry as in the industries of the developed world. Questions about why women as a group share a common fate, ending up at the bottom of job hierarchies, and about the relation between work performed, wages and skill categories do need to be asked.

This chapter will provide both background to the discussion of the sexual division of labour in Brazilian industry and also support for some of the assertions which have just been made about the nature of that division. It starts with an account of industrialization in Brazil and the way 'expulsionist' writers have interpreted the impact of this industrialization upon female employment. This will be followed by a critique of the 'expulsionist' perspective and the proposal of a different interpretation of trends in female industrial employment. Particular attention is paid to the situation in São Paulo, which is the site of the rest of the analysis. Having established that women form a significant segment of manual workers in São Paulo industry, the chapter concludes by examining some indicators of the disadvantage women experienced in industrial employment.

INDUSTRIAL DEVELOPMENT IN BRAZIL

Unlike many Third World countries Brazil has a long history of industrial development. In the second half of the nineteenth century the rapid expansion of coffee production stimulated large-scale immigration from Europe, and the development of rail transport, import-export businesses, finance, and banking. Coffee's success also stimulated demand for manufactured products. At first this demand was met by a mixture of local artisanal production and imports from Europe, but in the latter part of the century local factory production began on a large scale. In particular, imports of textiles were replaced by the import of textile machinery, and in the last decade of the old century and the first of the new, the local textile industry supplanted England as the main source of supply for the Brazilian market. Other industries developed, too. While the textile industry was paramount, employment in the garment and food industries expanded, and artisanal production of metallurgical products also grew significantly.

Throughout this period, and right up until 1930, the development of industry was largely unplanned. The dominant political forces controlling the federal and state governments were linked to agricultural interests, and while the government invested considerable sums in the protection and expansion of agricultural production (particularly coffee), little was done for industry. Such tariff barriers as existed resulted more from the state's need for revenue than the planned protection of industry, and they were never systematized. Although the state did provide some limited protection for the textile industry in times of crisis (Leme 1978: 82), agricultural tariffs were much higher than industrial ones even in 1930. In spite of this, the dynamism of the agricultural economy was great enough to stimulate industrial advance across a broad spectrum. As Tavares has suggested:

> 'When the Great Depression came, the country already had a relatively large internal market and an industrial structure which, if still in its infancy, was already relatively diversified. This was due to the nature of the export sector. . . . Within the primary-export model itself there was a vigorous . . . development of a series of "traditional" industries such as food, beverages, garments, furniture etc. Metal-working itself, although in artisanal form, is quite long established in the country.'
>
> (1974: 59–60)

The coffee-centred, primary-export pattern of development received a severe shock at the time of the Great Depression. The collapse of demand in Brazil's major export market, the USA, led to a dramatic fall in foreign exchange earnings. The buying power of exports fell by 45 per cent between 1928–29 and 1932 (Tavares 1974: 64), and there was little sustained improvement in export earnings for the rest of the decade.[1] The crisis of the export economy had three major effects on industry. First, devaluation of the currency and restrictions on imports, which were required to deal with Brazil's balance of payments problems, gave industry a considerable degree of protection against competition from imported manufactured goods. Second, the government's measures to protect the incomes of the coffee sector (and the financial system dependent upon it) also helped industry by partially reflating the economy and increasing demand for industrial products (Tavares 1974: 32–5). Third, the economic crisis led to a political shift, with the oligarchic alliance which had controlled the state since the foundation of the republic in 1889 being swept away in 1930.

The new government of Getúlio Vargas centralized and modernized the state and intervened much more decisively to promote industrial development. Much closer relations between the state and industrial employers developed, with the latter declaring in 1936 that their priorities were 'defending the nation, strengthening its economy and conquering the internal market' (Leme 1978: 58). Foreign trade was subjected to more detailed scrutiny and planning, and in key areas such as steel, the state sought actively to build up internal capacity. In this period the textile industry remained the largest single employer in manufacturing industry, accounting for just over one-third of all industrial labour in the key industrial state of São Paulo in 1940, but the metal-working and chemical industries were growing rapidly. In the long term import substitution industrialization was to lead to a displacement of the longer-established (or 'traditional') sectors from their position of dominance within manufacturing industry.

The impact of the Great Depression and, following it, the trade restrictions resulting from the Second World War, would have led to industrialization in Brazil without any conscious planning by the state at all. Industrial growth was an almost automatic response to external difficulties. After the war, however, the Brazilian government was faced with the need to make a choice between deepening industrial development or reintegrating its economy into world commerce on the basis of liberal trade policies which would hamper industrial development. The latter policy was tried briefly in the post-war period, but it caused such a drain on foreign exchange reserves that it had to be abandoned. From this time on, the only question to be posed concerned the way in which increased industrial development was to be achieved.[2]

Given the state's active role in the promotion of industry after 1950, the issue arose as to methods and priorities. Two main choices appear to have been considered. First, priority could have been given to the development of heavy industry, which would have meant a significant expansion of the state sector and further restrictions on trade. Second, emphasis could have been placed on the development of consumer durables industries and the involvement of foreign capital and multinational companies.[3] A clear choice was not made until the mid-1950s, when the Target Plan of President Kubitschek outlined a strategy of rapid industrialization and modernization of energy and transport. Foreign firms were encouraged to set up or expand operations in Brazil, and particular emphasis was given to road transport. The short-term results of the strategy were impressive, with manufacturing output growing by 62 per cent between 1957 and 1961. The consumer durables industries grew particularly rapidly as a result of this policy (Singer 1976: 63), but there was also considerable modernization of the more traditional sectors.

This pattern of development was not reversed after the military coup in 1964. In spite of changes in such areas as wage policy, banking, and taxation, the pattern of sectoral growth seen in the period of the 'economic miracle' (1967–73) was very similar to that seen in the 1950s. The consumer durables sectors – particularly passenger cars and consumer electrical items – expanded rapidly, while the more traditional industries lagged behind. Change in the sectoral pattern of manufacturing growth came only after 1974, when the oil crisis, balance of payments problems, and the availability of low-interest foreign loans led to a considerable expansion of heavy industry and infrastructural investment on a large scale.

The sectoral transformation of manufacturing industry between 1950 and 1980 is presented in *Table 1*.[4] In the thirty-one-year period from 1 January, 1950 to 31 December, 1980, employment in manufacturing industry grew at the respectable rate of 4.3 per cent per annum, increasing from just over 1 million to nearly 4 million. Over the period as a whole, the textile industry shows a small rise in total

Table 1 *Increase in employment in selected sectors of industry: Brazil 1950–80*[1]

industry (selected)	*employment 1950*	*employment 1980*	*per annum increase 1950–80*[2]	*increase in employment*	*distribution of increase (%)*
metallurgical	89,682	456,265	5.4	366,583	12.7
mechanical	22,281	471,990	10.4	449,709	15.6
electrical equipment	13,939	213,986	9.2	200,047	6.9
transport materials	15,659	250,281	9.4	234,622	8.1
chemicals and related[3]	59,060	174,664	3.6	115,604	4.0
plastics[4]	—	102,440	—	—	—
textiles	308,501	346,562	0.4	38,061	1.3
clothing and footwear	65,725	404,440	6.0	338,715	11.7
food	178,476	457,916	3.1	279,440	9.7
all twenty-one industries	1,095,059	3,983,182	4.3	2,888,123	100

Sources Industrial censuses, Brazil, 1950 and 1980, data referring to all establishments.

Notes

1 For 1950 figures are for 'workers and foremen', and for 1980, 'persons linked to production'.

2 There is a thirty-one year gap between the two censuses because the date of the census was moved from 1 January to 31 December.

3 Chemicals, pharmaceuticals, and toiletries were aggregated into one sector in 1950.

4 In 1950 the plastics industry was included in the miscellaneous industry category.

employment, while some other sectors show large increases in the number of workers employed. Among the eleven major industries selected for the table, the greatest increases in employment are found in the metal-working sector.[5] Among the longer-established industries, there was strong growth in the clothing and footwear sector, slower growth in the chemical and related industries and the food industry, and little growth at all in textiles. The result of these changes was a major shift in the relative importance of the various sectors of industry over the period. The textile industry's share of total manufacturing employment fell from 28 per cent to under 9 per cent, while the four metal-working industries expanded their share from 13 per cent to 35 per cent. The stagnation of the textile industry was only partially compensated by the steady expansion of the food industry and the vitality of the clothing and footwear industry: the share of these three sectors together fell from just over 50 per cent to just over 30 per cent.[6]

These figures for the period as a whole conceal the fact that the rate of growth of industrial employment varied considerably from one decade to another. In the 1950s manufacturing employment grew at an average annual growth rate of 2.2 per cent, which was below the rate of growth of the population as a whole. Employment in what were the two most important sectors in 1950 – textiles and food – grew by just one-half of 1 per cent in the following decade, and in the so-called 'traditional' industries as a whole rising productivity meant that rising output created relatively few jobs.[7] Employment per unit of output in these industries fell by 23 per cent between 1949 and 1958, and by 46 per cent between 1949 and 1969 (Mata and Bacha 1973: 307). While the output of the 'traditional' sectors of the economy grew by 4 per cent per annum, employment increased by just 1 per cent (Mata and Bacha 1973: 310). Not surprisingly, when figures for the 1950s became available, both import substitution industrialization and the Kubitschek rapid development plan were regarded as having been failures in the crucial area of employment creation. However, this judgement turned out to be somewhat premature. In the 1960s manufacturing employment grew at a rate of 4 per cent per annum, with a much better performance in the food and clothing and footwear industries, and a strong showing from the more dynamic industries.

The acceleration of employment creation continued in the 1970s when the annual rate of growth of employment in manufacturing reached 6.3 per cent per annum, creating jobs on a large scale. The total number of jobs registered by the industrial census rose from 1 million to almost 4 million between 1950 and 1980. According to the figures from the demographic census, the number of people registered as working in industrial activities rose from 2.4 million to 10.8 million between 1950 and 1980.[8] The proportion of the economically active population in industrial activities rose from 14 per cent to 25 per cent.

INDUSTRIAL DEVELOPMENT AND WOMEN'S EMPLOYMENT IN MANUFACTURING

The growth and transformation of industrial employment in the post-war period had a profound impact on the sexual division of labour and female employment. However, it is perhaps not surprising that none of the authors mentioned so far in this analysis of trends in industrial employment paid any attention to the issue of the sex composition of the labour force. The industrial censuses themselves reflect this lack of interest: only one of the sixteen major tables in the 1970 census had a breakdown by sex. However, Brazil was perhaps exceptional in so far as the issue of industrialization and its impact on women's employment was raised as early as the mid-1960s by Heleieth Saffioti. Although her pioneering work, *Women in a Class Society*, was published in English only in 1978, it first appeared in Brazil a decade earlier.

Saffioti's work has been influential in Brazil and many of its ideas on women's participation in the labour force have been taken up and developed by later authors. Her main line of argument was that the development of capitalism in Brazil had led to a marginalization of women from the economically active population, and in particular from industrial activities. Her arguments divide the past century into two distinct stages. The first covers the period from 1870 to 1920, when female participation rates declined sharply. The second concerns the period after 1920, when the share of female employment in the economy as a whole and in industry remained rather stagnant. These two periods should be distinguished for reasons outlined below, even though writers such as Arizpe (1977: 291) have interpreted Saffioti's figures as proof of a single, long-term trend towards the marginalization of women. For the earlier period

Saffioti cites data from the 1872 census showing that women formed 45 per cent of the economically active population and that they constituted the majority of the labour force in industry because of their importance in textiles. The census for 1900 showed that women still constituted 45 per cent of the economically active population, and in *Women in a Class Society* this is taken to indicate a continuation of the importance of female labour. However, in another work Saffioti refers to the fall in the proportion of women in agricultural employment and the rise in prominence of domestic activities as evidence of 'a strong movement from 1872 to 1900 toward expulsion of women from productive economic activities and even from commercial activities' (1976: 149). By 1920 the expulsion is much more clearly established, and there is no uncertainty in Saffioti's argument. The census of that year registered women's share of the economically active population as having fallen to 15 per cent, and this is attributed to the capitalization of social relations in Brazil. For the purposes of our analysis, the period up to 1920 is not important, although it plays an important role in sustaining Saffioti's overall thesis of marginalization.[9]

The second stage of Saffioti's argument is more directly relevant to this study. It refers to the period after 1920, and in particular to the effects of import substitution industrialization after 1930. She suggests that women were marginalized from economic activity, and in particular from industrial jobs, as a result of the combined effects of a shift in the structure of industry and the tendency for new industrial jobs to be taken by men. According to Saffioti, 'contrary to general belief, industrial development did not bring about a substantial increase in the employment of female labour' (1978: 185), and she offers two reasons why the changing nature of manufacturing production favoured male employment. First, in so far as the development of industry involves the substitution of handicraft and domestic production of manufactured articles by factory production, this also means that female-dominated forms of production are replaced by male-dominated ones. This argument is similar to that advanced by Boserup (1970: 109). In the case of Latin America, the replacement of artisanal production by factory production was still going ahead after the Second World War, and it has been suggested that this is one of the factors contributing to the decline in female employment and the poor overall growth of employment in the 1950s.[10] Saffioti refers specifically to this problem in her account of the decline of female employment in the textile industry (1981: 29–30), but it is not of direct concern to the present study, which is specifically focused on factory employment.

The second reason offered by Saffioti to account for the decline of female jobs concerns the changing sectoral composition of factory production itself. She argues that the new, predominantly consumer-durables industries which developed after the Second World War tended to employ men. Their expansion, combined with the relative decline of some of the more traditional sectors which employed a high proportion of women workers, shifted the balance of employment markedly in favour of men. 'Female' industries such as textiles lagged behind, while the 'new working class' created by the growth of the dynamic sectors of industry was predominantly male. Evidence for this effect is provided in *Table 1.* The slower-growing industries, such as textiles and some of the chemical-related sectors, employed relatively large proportions of women (60 per cent of workers in textiles and one-third of those in the chemical-related sectors were women in 1950), while the female share of employment in the fast-growing metal-working industries was only 8 per cent in 1950. This alone was sufficient to lead to a decline in the share of total manufacturing employment accounted for by women workers. In 1950, in fact, the female share of manufacturing employment was 28.9 per cent, and by 1980 it was only 23.7 per cent.

In addition to the effects of these changes in sectoral composition of industry, Saffioti suggests that two other factors would also shift the balance of employment in favour of men. First, she argues that a major problem of import-substitution industrialization is that it creates few jobs overall, and that as a result, they are commandeered by men. Women, therefore, are left with little option but to stop seeking work altogether or look for marginal forms of employment. They form a reserve army of labour, and this army can be demobilized, or marginalized, when industry needs few workers. This problem was particularly acute in Brazil in the 1950s, as was noted above, and on the basis of that period, Saffioti wrote that:

> 'the problem of unemployment, both apparent and concealed, is much more serious in countries with dependent economies than in the centre of the international capitalist system. The marginalisation of female labour . . . turns out to be a consequence of the full development of capitalist relations of production.'
>
> (1978: 188)

A similar argument has been advanced by Ruth Sautu, who suggests that an overall shortage of jobs in industry, resulting from the application of labour-saving technology, leads to women being forced into either the industrial reserve army or low-wage, informal sector employment (1980: 152). In other words, the few good jobs available would be taken by men.

Second, Saffioti argues that modernization of industry destroys the unskilled jobs that women generally perform and replaces them with skilled jobs, which are normally the preserve of men. Chaney and Schmink provide a good summary of this general argument:

> 'those countries now industrialising may invest in such advanced technology that women never leave the home for the factory. They may simply have no part in the process at all, since nations whose development is dominated and controlled by large corporations often skip the labour-intensive stages of industrialization where women formerly found opportunity. Even in societies where women enter the factories in large numbers as industrialization proceeds, the proportion of women employed in the secondary sector declines. . . . According to our thesis, the demand for skilled labour to manage complicated machines is explicitly a "male-favoured" demand.'
>
> (1976: 168)

The decline of female employment in the Brazilian textile industry appears to provide an excellent illustration of these arguments, and Saffioti uses it as an indicator of general trends in female employment. She is able to point to the decline of artisanal production, particularly in the north-east, the stagnation of total employment in the industry in the 1950s because of rising productivity, and the gradual but constant displacement of women by men in the industry in the post-war period. On the latter point, she argues:

> 'women are being replaced by men to the extent that manual looms are being replaced by mechanical looms, and simpler looms are replaced by more sophisticated machinery. The requirements of firms for skilled maintenance personnel rise, while the greater productivity achieved by the new technologies expels large numbers of workers directly linked to production.'
>
> (1981: 26)

Textile employment rose by just over 12 per cent between 1950 and 1980, while industrial employment as a whole rose by 260 per cent. At the same time the industry was 'de-feminized', with the female share of textile employment falling from 60.4 per cent in 1950 to only 46.5 per cent in 1980.[11]

WOMEN'S EMPLOYMENT AND INDUSTRIALIZATION RECONSIDERED

Saffioti's arguments concerning the marginalization of women from economic activity and industrial employment find a considerable degree of support in the statistical data for the period. The 1950s appeared to confirm that dependent development could not create enough jobs to occupy the fast-expanding labour force, and there was an unmistakable decline in the share of industrial employment taken by women between 1950 and 1980, as was noted above. The trend of industrial development seemed inexorably to marginalize women workers. However, this trend was neither monolithic nor unchanging, and the accuracy of these arguments are cast into serious doubt by employment trends in the 1970s. Demographic census data for the 1970s showed the number of women employed in 'industrial activities' increasing by 181 per cent in the decade, double the rate of increase in both the female economically active population (95 per cent) and the male labour force in industrial activities (91 per cent).[12] The industrial censuses tell a similar story: female employment in manufacturing rising by 120 per cent, compared to 74 per cent for men. Far from being forced to seek work in the service sectors, women found work in large numbers in both industry and commerce in this period. Clearly this invites a reconsideration of the general development of male and female employment in the post-war period, and also close examination of the factors which might have led to a surge of women's employment in industry.

The figures in *Table 2* show just how great was the contrast between the situation in the 1950s described by Saffioti and that in the 1970s. In the 1950s male employment grew at a rate of 3.3 per cent per annum, while female employment declined very slightly over the decade between the two censuses. In large part this decline was the result of the stagnation of overall textile employment and

Table 2 *Growth of labour force in manufacturing industry: Brazil 1950–80 (% per annum)*

	1950–60[1]	*1960–70*[2]	*1970–80*[3]
all manufacturing			
men	+3.3	+4.2	+5.7
women	−0.1	+2.8	+8.2
manufacturing, excluding textiles			
men	+3.6	+4.6	+6.1
women	+1.8	+5.3	+10.9

Sources Industrial censuses, 1950, 1960, 1970, and 1980, for all establishments.

Notes

1 The growth rates are for 'workers and foremen' for the years 1950, 1960, and 1970.
2 In 1950 and 1960 the census was on 1 January, whereas for 1970 and 1980 the census date was 31 December. Therefore there is an eleven-year gap between the 1960 and 1970 censuses.
3 The 1970–80 growth rates are for workers, foremen, and technical staff.

the de-feminization of the industry, which resulted in the loss of 37,000 female jobs. In 1950 this one industry accounted for 58.8 per cent of all female industrial employment, and its decline was sufficient to offset the growth registered in all the other twenty sectors of manufacturing put together. But even outside the textile industry, male employment grew at twice the rate of female, which would seem to give clear support to Saffioti's line of argument.

In the 1960s female manufacturing employment did increase, but more slowly than male. However, the continued lagging behind of female employment is clearly due to the poor performance of the textile industry and its de-feminization. Outside textiles, female employment grew at a healthy 5.3 per cent per annum, compared to the figure for men of 4.6 per cent. However, this improvement in female employment growth pales into significance when compared to the figures for 1970–80. Over the latter decade female manufacturing employment grew by 8.2 per cent per annum, compared to 5.7 per cent for male employment. If the textile sector is excluded from the calculations, the female rate rises to 10.9 per cent, well above the male figure of 6.1 per cent per annum growth. In spite of female employment in the textile industry growing by only 11,000 over the decade, the number of women employed in manufacturing as a whole rose from 428,000 in 1970 to 945,000 in 1980.

Some doubts have been raised concerning the reliability of these figures. Writers adhering to the 'expulsionist' school have raised three areas of doubt in particular. First, it was argued that the rapid rise in female employment in the 1980 demographic census was the result of changes in the recording of female employment designed to correct earlier underestimations of female participation rates. Costa, for example, suggests that:

> 'a significant part of the growth of the female economically active population in the State of São Paulo . . . might be illusory, a product only of the way the data was collected.'
>
> (1982: 266)

However, this caveat should be applied only to agricultural employment. The census-takers certainly did change the phrasing of questions about economic activity, but this seems to have affected the result for agriculture more than other sectors.[13] Figures for industry and commerce do not seem to have been unduly affected by this, and yet it is precisely in these sectors that the greatest rises in female employment in the decade were registered. The growth of female employment in these sectors is confirmed by the industrial and commercial censuses, which are establishment-based and do not suffer from the same problems of under-registration of female employment as the demographic census. The rise in female employment was genuine, and there seems to be little doubt that in spite of a decline in agricultural employment, women were able to find plenty of jobs outside the service sector.

Second, it was argued that the rise in female industrial employment in the 1970s was the result of the so-called 'tertiarization' of industry – the increased use of women in office work in industrial establishments. Saffioti has argued that during the 1960s this was a major factor increasing female industrial employment (1981: 30). However, the data for the 1970s should not be interpreted in this way. While it may have been the case that the number of women working in offices (including offices attached to industrial establishments) grew very rapidly, the number of women working on the shop floor also grew at great speed. The figures presented in *Table 2* refer to women and men in 'occupations linked to production' – first-line supervisors, technicians, and workers. The vast majority (98.7 per cent in 1970) of female employees in this category were classified as 'workers', and female employment in this category certainly rose very rapidly.

A third explanation of the rise of women's industrial employment centred on the rapid growth of semi-artisanal manufacturing industries, such as the clothing sector. Saffioti refers to this when considering female employment in the 1960s, and Bruschini and Rosemberg took up the same theme when considering the expansion of female employment in the 1970s (1982: 15). This argument certainly has more foundation than the previous two considered. Between 1970 and 1980 the continued stagnation of employment in the textile industry was offset to a large extent by the dynamic growth of the clothing and footwear and food industries. Many additional female jobs were created in manufacturing as a result. However, in the country as a whole, and in each of the major industrial states, the dynamic industries were still growing much more quickly than the traditional ones, and the sectoral distribution of employment growth still favoured men rather than women. Women increased their share of total employment in manufacturing industry largely by increasing their share of employment within many different sectors of industry, not through the growth of traditional 'female' industries.

It remains a fact that none of the 'expulsionist' arguments can account for the most distinctive feature of female employment growth in the 1970s – the generalized advance of female employment shares across most sectors of industry. Whereas in the 1960s women's share of employment fell in some sectors and rose in others, during the 1970s female employment rose more quickly than male in almost every sector of industry. In those sectors where the female share of employment had already been rising in the 1960s the gap between female and male growth rates widened in the following decade. Three factors seem to account for this advance. First, it seems likely that as a result of strong growth in certain subsectors of industry (such as electronics) which employ significant numbers of female workers, women's share of employment in some sectors of industry rose. This tendency was already evident in the 1960s and partly accounts for the rapid growth of employment for women outside the textile industry. Unfortunately the figures from the industrial census are not disaggregated enough to provide clear proof of this point. Second, there was considerable vitality in some of the more traditional sectors of industry and women's employment, as was noted above. Third, shortages of labour, including unskilled labour, arising from rapid industrialization led to an extensive incorporation of women into industrial jobs, particular in the period 1970–75, when industrial growth was at its peak (Humphrey 1984: 236–39). In other words, tightness in urban labour markets in the period led to a more rapid incorporation of women than might have been expected. Women entered in particularly large numbers into those industries which could most easily recruit and use female labour, but the distinctive feature of the 1970s was the generalized shift towards women's employment.

Clearly in the absence of a detailed census breakdown of male and female employment by subsector or industry or occupation, it is not possible to rule out the hypothesis that female employment growth was merely the result of either greater than average growth in those subsectors of industry which employ relatively large proportions of women, or technical change which led to de-skilling and feminization. However, given the rise in female employment shares across almost all sectors of industry, and given persistent shortages of labour in the early 1970s, it seems plausible to suggest that a general factor such as shortages of labour had some influence on the growth of women's employment in the period.[14]

This explanation of the rapid advance of female employment has been offered as a variant of the industrial reserve army thesis. Miranda (1977: 261) argues that women were incorporated into some non-traditional forms of work in the early 1970s, only to be expelled again later in the decade. However, it will be argued in this book that there was no sign of an expulsion of women from industry up until 1980, and that the sexual division of labour in industry effectively prevents the easy mobilization and de-mobilization of women workers in accordance with demand conditions. Evidence from the crisis period after 1980 supports this point, as shown in Hirata and Humphrey (1984), and the issue will be examined in detail in Chapter 7. Even if labour shortages were a stimulus to the incorporation of women into industrial work, this incorporation produced profound structural changes which could not be easily reversed.

FEMALE EMPLOYMENT IN SÃO PAULO

The interpretation of female employment trends offered above has particular importance when the case of the state of São Paulo is considered. São Paulo is the most industrialized and developed state in Brazil. In 1975 it accounted for half of all industrial employment in the country, and the most dynamic and advanced industries were more concentrated there than anywhere else. It was the state where industrial advance and modernization of specific sectors had been taken furthest. If Saffioti and other writers were correct, one would expect São Paulo to show the highest degree of marginalization of women workers. The traditional industries had declined most, and the introduction of new technologies had been taken furthest. However, the data for the state show just the opposite picture. Female employment as a proportion of total employment in manufacturing in São Paulo has been consistently higher than in most other regions of Brazil. Even in the 1950s and 1960s when male labour was not in short supply, female employment accounted for a higher share of total employment in industry in São Paulo than in the rest of the country.

Two factors account for this. First, in São Paulo the female share of employment in each sector of manufacturing industry has been consistently higher than the national average in the post-war period, and higher than in most other states of Brazil. In all the eleven sectors selected for *Table 1*, the female employment share in São Paulo in 1970 was higher than the average for the country as a whole, and with one exception, higher than in the two other major industrialized states, Minas Gerais and Guanabara.[15] Female employment shares in São Paulo were also significantly higher than those found in the less industrialized states of the north-east.

Second, the decline of the traditional sectors has been largely offset by the growth of female employment in the more dynamic and modern sectors of industry. This can be seen very clearly in the metropolitan region of São Paulo, which is compared to the interior of the state and to the rest of Brazil in *Table 3*. The table shows that in the eleven industries cited in *Table 1* (aggregated on this occasion), a greater share of total employment went to women in the metropolitan region of São Paulo in each of the sectoral groupings than elsewhere in the country. It also shows that the newer industries expanded and absorbed women displaced from the more traditional sectors. Thus, for example, in the metropolitan region, the three traditional sectors accounted for 39.2 per cent of female employment, and the four metal-working industries 29.9 per cent. In Brazil outside the state of São Paulo the figures were 57.4 per cent and 12.4 per cent respectively.

Table 3 *Female employees in industry by sector for selected areas: 1976*

sectors of industry (selected)	*metropolitan São Paulo*			*interior of São Paulo*			*rest of Brazil*		
	employment	*emp. share*[1]	*emp. dis.*[2]	*employment*	*emp. share*	*emp. dis.*	*employment*	*emp. share*	*emp. dis.*
four metal-working industries	112,860	15.7	29.9	20,749	9.8	14.9	54,840	11.2	12.4
chemical-related industries	28,054	27.2	7.4	5,034	16.8	3.7	21,007	20.7	4.7
plastics	20,203	33.8	5.3	2,260	30.0	1.6	11,509	28.4	2.6
three traditional sectors[3]	148,340	52.1	39.2	84,692	38.3	61.0	255,582	38.7	57.4
all twenty-one industries	378,130	25.6	100	141,812	19.5	100	445,099	22.1	100

Source Ministry of Labour *Relacão Anual de Informações Sociais*, 1976. All employees (see Appendix 2).

Notes

1 Female employment as a percentage of total employment in the sectoral groupings chosen.

2 Female employment in the sectoral groupings chosen as a percentage of total female employment.

3 Textiles, clothing and footwear, and food products. These sectors are the most important for female employment among the traditional industries.

Table 4 *Distribution of increase in female employment in manufacturing by industrial sector and by region: 1970–75*[1]

sectors	*region*		
	São Paulo[2]	*Brazil outside São Paulo*	*Brazil*
four metal-working industries	33.6	11.7	21.8
chemical-related industries	4.7	1.0	2.7
plastics	6.9	3.7	5.2
textiles[3]	(6.1)	(4.9)	(5.5)
clothing and footwear, and food products	43.3	65.9	55.5
other industries	17.5	22.6	20.3
all twenty-one industries (absolute numbers)	106,680	124,028	230,716

Sources: Industrial censuses, São Paulo and Brazil, 1970 and 1975.

Notes:

1 The figures refer to workers linked to production, in factories with at least five employees.

2 The data are for the state of São Paulo as a whole. The census does not produce figures for the metropolitan regions of the type shown in *Table 3*.

3 The parentheses denote a decline in employment. The textile industry has been separated from the other two major traditional sectors because of this decline.

The contrast between São Paulo and the rest of the country is taken further in *Table 4*. It compares the sectoral distribution of the increase in female industrial employment between 1970 and 1975, the period of most rapid employment growth, for São Paulo and the rest of Brazil. In Brazil outside the state of São Paulo, the expansion of female employment was heavily dependent on the performance of the traditional sectors. The clothing and footwear and food industries accounted for 65.9 per cent of female employment growth in the period, compared to just 11.7 per cent in the four metal-working industries, and 4.7 per cent in the chemical-related and plastics industries. The growth of the clothing and footwear and food industries was so strong that it totally dwarfed the continued decline of the textile industry. In São Paulo the situation was quite different. The metal-working industries were much more significant, accounting for one-third of all the growth in female employment, and the chemical-related and plastics industries accounted for a further 11.6 per cent. These industries together provided more new jobs than clothing and shoes and food, and even the inclusion of beverages and tobacco would lift the share of the traditional industried by only another 0.4 per cent. In other words, while the more long-established sectors of industry remained important for women, in the State of Sao Paulo they were only as important as the new industries.

THE SEXUAL DIVISION OF LABOUR IN INDUSTRY

Clearly the problem facing potential female industrial workers in Brazil, and particularly in São Paulo, during the 1970s was not lack of jobs. Far from being marginalized, they were being incorporated into industrial employment in large numbers. The problem facing women was not incorporation as such, but rather the nature of their incorporation. The existence of jobs for women, by itself, is no guarantee of equality, and in Brazil there is ample evidence that women, in general, worked for low wages and were denied access to many areas of work, and that married women and women with children had particular difficulties in obtaining jobs in industry. These problems were not the result of the preponderance of traditional sector employment. In São Paulo the massive entry of women into non-traditional sectors of industry neither improved their work situation nor challenged the established bases of the sexual division of labour.

The study of women workers in industry and the gendered structure of the labour force is made imperative by the fact that women have been incorporated into such work on the basis of a pervasive and unequal sexual division of labour. The following chapters of this book are devoted to a detailed examination of this issue. At this point, the exposition will be confined to a consideration of some of the most general indicators of the sexual division of labour and women's disadvantage in São Paulo industry. Three areas will be examined: the exclusion of women from managerial and skilled work, wage differentials, and the selection of women for industrial work on the basis of age and marital status.

In industry men and women are segregated by occupation, sector of work, department, and skill, and these aspects will be considered in detail in the next chapter. There is also a pronounced vertical division of labour by gender, with women generally concentrated in low-status work and high-status jobs largely monopolized by men. Very few women gained access to managerial, technical, supervisory, and skilled jobs. One study of large firms in Rio de Janeiro showed that there were sixteen men in managerial posts for every woman (Ministério do Trabalho 1976: 90–1), and SENAI's survey of manufacturing industry in the city of São Paulo (see Appendix 2) showed that in technical occupations there were twenty-four men employed for every one woman. Similarly all the data available on the distribution of men and women in supervisory posts show that women workers are very much under-represented. Finally, women are largely excluded from jobs classified as skilled. The SENAI survey found virtually no women in tool-room and maintenance functions, and that skilled women workers were to be found in significant numbers only in the textile and clothing industries. Outside these two industries there were seventy-seven skilled male workers for every one woman worker classified as skilled. Women were concentrated in so-called 'semi-skilled' occupations, defined by SENAI as:

> 'occupations characterised by the use of manual dexterity limited to operations subjected to automatism, whose execution normally requires attention, motor coordination and rudimentary technical knowledge.'
>
> (Faraone 1978: 18)

This division of labour has a clear impact on the relative wages paid to men and women. All the available wage and earnings data show that men earn considerably more than women. For example in 1979 the average yearly pay in both the four metal-working industries and the three largest traditional sectors was twice as great for male employees as for female employees in São Paulo.[16] Wage differentials are also indicated by the demographic census. According to the 1980 census for the state of São Paulo, 73.5 per cent of women working in industrial activities earned less than twice the minimum wage, compared to 36.3 per cent of male workers. These differences are only partially explained by the slightly longer hours worked by men. Average hourly wage rates, too, are much lower for women than for men. Among 3,615 employees in five plastics establishments in the city of São Paulo, for example, average hourly wage rates for women were only 57 per cent of those for men. Even among unskilled and semi-skilled production workers, wage rates for women were, on average, only 75 per cent of the level for men.[17]

Finally, it should be noted that the incorporation of women into industry was based upon clear employer preferences for certain types of women workers. A notable feature of the rise in female employment in the 1970s was the sharp rise in participation rates for women in the 25–40 age range and the considerable increase in the number of women with children registered as being economically active (Humphrey 1984: 241–43). In spite of this, the female *industrial* labour force remained predominantly young, unmarried, and childless. Although the number of older, non-single (married, divorced, separated, or widowed) women in industrial activities increased rapidly from a very low base, firms still favoured employing single, childless women.[18] Non-single women accounted for 58.2 per cent of the increase in the female labour force in non-agricultural economic activities in the decade, but their share of the increase in industrial employment was only 43.7 per cent. A similar pattern is seen for women with children. These two categories were more likely to find employment in the personal services (mainly domestic service) and in schools and hospitals than in industry (Humphrey 1984: 242). While this might have been due, in part, to women's own needs to find work which might be compatible with domestic obligations, evidence of widespread employer prejudice against married women and women with children will be shown in Chapter 3.

CONCLUSIONS

The evidence from Brazil shows that a considerable growth in female industrial employment took place in the 1970s. Women were not marginalized from industrial employment in the state of São Paulo, nor did they find jobs overwhelmingly in the 'traditional' sectors of female employment such as textiles and garments. Similarly their employment was not confined to secretarial and clerical occupations. Women were employed quite extensively in blue-collar production work, and the range of industries in which they were employed went considerably beyond the traditional areas of women's industrial work, textiles and clothing. They were to be found in significant numbers in such sectors as pharmaceuticals, toiletries, light chemicals, plastics, motor components, leather goods, and electrical products. At the same time, the rapid growth of female employment was not associated with an export-oriented pattern of industrialization. While electronics was one of the new industries into which women were recruited, the women workers in São Paulo produced products for the local market, in factories which very often engaged in the complete cycle of production.

While the extent of industrial employment for women in São Paulo was greater than elsewhere, their conditions of employment continued to be much the same. Women continued to be concentrated in low-wage, unskilled, or semi-skilled work, and segregation and inequality were still the dominant features of the sexual division of labour in industry. Even in factories which had a wider range of jobs than seen in the export-processing zones of south-east Asia and the Mexican border, broad areas of work seemed to be monopolized by men, and women remained confined to what was considered 'women's work'. At the same time, the census data indicate that firms in manufacturing continued to be very selective about the kinds of women they employed. While a significant minority of older women, married women, and women with children were to be found in industrial activities, employers seemed to prefer their female workers to be young, unmarried, and childless.

Clearly women's employment and the sexual division of labour in Brazil is as complex as that in Europe or North America, and the remainder of this book will attempt to analyse and explain some of the many facets of the sexual division of labour in industry. Before addressing the theoretical questions directly, the next chapter will examine the sexual division of labour and the segregation of men and women in the factories studied in São Paulo so that the terrain can be defined more clearly.

2

Gender, hierarchy, and segregation in industry

INTRODUCTION

Women workers were certainly incorporated into employment in the manufacturing sector in São Paulo in the course of the 1970s. Their problem was not marginalization from industrial employment as such, but rather the nature of their incorporation into industrial work. As one might expect on the basis of experience in many other countries, men held a virtual monopoly on managerial and technical occupations. Female managers were rare and very few women were found in engineering and technical occupations. According to the SENAI survey of establishments in the city of São Paulo, there were twenty male technical workers employed for every one woman. Even among the workers who are the focus of this study, blue-collar manual workers, there was a well-defined sexual division of labour.[1] In addition to the exclusion of women from many functional areas – such as stores and maintenance – and the concentration of women workers at the bottom of job hierarchies, a considerable segregation of the male and female labour forces along occupational and departmental lines was also found, even when women and men worked in the same functional areas, typically in production and quality control work. This chapter will only describe the extent of the divide between male and female and the hierarchy established between them. In subsequent chapters these phenomena will be explained.

The chapter begins with an examination of SENAI's survey of industrial establishments in the city of São Paulo and the information it contains on the sexual division of labour.[2] This will be followed by a detailed study of the occupational structures for hourly-paid workers in seven manufacturing plants. Details of the establishments and the firms which owned them can be found in Appendix 1. In addition to the information from these plants, reference will also be made to information on occupational structures in five large firms in the plastics industry. The source of this information, too, is specified in more detail in Appendix 1.

THE SEXUAL DIVISION OF LABOUR

Detailed survey material on the sexual division of labour in Brazilian industry is very rare. Fortunately the Sao Paulo office of the National Industrial Apprentice Scheme, SENAI, carried out a survey of industrial establishments in the city of Sao Paulo in the late 1970s. As might be expected, the survey was mainly concerned with women's employment in relation to SENAI's training schemes. It concentrated attention on those occupations classified as 'characteristically industrial' (Faraone 1978: 18). Office and administrative work was given little attention, being classified under the general heading of 'administrative occupations', but detailed and specific attention was given to manual occupations and to the question of skill. This makes it particularly valuable for the current discussion. The survey's findings with respect to the distribution of male and female workers by SENAI's major categories of occupation are presented in *Table 5*. Women formed 29.4 per cent of the labour force in manufacturing industry, and their share of administrative jobs was roughly the same. In non-administrative, or 'characteristically industrial' jobs, women constituted approximately 30 per cent of the labour force, but they were distributed very unevenly across the categories used by SENAI to indicate training and skill.

The SENAI figures show very clearly that women workers were concentrated in the lower reaches of the job hierarchy, while men were spread more evenly across it. Men outnumbered women by twenty to one in technical and engineering occupations, and by almost eight to one in those jobs SENAI classified as skilled. Women were overwhelmingly concentrated in semi-skilled jobs, defined as 'requiring dexterity', 'repetitive', and needing 'concentration'. In effect the category includes any work with machines not requiring specialized training, and a lot of semi-skilled work is paid at the same rate as the lowest SENAI category, 'labouring'. Taking just the three manual categories (skilled, semi-skilled, and labouring) 83 per cent

Table 5 *Distribution of employees in manufacturing industry by sex and by type of occupations: city of São Paulo (absolute numbers and percentages)*[1]

type of occupation[2]	*women*		*men*		
	number	*distribution*	*number*	*distribution*	*women as % of total*
administrative	43,519	20.8	107,033	21.3	28.9
technical and engineering	1,130	0.5	23,910	4.8	4.5
labourers	16,471	7.9	62,087	12.4	21.0
semi-skilled	137,349	65.5	221,704	44.1	38.3
skilled	11,172	5.3	87,716	17.5	11.3
total	209,641	100	502,450	100	29.4

Source Unpublished survey data from SENAI. See Appendix 2 for details.

Notes
1 The data refer to all employees in manufacturing establishments of fifty or more employees. The table excludes data from the public utilities, construction, and industrial services, which were also included in the SENAI survey.
2 For definitions of the categories used by SENAI, see Appendix 2.

of women were employed in semi-skilled work. Male manual workers were distributed much more evenly across the skill categories. Approximately 24 per cent were skilled, 17 per cent in labouring jobs, and 60 per cent in semi-skilled work.

While these figures are revealing, they also hide further significant differences between female and male workers and the nature of the skilled work they perform. The global figures on skill underestimate the degree of difference in the situations of men and women workers in two significant ways.[3] First, the types of work performed by female and male skilled workers were very different. The female workers classified as skilled by SENAI were overwhelmingly concentrated in just two occupations and industries. Of the 11,190 female skilled workers registered by the survey, 9,821 (or 88 per cent) worked in the textile and clothing industries, mostly as overlockers and sewers (mostly on sewing machines). Outside these two industries there were 1,369 skilled women workers and approximately 80,000 skilled men. The large numbers of skilled women in textiles and clothing may be due partly to the demands of the work, but the possibility should also be borne in mind that overlocking and sewing were classified as skilled in order to attract industry training grants and enable firms to pay low wages to apprentices. Overall, almost all the women working in skilled work had production jobs. According to SENAI's figures, there were only 10 skilled women workers in tool-room and maintenance functions in the whole of the city of São Paulo, and a further 155 skilled women in production control, progress chasing, and related functions. Although the SENAI data do not provide a detailed breakdown for male workers, it can be assumed that they were distributed across a much broader range of skilled jobs and industries.

Second, the SENAI survey classified the skill of workers according to the general character of the occupations they filled. Radio-technician or overlocker, for example, were regarded as skilled occupations, and all the workers performing functions relating to such work were classified as skilled, irrespective of the degree of achievement or training reached. For each occupation SENAI distinguished five degrees of training or competence: assistant, apprentice, post-apprentice, fully skilled, and supervisor. Outside the clothing and textile industries, women were concentrated in the lower categories within each skill grouping. In an extreme case in the electrical industry, the survey found that all 255 women in the (skilled) radio-technician occupation were classified either as assistants (basically low-grade auxiliary workers) or apprentices. None of them had reached the higher levels of the SENAI classification – 'post-apprentice' (having completed their training but not having had the necessary experience to earn the full skilled rate for the job), 'fully skilled', or 'supervisor'. Similarly the sixty-two skilled women workers in mechanical engineering were grouped in the occupational categories of fitters and metal-finishers, but all were apprentices. In the paper and cardboard industry there were niney-four assistants and apprentices, and only fifty-two fully skilled workers. The survey also found eighty-five female apprentice glove-makers, but only one qualified female glove-maker. Only in the textile and clothing industries did skilled women workers outnumber the assistants and apprentices. It seems highly unlikely that this distribution was the result of either a sudden upsurge of training for women which would bear fruit at a later stage, or the result of enormously high rates of exits from the occupations concerned of skilled female workers. It seems certain that firms were either (1) using women only for inferior jobs relating to skilled work, or (2) classifying women as unskilled assistants and apprentices even when they were performing the skilled functions, or (3) employing women as apprentices merely in order to be able to pay wage rates below the statutory minimum wage. While comparable figures for male workers are not, once again, supplied by the survey, they would have been unlikely to show a similar pattern. Although cases of male workers being trained for skilled work and yet being employed in other jobs at the end of their apprenticeships were found in some of the factories studied, the practice did not appear to be widespread.

The SENAI figures give some idea of women's marginalization from skilled work, but they cannot convey the full extent of the sexual division of labour. The vertical division of labour, or the restriction of women's access to higher status occupations, was only one part of this division. There was also a significant horizontal division of labour between men and women in unskilled and semi-skilled work. The kinds of work the two sexes performed and the occupations to which they were assigned were quite distinct. This can be seen much more clearly through a detailed examination of occupational structures in one of the seven firms studied.

THE SECOND AUTOMOTIVE FACTORY

The depth of the division between male and female within manufacturing establishments, which was evident in all of the factories visited, can be illustrated by a description of the situation in the second automotive plant. This particular plant is taken merely as one example, and a similar description of the second electrical factory can be found elsewhere (Humphrey 1985). The second automotive plant belonged to a multinational company, being its largest establishment in Brazil. Its hourly-paid labour force consisted of 578 workers in September 1978, of whom 72 per cent were male and 28 per cent female. The plant produced automotive components and industrial ceramics. Its occupational structure incorporated a sexual division of labour which ran along functional, hierarchical, and occupational lines.

As might be expected from the results of the SENAI survey, male workers in the plant monopolized almost all of the skilled occupations within it. There were virtually no women working in machine-setting or the tool-room and maintenance sections of the plant, and men also monopolized the store-keeping work. In these four areas there were just 3 unskilled women employed, compared to 221 men – over half (53.4 per cent) of the male work-force in the plant. In effect women were confined to jobs in production, packaging, and quality control: 97.6 per cent of all women working in the plant were in such functions, compared to just 44.0 per cent of men.[4]

In common with many factories in Brazil, the plant had a wide variety of occupational titles which were grouped into a number of grades. There were twenty-two different grades for hourly-paid workers as a whole and fourteen for production workers. Although the grades overlapped in wage terms, each had its own starting wage and increments according to merit and length of service. As might be expected, the exclusion of women from many areas of skilled work meant that a much greater proportion of men than women held higher-grade jobs, as can be seen in *Table 6*. Of all male hourly-paid workers 72.8 per cent had jobs on grade eight or higher, compared to only 2.0 per cent of the women. Women were concentrated at the

Table 6 *Distribution of hourly-paid employees by sex and by grade: selected groups of employees, factory A2, September 1982*[1]

category of employee	*sex*	*grades*				
		1–4[2] *%*	*5–7 %*	*8–10 %*	*11 and higher %*	
all hourly-paid workers	women	97.3	0.7	2.0	0	n = 150
	men	13.2	14.0	27.7	45.1	n = 401
production workers	women	100.0	0	0	0	n = 102
	men	25.7	26.3	32.2	15.8	n = 152
quality control workers	women	90.9	2.3	6.8	0	n = 44
	men	0	0	72.7	27.3	n = 22

Source: Company records

Notes:

1 The figures exclude twelve female charge-hands and fifteen male apprentices who were not allocated to any one grade.

2 Grade 1 includes a small number of women working in the ceramics division of the plant who were paid a little below the bottom rate seen in other departments.

bottom of the job hierarchy, with 97.3 per cent of women being employed on the bottom four grades, compared to only 13.2 per cent of men. This concentration of women workers in the lower grades was not just the result of their exclusion from such skilled work as maintenance and machine-setting. *Table 6* shows that even in the production (which in this factory including packaging) and quality control functions, women were concentrated in lower-grade occupations, while men were distributed across a much wider range of grades. In production jobs almost half the men were on grade eight or higher, while all the women were on grade four or below. In quality control a small proportion of the women workers were on grade eight or higher, but this was the lowest grade for men in quality control work. Even within the production and quality control areas, therefore, women were concentrated on the bottom rungs of the occupational hierarchy and earning lower wages than men.

Even when the male and female workers were employed on the same grade, occupational segregation was still evident. The 578 hourly-paid workers in the plant were grouped into occupations which were almost totally single-sex. One male worker was classified as 'Machine Operator I', which was otherwise a female occupation, three women and sixteen men shared the title 'Quality Control Inspector I', and five cleaners (four men and one woman) shared the same occupation. Apart from these cases, all the other occupations were single-sex. Men and women were inserted into two segregated and differentiated occupational structures within the plant, each with its own jobs, wage levels, and patterns of mobility. Male workers in low-grade occupations were segregated from female workers in occupations of similar status, and such male workers had access to male-only higher-paid jobs. Even in those few cases where women gained access to higher-grade jobs, it was through specifically 'female' mobility chains into 'female' jobs.

SEGREGATION AND HIERARCHY

The second automotive factory was by no means exceptional in its occupational structure, sexual division of labour, and segregation of female and male workers. In the other automotive and electrical plants quite similar occupational structures were found. They all

Table 7 *Distribution of hourly-paid workers by grade and by sex: four factories*

category of workers	factory			
	E1	*E2*	*A1*	*A2*[1]
All hourly-paid workers				
number of grades	12	13	16	22
workers in bottom four grades (%)				
women	94.7	81.9	91.5	97.3
men	44.8	20.5	23.5	13.2
production workers only				
number of grades	8	10	7	14
workers in bottom four grades (%)				
women	96.3	86.6	94.1	100
men	92.0	33.6	48.6	25.7

Source Company records.

Note

1 The figures exclude charge-hands and apprentices because they are not assigned to a specific grade. In the other factories, charge-hands fall within the grading structure, but apprentices do not, and only the latter have been excluded. In A2, a small number of workers earning slightly below the grade 1 wage rate have been aggregated into that grade for the purposes of calculation.

showed a concentration of women in production jobs, low-grade work, and one or two broadly defined occupations, as well as segregation by department and occupational category, and distinct promotion patterns for men and women. In the pharmaceuticals and toiletries establishments the nature of the work resulted in a much less elaborate structure of occupations and grades, but the overall impact on the employment of men and women was the same.

Concentration in low-grade work and production jobs

Although grading structures differed somewhat in the four firms which had a limited number of clearly defined grades, *Table 7* has been constructed to show the degree of concentration of female and male workers in low-grade work. It gives the number of workers on the bottom four grades as a percentage of the total number of workers for the female and the male labour forces for production workers and for all occupations. The pattern seen in A2 was repeated in the other three plants. Between 81.9 per cent and 97.3 per cent of all women workers were concentrated in the bottom four grades, whereas for male workers the comparable figure ranged from 13.2 per cent to 44.8 per cent. Similarly, in production jobs women were heavily concentrated in the lowest grades. The proportion of men in low-grade production work varied considerably, and this was the result of two factors. First, the number of grades varied from factory to factory, and in the plants with fewer grades, a higher proportion of male workers could be expected on the bottom four grades. Second, there was a higher proportion of male production workers on lower grades in those factories which employed very few men in production. Where most of the production work was done by women, the men tended to be employed for general labouring work, which was unskilled. In E1, for example, where only twenty-four men worked in production, 92 per cent of male production workers were concentrated in the lower grades, while in E2, which employed hundreds of male workers in production, only one-third were on grade 4 or below.

The range of female work was also much narrower than for men in all five automotive and electrical firms: 90 per cent or more of hourly-paid women workers were employed in production, packaging, or quality control work, and very few women were found outside these areas in any of the factories for which information is available. Men could find work in areas such as maintenance, toolroom, and stores (which they monopolized), as well as in production and quality control. The only exception was E1, where men were almost entirely excluded from quality control and production work.

Associated with the concentration of women into low-grade production work was the grouping together of female workers into one or two broadly defined occupations situated at the bottom of the job hierarchy. *Table 8* shows that in four of the five electrical and automotive plants studied, between 59.6 per cent and 84.6 per cent of all hourly-paid female workers were grouped into a single occupation on the bottom grade of the job hierarchy. Typically this occupation was either 'production assistant' or 'assembler'. Even the one remaining case, A2, only appears to be different. The women worked on two very distinct product lines and there was a separate

Table 8 *Employment in the largest single occupation in relation to total hourly-paid employment and employment in production and quality control occupations by sex: five plants*[1]

		women			*men*		
plant	*date*	*largest occupation*	*as % of all women workers*	*as % of prod. and quality control workers*	*largest occupation*	*as % of all men workers*	*as % of prod. and quality control workers*
E1	May 1982	labourer	84.6	89.6	labourer	18.4	76.7
E2	May 1982	assembler	78.9	75.0	assembler	10.0	16.6
E3	Dec. 1980	assembler	67.9	71.8	labourer	11.9	16.3
A1	Dec. 1980	prod. assistant	59.6	63.7	prod. labourer	14.2	36.7
A2	Sept. 1982	prod. assistant	42.6	43.7	operator II	9.1	20.8

Source Company records.

Note

1 The data refer to all hourly-paid workers, including apprentices and charge-hands. Workers in packaging are included with workers in production.

job title for the unskilled women in each. Once again, the male occupational structure was very different. In the five factories surveyed, the largest single male occupation accounted for between 9.1 per cent and 18.4 per cent of all male workers. In part, this reflected the distribution of men across a wide range of functions, which was noted above, but even when the importance of a single occupation in production work alone is calculated, a clear difference between men and women remained. For women, between 43.7 per cent and 89.6 per cent of production workers were concentrated in a single occupation, while for men, the only factory where more than 40 per cent of male production workers were concentrated in one occupation was E1. As was noted above, this factory had very few male production workers.

Segregation by department and occupation

A considerable degree of segregation of male and female workers into single-sex departments was found in most factories, although not in A2. In E3, for example, five of the twelve production departments were overwhelmingly female (185 women and 2 men – excluding the male supervisors), and five departments were entirely male except for two women secretaries.[5] Generally speaking the only area in the factories studied where it was common to see men and women working together was quality control.

Even when workers were employed in the same department, it was common to find the sexes segregated along occupational lines. Job titles were almost entirely single-sex, and even in those plants where a common title for the lowest grade of worker was shared by the sexes, different kinds of work were performed by them (women assembling, while men did general labouring, for example). As a result it was extremely rare to find male and female workers doing similar work with the same job title. Just three exceptions to this rule were found. First, in F2 men and women were employed on the same work of filling the tubes and bottles with toiletry preparations. However, the male workers were paid a higher wage for this. Second, in the plastics industry there were a number of common titles in production work, such as ‘injection moulding machine operator’ and ‘silk-screen printer’ in the same factory, although it is not known whether or not their work was segregated. Third, men and women commonly worked together in quality control departments in the automotive and electrical industries, and there was often an overlap between male and female job titles. The highest-grade female quality control workers shared the same grade as the lowest-grade men, as was seen in A2.

Promotion patterns

Women's promotion opportunities relative to men were defined not by their stability but by the constitution of separate lines of advancement for them (defined by occupational segregation) and the very limited number of higher-grade occupations available. Women were recruited to lower-grade occupations, and they tended to stay there, irrespective of the length of their employment. In E3, for example, just over half of the women workers employed as 'assemblers' in December 1980 had been employed for over one year, and one-third of them had been employed for more than two years. Male workers experienced quite a different 'career' profile. They were often recruited to higher-grade jobs directly (as will be shown later), and when recruited into low-grade jobs they stayed for short periods, either obtaining promotion or leaving. In E3 there were a relatively large number of men doing low-grade 'assistant' work, but two-thirds of them had been employed in the plant for less than a year, and only 9.3 per cent had been employed for more than two years. A similar pattern was seen in E2. Only 17.0 per cent of men on the bottom grade had been employed for more than three years, compared to 46.6 per cent of women on the same grade.[6] As a result of these different patterns of advancement, the gap between male and female grades tended to increase with length of employment. Longer-service women tended to remain at the bottom of the job hierarchy, while men had much better opportunities to rise up the occupational hierarchy if they remained within the enterprise.

Pharmaceuticals and toiletries

The segregation of occupations and the differential vertical stratification of female and male workers took a somewhat different form in the pharmaceutical and toiletries sector. The factories studied were smaller, and the range of occupations among production workers much more restricted.[7] However, the same hierarchy existed. In F1 women were confined to production and packaging work. There were five grades for hourly-paid production workers; 89.5 per cent of the women workers were employed on the bottom two grades, and only group leaders and supervisors were put on grade 3. Just 1 woman out of 172 was employed on grade 4. The male workers monopolized the higher grades: there were three men employed as general labourers on grade 1, and five 'specialized packers' on grade 2 (the only job title shared between male and female production workers). The remaining thirty male production workers were employed on grades 3, 4, and 5, while male supervisors were salaried. In a different setting, therefore, a similar pattern to that seen in the electrical and automotive industries was found – limited overlap between the top female grades and bottom male grades.

In F2 the level of segregation was less. Women were confined to production work, but within production there were certain jobs performed by both sexes. Even so, unskilled male workers were paid 10 per cent more than female, irrespective of the work they did, and management even admitted to paying lower wages to women who did more demanding jobs on high-value product lines. One feature used by managements to distinguish men and women was shift-work. The men worked three shifts at periods of peak seasonal production, while women worked two all the year round. This pattern of shift-working and the resulting overlap in male and female work on day shifts can also be found in continuous process industries such as glass-making.

WAGE DIFFERENTIALS

The pattern of occupational hierarchy and segregation noted above has very clear implications for the wages and earnings of female and male workers. Differences in rates of pay between high-grade and low-grade jobs are considerable in Brazilian industry. In the second automotive factory already discussed at length in this chapter, the wage rate for a male 'machine operator IV' was 50 per cent higher than for the lowest-paid production job. When non-production occupations are taken into account, wage differentials reached two to

Table 9 *Average hourly wage rates for selected groups of workers by sex: E3 and in five plastics firms (female rate=100)*

group	*E3*	*plastics firms*
all employees	153[1]	174
hourly-paid workers	146	—[2]
production workers[3]	141	132
quality control workers[3]	129	143

Source For E3, company records for December 1980. For the plastics firms, data from the Trade Union Contribution Records submitted by firms to the Union and calculated for March 1981.

Notes
1 The male rate is 53 per cent higher than the female rate, which is taken as the index level for 100 for each category.
2 The data for plastics workers are not broken down by salaried and hourly-paid criteria.
3 Charge-hands have been excluded from these calculations.

one or more. In other factories wage differences were even higher. In E3, for example, a carpenter working on the production of television and speaker cabinets could earn two and a half times as much as a (female) assembler and a tool-maker three and a half times as much.[8] As a result, differences in the grading of male and female occupations led to big differences in wages for men and women. Hourly wage rates for male workers were much higher than those for women, even within the same areas of employment. In the case of E3, for example, average hourly wage rates for all men were 53 per cent higher than for all women, and 46 per cent higher for hourly-paid employees, as can be seen in *Table 9*. Even among production workers the average hourly rate was 41 per cent higher for men than for women, and for quality control workers the difference was 29 per cent. Figures for the five plastic firms revealed a roughly similar situation: overall, male hourly wage rates were 74 per cent higher than the average female rate, and in production and quality control the differences were 32 per cent and 43 per cent respectively.

Because of the patterns of promotion for male and female workers referred to above, wage differentials for male and female workers tended to increase with length of employment. Taking E3 as an example, once again, the wage differential for newly hired (less than four months in the firm) male and female production workers was 18.7 per cent. Average hourly wage rates for men were 118.7 per cent of average hourly rate for women. For workers with between one and three years' employment, the difference rose to 33.7 per cent, and for workers with more than six years' employment, the difference between average hourly wage rates for male and female production workers reached 44.9 per cent. Such widening wage differentials were not just the result of men entering the kinds of occupations which offered chances for training and advancement. Even when men and women were recruited to the same occupations, as could happen in the plastics industry, wage differentials widened over time. In mixed-sex occupations men and women employed for only a short time in the plant had roughly similar wage levels, but as length of employment rose differences emerged. Female wage rates remained roughly constant, while male rates rose. Even in low-grade labouring and 'production assistant' work, female wages rose less than male as length of service increased. Men gained in two ways, therefore. Within a given occupation, their chances of advancement up incremental scales were greater, and they also had a better chance of promotion to higher-grade occupations.

CONCLUSIONS

The detailed examination of employment of men and women in the factories shows the extent and rigidity of the sexual division of labour. The segregation of women and men was overwhelming at all levels, with the only significant exceptions being quality control work and the shift-workers in F2. Such a sexual division could also be found in many other industries and factories, even though it is far from universal. In very small firms, particularly low-wage firms, and also in certain industries (plastics being one example for Brazil in the early 1980s), the sexual division of labour was less pronounced, but in most of the factories and industries researched it provided a fundamental line of division within the labour force. The pervasiveness of the sexual division of labour and segregation of men and women raises a number of fundamental issues. First, why are women so overwhelmingly concentrated at the bottom of the job hierarchy? Second, why is there such a thorough-going segregation of men and women, which goes far beyond that which might arise from any concentration of women into low-grade work? In other words, why is occupational and departmental segregation so pronounced even at the bottom of job hierarchies? Segregation went far beyond the exclusion of women from skilled work and other specialized areas. If this were the sole basis of the division of labour, then one would expect to see mixed-sex occupations towards the bottom of the job hierarchy, but even in lower-grade production and quality control jobs, a remarkably rigid segregation of men and women prevailed. Third, what is the relation between segregation and low wages for women? Are women confined to low-wage occupations, which are low-wage irrespective of whether they are occupied by women or men, or do the jobs occupied by women acquire low status and low wages?

The segregation of men and women workers appears quite clearly to be a basic principle structuring occupational hierarchies in industry. It is not merely the effect of the application of non-gendered principles to female and male workers with differing qualities of labour to offer. Occupational structures themselves quite clearly institutionalized a gendered labour force, defining quite distinct female and male labour forces, each with its own areas of work, wage rates, patterns of recruitment, and promotion practices. The bases upon which these separate female and male spheres are constructed and maintained, and also the types of employment practices operative within them is the subject of the remainder of this book.

3

Work and home: domestic situation and waged employment

INTRODUCTION

The analysis of occupational structures in Chapter 2 reveals a huge divide between the male and female manual labour forces in the seven plants studied. An examination of other aspects of factory life – such as discipline or types of work performed – would have revealed equally significant differences, as will be seen in Chapters 4 and 5. Upon entering the factory, workers are incorporated into a system whose basic structure is gendered. Two separate and opposing groups are defined – the female work-force and the male. They have different occupations, different promotion prospects, and are supposed to do different types of work. More than any personal characteristic (age, education, experience, and so on) a person's experience of factory life will be influenced right from the outset according to whether they fall into the masculine category or the feminine category. Women and men are treated differently, and women are treated as inferior to men.

Clearly the basic features of the gender identities constructed in factories – the separation into two and only two genders, the stereotyped masculine and feminine attributes, and the superiority of the masculine over the feminine – do not originate within the factory environment. On the contrary, these are the basic traits of the sex/gender system dominant in Brazil and other societies. Following Rubin, Chodorow defines such a system as including:

> 'Ways in which biological sex becomes cultural gender, a sexual division of labour, social relations for the production of gender and of gender-organised social worlds, rules and regulations for

sexual object choice, and concepts of childhood. The sex-gender system is, like a society's mode of production, a fundamental determining and constituting element of society, socially constructed, and subject to historical change and development.'

(Chodorow 1979: 84–5)

Following this abstract statement about the nature of the sex/gender system, Chodorow goes on to describe certain features of the sex/gender system 'in our own society' (presumably the USA). She points to a system which creates 'two and only two genders . . . and maintains a heterosexual norm', has a largely nuclear family, assigns primary parenting functions to women, has a sexual division of labour in which women's first duty is in the home and men's outside it, and is characterized by male dominance. In this sex/gender system women have access to a narrower range of jobs and earn less than men (1979: 85).

These features adequately characterize the family and occupational structures seen in São Paulo, and they determine the range of gender identities possible within factories in the region. When men and women enter a factory, or take up paid employment, they find that the principles of gender construction established in families and prevalent in society as a whole are also operative at work. Far from subverting male dominance and the rigid division into two genders, the organization of work incorporates it. Men are defined as 'breadwinners' – actual or potential – while women are seen as temporary and uncommitted workers. The work men do is over-valued, and that done by women devalued. Women's general experience of 'being always perceived and treated as members of a gender category about which there are all kinds of stereotyped beliefs, and which is inferior to the alternative gender category, that of men' (Whitehead 1978: 11) is maintained in the factory. Women's labour is regarded as inferior precisely because it is women's, and their right to work and commitment to it are questioned because of the assignment of primary parenting functions to them. While the seat of women's subordination may be the family, sexuality, and reproduction, the factory offers a further site for subordination. In Cockburn's elegant description:

'the family, as the throne of "patriarchy", has its own malevolent effectivity within capitalism and capitalist relations, it pursues women out into waged work.'

(1981: 54)

The general parameters of gender identities, then, are established in the domestic sphere. However, specific gender identities have to be established at work, too. Male and female forms of being workers are constructed in such a way as to preserve male dominance and regulate and limit women's access to the public sphere. More accurately, numerous masculine and feminine identities have to be constructed and maintained, reflecting differences not only of gender, but also of age, skill, race, marital status, and so on. In the factory such identities are subject not only to the gender hierarchy prevailing in society as a whole, but also to the pressures of capital–labour relations, the demands of the labour market which vary the extent and nature of women's access to paid employment, and the notions of equity which link effort with rewards and status. As Barrett and McIntosh have noted:

> 'More recently, feminists have emphasised how gender identities are not merely transported into the workplace but are created and structured there in definitions of feminity and masculinity that in turn feed back into the domestic meaning of gender.'
>
> (1982: 89)

The creation and maintenance of gender identities in the work-place can involve conflict and struggle. Male dominance has to struggle to maintain itself not only in the face of ideas of sexual equality, which may be more or less prevalent depending upon the strength of the women's movement and its influence on women workers and trade unions, but also against notions of justice, merit, and achievement.

Women as workers may largely accept notions of the male bread-winner and the female supplementary wage, or of men's innate capacities for certain kinds of work, but this does not mean that they will accept blatantly unequal treatment without resentment or protest. Men 'manage' the sexual division of labour so that such blatantly obvious inequalities are minimized. Male domination is most secure when the categories of familial ideology, such as the bread-winner, are coupled with work categories, such as skill, strength, and technical competence. In order to maintain male superiority in the factory men diminish women as workers, largely through stereotyping their work and identifying it as 'feminine'. This is a continuous process. Established places and identities can be challenged or undermined by shifts in technology and the tides of employment and unemployment that sweep economies periodically. At such times, the conflicts can become open and sharp, as examined, for example, in Cockburn's work on the printing industry (1983) and Milkman's study of female employment in the USA at the end of the Second World War (1983). But even apart from such sea-changes in employment, the establishment of gender identities in factories is a constant and complex activity. It involves a series of controls over what people do, how they relate to each other, how their work and wages are evaluated, and so on. The extent of such practices tends to remain hidden until such time as they fail, and even then conflicts over equal pay, employment rights, and access to certain types of work are rarely reported or discussed.

Attention will be focused on the work women and men do in factories, and the construction of stereotypes of masculine and feminine work in Chapter 4. In the current chapter the focus will be on the identities of women and men as employees in general and the relationship between home and work. In particular, we will explore (1) the domestic division of labour and the performance (or non-performance) of domestic labour by men and women according to their differing domestic situations at differing points in the lives, (2) parenthood, familial ideologies, and access to paid employment, and (3) management strategies with regard to the employment of men and women according to their marital and parental status and how managements shape their employment policies for men and women in accordance with both their perceptions of family life and the constraints of the labour market.

The analysis starts off, therefore, by distinguishing 'between the role of familial ideology, which asserts that a woman's primary responsibilities are those of housewife and mother, and the concrete constraints which caring for children and other dependants impose on certain women' (Beechey 1983: 42). The latter aspect is considered first, followed by the former. The implications of domestic labour for the meaning of work and employment strategies for men, unmarried and childless women as well as for wives and mothers will be given full consideration. It will be seen that women's situations vary significantly over their lives and that women's and men's working lives (in paid employment) are shaped by power relations within families, ideologies, practical necessities, and the opportunities opened up by managerial practices. It will also be seen that the working 'careers' of both men and women in Brazil are somewhat different from those in Europe. It will further be shown that managements do not merely respond to these differences passively, but rather mould the opportunities of different categories of men and women in accordance with their own perceptions of work and home.

DOMESTIC LABOUR

A full examination of the complex issues arising out of domestic labour and household structures would require a study of both domestic situations and paid employment starting from the household and then following its members into paid employment of all kinds. A factory study is limited by its lack of access to those who are not in paid employment and this is a particularly severe problem in Brazil because the overwhelming majority of married women do not work in factories. However, a factory study can still learn a considerable amount about the interrelation of domestic situation and paid employment, particularly when workers are interviewed in depth. The interviews in E3 provided information about performance of domestic labour in 100 households.[1] All the workers were asked about the nature of their households and the performance of domestic tasks within them. A sophisticated measure of domestic labour was unnecessary for this analysis, and emphasis was placed upon who was *responsible* for domestic tasks. All the workers interviewed were asked about the performance of a series of basic domestic chores in their household: washing clothes, ironing, cooking, washing dishes, cleaning the house, and shopping – the six tasks defined as core household duties by Oakley (1974: 49). In addition, workers in households with children were asked about childcare and education. For all the questions, workers were merely asked to state if the named tasks were (1) the sole responsibility of the respondent, (2) shared between the respondent and another household member, or (3) solely the responsibility of someone else in the household. The six non-childcare tasks were scored by awarding two points for sole responsibility, one for shared responsibility (including cases where workers did some of the work, such as washing their own clothes), and no points if the worker did not perform any labour in relation to that specific task. For the six tasks, therefore, a minimum of zero and a maximum of twelve points could be scored.[2]

Male domestic labour

The interviews in E3 revealed very little evidence of men performing anything more than cursory amounts of domestic labour. Whether as sons living with their parents, or as husbands living with wives, or as single, separated, or divorced men living in non-nuclear-family households, the male workers did very little domestic work. The five male workers living in households with adult couples (parents or uncles and aunts, for example) claimed to make no contribution to domestic labour whatsoever as can be seen in *Table 10.* All five were aged between 19 and 23 and they were serviced almost entirely by married women not in paid employment. The eight men who had neither wives nor mothers to service them made slightly greater contributions to domestic labour. The three men living with their sisters (but no other female relatives), for example, scored 3.3 points, but still devolved the majority of domestic labour on to these women (two of whom had paid employment), while the five male workers living in households without female members depended heavily on female help, using paid labour.

Table 10 *Performance of domestic labour by men according to their position in the household*

position in household[1]	*shopping*	*points scored*[2]						
		0	*1*	*2–3*	*4–6*	*6+*	*mean*	
son living with	included	5	—	—	—	—	0	= 5
both parents	excluded	5	—	—	—	—	0	
husbands living								
with wives	included	8	6	8	4	—	1.7	= 26
(and children)	excluded	18	3	4	1	—	0.7	
brothers living	included	—	—	2	1	—	3.3	= 3
with sisters	excluded	—	1	2	—	—	1.7	
men living alone								
or with other	included	1	—	—	2	2	5.4	= 5
men	excluded	1	—	2	1	1	4.0	

Source: Personal interviews.

Notes
1 Excludes one single parent.
2 For details of the scoring system, see text.

The married male workers made even more limited contributions to domestic labour than those living with their sisters. Eight of the twenty-six married men claimed to make no contribution whatsoever to the six specified domestic tasks, six claimed nothing more than a share in the shopping with their wives, and a further four said that they did all the shopping but nothing else in the house. The average score over the six tasks was 1.7 points out of a possible 12 or 0.7 out of 10 once shopping is excluded from the calculations. As shown in *Table 10*, 70 per cent of the married men did nothing other than the shopping. The contributions of the remaining 30 per cent were almost entirely confined to sharing a limited number of tasks with other family members, mainly wives, but even this statement may well overestimate their contributions to domestic labour. Surveys have shown that when tasks are 'shared' between husbands and wives, the woman does considerably more than the man (Hartmann 1981: 381), and Sarti's research in São Paulo indicated a similar situation. She confirms that a man's part in domestic labour is qualitatively different from a woman's, being complementary and irregular and having none of the continuous nature of female domestic labour (1983: 23). Only one of the twenty-six married men claimed to take full responsiblity for any one task other than shopping (cleaning in this case). Washing and ironing were left almost entirely to women, and only two men even claimed to share responsibility for them. In six of the twenty-six cases the workers' wives had some income-generating activity, but this did not seem to increase the men's contributions to domestic labour. This confirms the results of other studies, including that by Sarti mentioned above. Women are expected to perform most or all of the domestic labour, and paid employment for women does not lead to any of this responsibility being put on to men.[3]

The husbands and fathers also took very limited responsiblity for their children. Only two of the twenty-four married men with children claimed to play any role at all in taking care of them, and among the fifteen men with children of school age, only four claimed even to share in the supervision of the children's education – supervising homework or attending the school when required. Even though some men do certainly take children for walks or on trips at the weekend, none of the male workers ever mentioned any problems with childcare which might have affected their paid work. This was not the result of any nonchalance with respect to education and childcare on the part of the workers interviewed. They considered it to be an important matter for their wives to look after.

Overall then, the male workers made a very limited contribution to domestic labour. Certainly a wider definition of domestic labour, which included house construction and maintainence, would produce a higher figure for male domestic labour, given that many working-class families build (or participate in the building of) their own houses, but such work has the hallmark of male labour, irregularity and discontinuity. The only male worker who serviced other family members and clearly took responsibility for the running of the household was the sole single parent. Even this case may have been exceptional. The man lived with his five children aged between 6 and 12, and for some time much of the domestic labour had been performed by the eldest daughter, aged 13. She had recently left the household to go and live with her mother, and so the father was left with most of the chores. On the scoring system outlined earlier, he scored ten points, claiming to be responsible for everything except the washing up. However, the children were left to look after themselves in other respects and he did not claim to do any childcare or supervise their education.

Female domestic labour

Irrespective of their family situation, therefore, men performed little or no domestic labour. Such labour fell to women, and the women always did more domestic labour than males in similar household circumstances. However, domestic responsbilities differed considerably from one group of women to another. There was a clear 'circulation of domestic tasks' between women (Chabaud-Rychter, Fougeyrollas-Schwebel, and Sonthonnax 1985: 75–102). The extent of domestic labour performed by women working in the factory varied according to their status (daughter, wife, niece, for example) within the household, the presence of other adult women, and the number of people to be serviced. Women in households where other adult women were available for domestic labour did relatively little, while women who were the sole adult females in households performed large amounts of domestic labour.

The principles governing the allocation of domestic labour can be illustrated by reference to the eighteen women who *did not* live in nuclear families.[4] The seven women in this group scoring three points or less in *Table 11* all lived in households where one or more other women were available to do most of the domestic labour. In five cases mothers or sisters living in the household did most of the work, while in the other two the work was done by a domestic servant and a niece who was the daughter of the head of the household. At the other extreme, scores of 9 or more were scored by the women living alone and by two women who had to assume a leading role. One was a single mother of twins who lived with her frail mother, and the other lived with her brother and aunt, both of whom were in paid employment.

The forty-two women living in nuclear families fell into two very distinct groups. First, there were the daughters, twenty-five in all, who lived with both their parents and in many cases brothers and sisters as well.[5] Second, there were those women who were wives and/or mothers and the sole adult females in households where there were males or young people who might expect to be serviced by them. Nine of the women in this group were married and lived with husbands and children, and a further four lived just with their husbands. Four single parents with children under the age of 14 will also be considered as part of this group.

Table 11 *Performance of domestic labour by women according to their position in the household*

position in household	*points scored*[1]							
	0	*1*	*2–3*	*4–6*	*7–8*	*9+*	*mean*	
women living in non-nuclear households	2	1	4	4	3	4	3.8	= 18
daughters living with both their parents	7	7	3	8	—	—	2.0	= 25
wives/mothers as a sole adult female in the household								
married	1	—	—	—	4	8	7.9	=13
single parent	—	—	—	—	3	1	8.5	= 4

Source Personal interviews.

Note

1 For details of scoring system, see text.

The women living with both their parents made very limited contributions to domestic labour. Mothers and sisters performed most or all of the domestic work. Fourteen of the twenty-five 'daughters' scored either 0 or 1 point for their contributions to the six basic domestic tasks outlined earlier, as can be seen in *Table 11*. Their attitudes were summed up by the comment, 'When I get home from work I just rest and watch the soap operas.'[6] However, unlike male workers in similar circumstances, these women workers were not totally exempted from domestic labour. When the other women in the household could not take all the responsibility for domestic labour, the daughters were expected to help out. As *Table 11* shows, one-third (eight out of twenty-five) of the 'daughters' groups made some definite contributions to domestic labour, scoring between 4 and 6 points. In six of these cases the help provided by the daughter in paid employment was clearly related to the burdens of the mother, who was either in paid employment herself or had to service a particularly large household. In such cases working daughters were expected to help out (while sons and husbands were not), even though such contributions were restricted to helping at weekends or looking after their own things (washing just their own clothes, for example). Continuous availability to service household members was not required, and no major responsibilities for childcare were assumed.

Much more domestic labour was performed by the women workers who were the sole adult females in their households. They had to take overall responsibility for the six domestic tasks and also for childcare, combining this with nine hours and thirty-six minutes of paid work (starting at 7.30 am), a one-hour lunch break, and an average of forty minutes travel each day between home and the factory. Wives without children could just manage. Three of the four married women without children scored 10 or more points out of a maximum possible of 12 for the six tasks, as did a single parent whose son was aged 19. However, for women with children of school age or below, paid employment was only possible if some help with domestic labour was available. This necessary additional help tended not to come from husbands (among the married women) or other males in the household. Of the nine married women with children under the age of 15 included in the sample, six had husbands who did nothing but help with the shopping, and only one husband took complete responsibility for a domestic task other than shopping (according to the women interviewed). The three single parents with school-age children relied heavily on the labour of the elder daughters, who did some domestic labour and took care of the younger children during the day, and this pattern was also seen in the case of a married woman who had worked in the factory for six years as a single parent prior to marrying. In general, however, the married women relied more on the work of other relatives – sisters, mothers, mothers-in-law, and so on – and in two cases paid help. Four of the nine had their washing done by relatives or paid female help, and four had the ironing done. Even so, the average score for married women was still 8.1 points out of a possible 12, and only the woman whose daughter did all the domestic work scored less than 6 points.

Clearly women with children had to make arrangements for them during the day. Those living with their mothers and those with older children were able to leave childcare to them. The others had to resort to the labour of relatives, who ranged from sisters and sisters-in-law to mothers-in-law and stepmothers. Such help was crucial in determining the availability of women to continue or take up paid employment, and it was mentioned by men and women alike as a key factor in influencing decisions about paid employment of mothers. Sarti's assessment of the situation was amply confirmed by the research in the third electrical factory:

> 'When women have a job . . . they generally leave household jobs till the weekend. . . . However, the care of small children requires a constant presence of at least one person in charge of them – to keep an eye on them, to clean them, and to feed them. If arrangements can be made for the woman herself to look after the house, this is not the case with small children. She has to be substituted. It is for this reason that women in the Jardin das Camelias systematically mention the fact of not having anyone with whom to leave the children as the major impediment to working outside of the house.
>
> (Sarti 1983: 21)

None of the women interviewed used a crèche, and once again, men played no part.[7] The only exception to this was a woman whose husband took a month's holiday to look after the baby when she returned to work after maternity leave.

The information from the third electrical factory matches that presented by Sarti. She found that 34.9 per cent of the children of women in paid employment were left with relatives, 33.7 per cent with older children to look after them, 19.3 per cent were left on their own, and just 1.2 per cent were left with paid minders or domestic servants (Sarti 1983: 21). Although none of the women interviewed in the factory admitted to leaving young children on their own during the day, this seems likely to have happened in at least some instances, and domestic arrangements were precarious for all mothers. They broke down if relatives became unavailable for any reason and when problems such as child illness arose. In such circumstances the mother (never the father) was expected to cope.[8] Many women were just unable to continue work, although equally some women did not have the option of stopping work, even if they wanted to, as will be seen in the next section.

In E3 a number of women reported the difficulties they encountered when their children were ill or needed to be taken to clinics for vaccinations, and so on. The firm made few concessions for lateness and absenteeism, which were punished quite rigorously through the loss of the 'paid weekly rest-day',[9] and also by warnings, suspensions, and eventual dismissal. This could lead to serious problems as the following two cases can testify:

> 'If I have to take the child to the doctor, and I have a certificate to prove it, they shouldn't deduct the Sunday, but he [the manager in charge of the department] will not let me keep it. I was given a verbal warning. I've already had a written warning and a suspension. The lady who looks after my daughter is elderly, and she cannot take her to the doctor. Lately, [the daughter] has been ill. . . . I'm working here because I'm poor. My husband doesn't earn very much. I've asked to be sacked, but the boss won't sack me. I can't afford just to give in my notice, I need the money. With two suspensions now, if I'm absent a third time they'll sack me with due cause and I'll lose the money anyway.'
>
> (quality control worker)

> 'They think that we have too many problems, that we are absent from work too often. It's true, but we need to work, don't we? We need to buy things, don't we? We need milk, we need to pay people to look after the baby. They think it's just me, and that I

miss work too much. There's another woman with a child who never misses a day. But each of us looks after our children in our own way. It makes no difference to me. If my child is ill, I don't come to work. My boss says, "If this happens and the baby is ill, you can leave him with a neighbour." Me and my boss just don't get on.'

(assembler with a child of 13 months)

For purely practical reasons it was difficult for many women to combine responsibility for children and paid employment.[10]

FAMILIAL IDEOLOGY

The analysis of domestic labour shows that it is performed by women, and that married women are obliged to do it irrespective of whether they have paid employment outside the home. Clearly the weight of familial ideology assigns domestic labour to women, particularly wives and mothers. Married women have to combine domestic labour and paid employment, and young unmarried women know that this future is most likely to await them, if they marry (as most do). However, familial ideology involves not only the performance of a given amount of domestic work, but also notions of correct standards of domestic servicing, the proper order of household affairs, 'proper' care of children and rights of access to power, money, and the social world by men and women. Particularly important here are the ideologies of motherhood and the bread-winner, which assign definite priorities to adult males and females in households and also define paths to be followed by younger household members. These ideologies had a strong hold on both sexes, although there were also differences and contradictions between them.

The male workers in the third electrical factory had a clear view of the correct order of things. Their responsibilities lay in the factory and in supporting their families, while women were to look after the house and children. The married men saw themselves as the bread-winners, and the unmarried expected to assume this role. They ought to provide most or all of the family income through their 'family wage'. One man with eight children whose wife had had no paid employment since marriage said quite plainly, 'My duty is to work and take home the money. I provide the money. The duty of a woman is to stay at home.' Another man, whose wife had also never worked outside the home, was adamant about the reasons why women should not go out to work:

> 'In the first place, where is she going to leave the children? It's not right to leave them with other people. With this crèche thing you don't know if they will be very well looked after. And in the second place, she'll only be a mother in the evenings. She's got married and she should stay at home. If not, who's going to do the work in the home?'

In such circumstances a working wife would not only threaten the male's domestic comfort, but also provide an indictment of his earning power. Therefore the male workers sought the jobs and promotion that would give them enough money to finance the whole household. Such ideas were not confined to the married men. Six of the eleven single men interviewed were of the opinion that it was not good for women to 'work' (that is continue in paid employment) after marriage at all, and the other five felt that women should definitely stop work after the birth of their first child.[11]

The overwhelming majority of married men in E3 considered paid employment for married women to be dependent on suitable arrangements for domestic labour being made, but their notions of what might be suitable were so demanding that in effect women with children would be discouraged from paid employment altogether. Paid employment would be limited to the period (often quite short) between marriage and motherhood:

> 'I think that both [husband and wife] should work at the beginning, before having children, so that they get themselves on their feet. . . . To help the husband out, she should work, and then stay at home. It's wrong to work when you have children because they are left without proper care.'

> 'In my view, a woman shouldn't work if she has children, because you really have to trust someone if you are going to leave your children with them. You could arrive home and the child might be ill or running around without any clothes on. The mother should look after them. If there's no children, it's better for her to work and put some money together for emergencies etc.'

Once children arrived, the men expected their wives to stay at home, and in many cases this cessation of paid employment was seen to be long term. The men did not expect their wives to return to paid employment when the children grew older. Less explicitly, the men seemed to think that women had no right to work outside the home, irrespective of the age of children.

In spite of such attitudes, six of the twenty-six married men interviewed in the plant had wives who had income generating work, and the wives of the other twenty had worked outside the home at some point after marriage. There were two main reasons for this. First, the male workers did not always get their own way on these matters. There was quite a lot of evidence of conflict on this question, from both the men and women interviewed, and some wives did appear to have insisted on working after having children:

> 'A woman should not work if she has children. My wife wanted to work. She didn't need to, but she wanted to, and she fixed up a job.'

In this case the worker reported that his wife had been depressed and sleeping badly and had wanted to get out to work again, even though they had children aged 4 and 2. It was not clear if the worker saw this desire for paid employment as a solution to the problem or as a further sign of it. However, just as many husbands explicitly said that they had actively prevented their wives from taking paid employment, and this may well be the more usual situation.

Second, the men accepted that financial circumstances might oblige their wives to go out to work, even if this had undesirable consequences (from the men's point of view) for childcare and domestic labour. This could be couched in terms of an extreme case, 'My wife will only return to work if I am completely unable to work.' It could also be seen as a regrettable but common occurrence:

> 'It depends on need. Sometimes the husband earns the minimum wage, and it [the wife's wage] pays the rent. If the husband earns enough to keep up the house, pay the rent, then it's better for the woman to stay at home, because when she arrives at home after work, a lot of jobs build up for her to do. She doesn't have time to give a mother's care and affection. When a woman has children,

it's better for her not to work. My wife worked when our children were very small.'

In this case, then, a woman's income is seen as essential by the man. Far from being 'pin-money' in the man's eyes, the woman's wage is vital, even if not always very large, and it is only this necessity which justifies her working. Very few of the men thought that women had a clear right to work, and they did not consider that women might want to take up paid employment for reasons unconnected with the household budget. Basically the men saw domestic labour as a female responsibility, and paid employment as a temporary and unfortunate necessity which might endanger childcare and also proper servicing for themselves (mentioned by some male respondents). It was to be avoided wherever possible.

Male attitudes and the sexual division of labour in households severely circumscribed women's choices about paid employment. When unmarried, they were more or less free to work, having little responsibility for domestic labour, and the money they earned was their own. Most of the unmarried women contributed well under half their earnings to the household budget, and they enjoyed both the social side of work friendships and the money they received at the end of the month. But even as single women, the workers in the third electrical factory were well aware of the conflicting pressures of male control, domestic labour, childcare, financial necessity, and financial independence which could affect their chances of working or not working if they married and had children.

There was every indication that the single women in the plant (unlike many of the men) did not regard marriage in itself as a reason for stopping work. As can be seen in *Table 12*, over 70 per cent of the single women thought that it would be a good thing to work after marriage, and nearly 80 per cent expected to continue work. The reasons for this were quite often financial – helping out with the household budget, getting a new home established, and in some cases the need to continue supporting other relatives – but women also mentioned a positive attachment to work outside the home, reluctance to be stuck at home all day, and also the advantages of having a separate source of income.

'It's good to carry on working after getting married because sometimes the husband's wage just isn't enough to look after the

Table 12 *Women's attitudes to work after marriage: single women, E3*

1 'Is it good or bad for women to continue working after marriage?'
2 'Do you intend to continue work after marriage?'
3 'Is it good or bad for women to continue working after having children?'

	good/ yes %	*depends* %	*bad/no* %	*don't know* %	
1 good to work after marriage	71.9	1.6	23.4	3.1	=38
2 intend to work after marriage	79.7	14.1	6.3	0	=38
3 work after having children	26.6	14.1	54.7	4.7	=38
4 qu. 3 for those answering good/yes to qu. 1 and 2	28.3	8.7	56.5	6.5	=28

Source Personal interviews. The responses have been weighted to reflect the sample, as specified in Appendix 1.

house. And women like to buy their own things. Asking your husband for money all the time is rotten.'

Rather more forcefully, another woman suggested:

> 'You could separate in the future, and until the divorce came through things would be difficult. If you're already working, you've got something to fall back on. It's a lot easier to carry on working [than start afresh].'

Such independence had to be fought for, however. Some of the women mentioned that their boyfriends wanted them to stop work even before marriage, and others told of cases of conflict:

> 'My sister, who worked at Wapsa, got married. She wanted to work, but her husband wouldn't let her. I think it's quite common. Chauvinism, you know. Take my boyfriend. I say to him, "When we marry, I want to work" and he says "No". I reckon I'm going to work. I'll only stop if the firm sacks me and I

can't find another job. I'll sort something out, and he [the boyfriend] will end up agreeing to it.'

In most cases the desire for independence did not extend to a wish to continue working after the birth of the first child. Among the 70 per cent of women who thought it was good to continue work after marriage and intended to do so, only 28.3 per cent intended to work after the birth of their first child, while over half definitely intended to stop work. Typical feelings are expressed in this comment from a quality control worker interviewed in the second automotive factory, who was willing to resist pressure to stop work only until her first child came along:

'I'm getting married in December. I'd like to work for six more months after that and then leave when the children come along. My boyfriend doesn't want me to work at the moment, but I like it. When you first get married, staying at home all day must be horrible for those women who are used to working.'

Paid work for most women in the plant was something to do up to, but not after, the birth of children.

The reasons for this are not hard to find. First, combining paid employment and motherhood in the plant was extremely difficult, as was seen earlier. No concessions were made for women with children. Second, many women positively wanted to devote time to bringing up their children, and there were strong pressures on all women with small children to stay at home and look after them, unless other reliable close relatives could be found to do it. Finally, it was seen in the previous section that men expected women in paid employment to perform almost all the domestic labour. If they could not arrange childcare and off-set some domestic labour, paid employment would be impossible, and even if this could be arranged, a full-time job would mean all the exertions of a double day in the factory and in the home.

In spite of all this, a significant number of women working in the third electrical factory had children under the age of 14 as can be seen in *Table 13*. More importantly, many of the mothers had young children. A 50 per cent sample of production and quality control workers in E3 (see Appendix 1 for details) showed that 30 out of 121 women had children under the age of 14. Eighteen of these women

Table 13 *Women workers and children born before and after entry to plant: E3, October 1982*

parental status when hired	*number of children born while employed in E3*			
	0	*1*	*2*	*total*
no children	91	10	2	103
one child	7	3	—	10
two children	3	1	—	4
three children	4	—	—	4
total	105	14	2	121

Source A sample of sixty-one cases selected from personnel department records in addition to the sixty women interviewed. The 121 women represent a 50 per cent sample of all women in production and quality control work, stratified by department and length of service.

entered the plant with children, and twelve of them had at least one child under the age of 6 (school age) at that time. Four of this group of women also gave birth to a second child while working in the plant. The other twelve women entered the plant childless but gave birth to one or more children while continuing to work in the factory. Clearly a significant minority of women combined paid employment in the factory with the raising of young children. Over 20 per cent had worked while their youngest child was under school age, and 13 per cent had worked through and after at least one successful pregnancy.

A significant minority of mothers working in the factory were divorced, separated, widowed, or single parents, but financial pressures could also be felt by women living with men. The single, childless women in the plant were well aware of this. Although almost a quarter of them did not want to continue paid employment in the factory after marriage, only two of the eight women concerned felt certain that they would be able to. Some of the women had a far less optimistic view of male earning power than that taken by many men:

> 'I don't think it's nice to carry on working. When I marry, the responsibility for the home will be mine. . . . I'll work to help out, but only if I have to. But it is hard to find a man who earns enough to keep his wife at home.'

In fact this statement may be unduly pessimistic. Factory workers are probably more likely to earn a 'family wage' than other workers, and women in factories are probably more likely than others to find factory-worker husbands, both because of work-place meetings, and because of the high social status enjoyed by women workers in industry relative to, say, domestic servants.

Financial pressure, then, is likely to play a major role in decisions about returning to work with young children or continuing to work through and after pregnancy. While there may be other reasons, such as the desire for independence mentioned by some of the single women above, and while women may well not reveal such reasons because of the pressures of familial ideology (as Karen Stone rightly points out – 1983: 36) a husband's low wage or the lack of a male wage-earner altogether appear to be very important factors. As one of the single parents made clear:

> 'One thing you can be certain of, women don't work because they like it, but because they need to work. They don't work for fun. It's because they really need to. It's not out of choice that they leave their children with other people. These days a woman has to struggle to live, helping her parents before she marries and helping her husband afterwards.'

Similarly most of the married women interviewed stated that they would have to make cuts in purchases of essential items if they were to lose their income. As one woman assessed the importance of her wages for the household budget:

> 'It is very important. Can I tell you something? None of the girls in my department work for fun. Their husband's wages are just not enough. Or they have to help their parents, or they need money for education. Each one has her own reason for being at work.'

Although the women continued to use the language of 'helping out' and 'supplementing' their husbands' incomes, the reality was that their contributions were often much more substantial and fundamental. Giving up working in the factory was out of the question:

> 'Without my wages things would be impossible. I'd quickly have to find another job. I can't even bear to think about it. On his wage alone there wouldn't be enough to live on.'

'I'd have to take up domestic service. We couldn't manage at all without my wages.'

As a result women made arrangements for their children to be looked after and stayed at work, even if this meant, for example, leaving the children from Sunday evening to Friday evening with a grandparent in a distant part of the city. Whatever arrangements were made, they had to allow the women to be in the factory from 7.30 am to 5.45 pm five days a week.

Women, then, may find that the 'option' to stop work is not available, whether they want to take it or not. As a result it was not unusual to find mothers working in the factory. However, the pattern of work for mothers was not that of a return to work when children were of school age. Among the thirty women with children found in the sample of half the production and quality control workers, only three had entered the plant as married women with their youngest child over the age of 5, and at least one of these had first returned to work in another factory when her child was aged 3. The remainder were split into three groups of equal size: (1) single parents and divorced, separated, and widowed women, (2) married women who entered E3 when their youngest child was aged 5 or younger,[12] and (3) women who had entered the plant without children, and subsequently had children and continued to work. Part of the explanation for this may lie within family structures. Once women stop work, their husbands pressure them not to resume, and once men can show that the household can manage to live on one income, they will try to stop their wives resuming paid employment. Similarly men's wages are likely to rise or remain constant over time rather than fall, and so the financial pressure for women to work is more likely to ease as time goes on, thereby making returns to work for financial reasons unlikely. Married women might also prefer work which is possibly easier to combine with domestic labour, such as daily cleaning jobs. At the same time managements also played a role – in E3 specifically, and in industry generally. This was not confined to a failure to take positive steps to encourage mothers into work: part-time jobs or short shifts, for instance. Managements actively structured their recruitment strategies around the marital and parental status of both male and female workers, and it is to this that attention is now turned.

MANAGEMENT STRATEGIES

In general managements adopt policies with regard to wage rates, training and promotion, stability, and so on, with the aim of fulfilling the labour needs of the enterprise in terms of quantity, control, motivation, and cost. The marital and parental statuses of workers are relevant factors in their calculations, both for women and for men. Managers have clear preferences for different types of workers, which have to be put into practice within the constraints posed by labour markets and the internal operation of the enterprise. A considerable degree of specialized and differentiated hiring of men and women was found in some of the factories, as well as differences between one factory and another.

Management and male workers

The assumption of the bread-winner role by men has certain advantages for managements. It may make the bread-winner more responsible and careful to keep his job, and it may also make him available for overtime in the evenings and at weekends. The bread-winner is a person cut out for paid employment: he is not encumbered by domestic work or children. His mind will be on the job. However, the bread-winner is also required to earn sufficient money to sustain the household, and he wants to provide most or all of its income. This places him under financial strain, as many writers have noted.[13] By far the largest group of male workers in industrial employment is aged between 20 and 30, and this is the time when financial responsibilities tend to increase. If men want to avoid their wives taking regular paid employment and support both them and the children as they come along, then they need something approaching a 'family wage'. This puts pressure on wage levels, which are rather low in Brazil, and it can lead to frustration for workers and high rates of turnover as workers seek jobs which pay enough to support a family.

In some industries this problem hardly arises because male wage rates are relatively high, or because opportunities for training and promotion are good. In the case of the first pharmaceutical firm, for example, the workers earned rates of pay for basic production work which were well above those prevailing in the electrical and automotive firms. The basic male production grade in F1, grade 3, was paid about the same as the most skilled production jobs (radio and television technicians, carpenters, and shapers) in E3. The higher-grade production workers in F1 were paid wages equivalent to maintenance workers in E3. Most of the pharmaceutical workers presented few problems for management. They earned relatively high wages, and their skills were not very transferable; 45 per cent had been employed for more than five years, and the labour force was older and better-educated than those in some of the electrical and automotive plants. No special hiring policies were required. However, there is some evidence to show that F1 took steps to avoid problems with the few male workers restricted to the bottom two grades. The eight workers concerned fell into two equal-size groups: (1) workers hired in their 40s and having been employed for three years or more, and (2) younger, recently hired (approximately one year) workers. The three workers on grade 1, and one of those on grade 2 had an average age of 49 and an average length of employment of four years. They were older workers in dead-end jobs, hired when at least 40 years old and probably already resigned to low-paid, unskilled work. In contrast, the second group of four had been hired only recently. While this may reflect merely the timing at which management decided to use men on packaging machinery, it may also arise from a tendency seen in industry for younger men to remain in low-grade jobs for a relatively short period of time. Managements are aware that men in their 20s will push for promotion out of low-wage employment, and so they deliberately seek older men for dead-end jobs and try to provide promotion prospects for younger men. This pattern was seen more starkly in low-wage plants.

Some of the firms studied were 'low-wage' enterprises and this meant careful planning in the employment of male workers. In such firms unskilled production pay was insufficient to support a family. Workers looking for a 'family wage' needed promotion to higher-grade jobs, which carried significant increases in pay. An unskilled male production worker in the electrical and components firms studied could have expected wage rises of 50–100 per cent through internal promotion and on-the-job training over a period of three or four years. As a result workers pressed very hard for promotion, and managers were well aware of the strong expectations of promotion among the less skilled male operatives; failure to achieve promotion led to frustration, dissatisfaction, and high rates of turnover in the work-force.

The most obvious signs of such frustration and turnover (apart from managerial comments on the problem) came from the leaving interviews conducted by many personnel departments. In three factories records were kept which showed the circumstances in which workers left their jobs. Excluding those cases where the reason for leaving was either cut-backs in staff or unknown, the major causes of male turnover were 'seeking better job opportunities', 'low wages', and 'lack of interest'. These three categories accounted for 58 per cent of male exits in E2 and a similar proportion within a much smaller sample of workers in A2.[14] The first two categories indicate workers leaving on their own initiative because of frustration over promotion, while 'lack of interest' was a common term used by personnel departments to denote workers who provoked their dismissal by being uncooperative.[15]

Managements sought to minimize such turnover by matching workers' earning power and expectations with different job prospects. They wished to avoid problems with men pushing for higher wages, while maintaining low wages for some men. The managers in E3, an avowedly low-wage firm, expressed the problem succintly:

> 'If we are hiring an unskilled [male] worker, then we would tend to give preference to an unmarried man. His wages are lower, and he has a longer time in which to move upwards. For skilled labour, we prefer workers with more responsibility. Married men. It's a question of their age etc.'
>
> (head of the personnel department)

Young men could be paid low wages as long as their promotion prospects in the longer term looked reasonable. But for dead-end jobs a different approach was required:

> 'Their age varies a lot according to the area which needs them. For example, in an area where there is no career, no future, where the work is always the same and will be in ten, twenty or thirty years' time, a young man will soon feel that he has no chance of promotion. So I prefer to hire people who cannot find a job, who understand their situation and have adapted to it. Where there is a process of training and learning, I go for people of twenty to twenty-two years' old, but we take on people of thirty-five to

fifty, and even fifty year olds, if they can show that they are good.'

(manager, woodworking department)

A typical example of a 'dead-end' worker in the woodworking department was a cleaner interviewed in 1982. Hired as a cleaner at the age of 50 after a lifetime of work in agriculture, he was still a sweeper ten years later. His case was similar to the grade 1 male workers in F1.

This cleaner in E3 was exceptional. He was the only male worker interviewed in the plant who was still classified as unskilled after having worked in the plant for more than one year. Similarly he was one of only three workers out of a total of sixteen men hired in the production departments as unskilled labourers who had had children at the time of hiring. One interpretation of these figures would be the conclusion that the firm genuinely tried to create promotion opportunities for younger male workers, treating the 'labourer' category as a temporary entrance grade. As a result there would be few longer-service unskilled workers. However, it seems just as likely that the firm could not, generally speaking, provide such promotion opportunities for everyone and that the absence of longer-service unskilled male workers was due to frustration and turnover along the lines found in E2 above.

Such patterns of hiring, promotion, and turnover produced quite distinctive age profiles for different sections of the male labour forces in low-wage firms, as can be seen in *Table 14*, which presents data for men (and also women, whose situation is discussed below) in two plastics firms. In skilled work – setting, tool-room, and maintenance – the labour force was relatively old, with well over half being over 30 years of age. This is because it takes time for them to train, and even if they leave one job, they can find work with other firms, who will hire trained and experienced workers even if they are in their 30s and 40s. The ancillary workers were even older, and in part this is accounted for by the use of workers with no ambition in portering and cleaning work, and in part by the use of mature men for security work. The production workers, on the other hand, were very young – only 26 per cent over the age of 30. Among unskilled production the figure was even lower – 16 per cent. As was noted above, managers were reluctant to recruit men

Table 14 *Proportion of workers over 30 years old by functional category and sex: two plastics factories, March 1981*

functional category	*men* %	*women* %
production	26.1	20.2
quality control	38.4	23.4
tool-room and maintenance	59.6	—
machine-setters	72.0	—
ancillary workers[1]	85.1	81.8
total	42.5	27.6

Source Employers' documentation accompanying the payment of the annual Trade Union Contribution to the union.

Note[1]

1 This category includes security staff, cleaners, canteen workers, and other hourly-paid workers not working in technical, administrative, or clerical occupations.

with families to support into low-wage work, unless such men were already resigned to earning low pay. At the same time, younger workers who failed to gain promotion from low-grade production to higher grade work would tend to move in search of other jobs. At some point, however, other jobs become impossible to find, and they leave industry altogether, to be replaced by younger and fitter male workers. Even when men do not move jobs of their own accord, such replacement is likely to occur through normal labour turnover on management initiative.

Given that transfers from production to non-production work seemed to be quite restricted, the relative youth of the male production labour force suggests that a large number of male workers are forced out of industrial employment altogether as they failed to obtain the promotion and skill which made industrial work attractive to them and their abilities attractive to employers as they grow older. In low-wage industries, then, the male labour forces could be quite young. The 1979 RAIS data (see Appendix 2, p. 208) for the state of São Paulo showed that 68 per cent of manual workers in the plastics industry were 30 years old or younger. While a rapidly expanding labour force and population in Brazil will tend to skew the labour force to the younger age groups, it seems to be the case that management policies skew the distribution even further.

Management and women workers

In the 1970s and 1980s industrial employers in Brazil generally had a large pool of available female labour from which to recruit. This pool included both married and single women. As we have seen, married women did make themselves available for industrial employment for a variety of reasons, and in some factories significant numbers of married women and mothers were employed. When factory E2 was hiring workers in 1982, 40 per cent of those filling in application forms admitted to having children under the age of 14, and a further 6 per cent to being married, but without children.[16] However, managements had strong prejudices against older women, and above all those with children. Some firms were reluctant to allow women who married to continue in employment, while others allowed their female employees to have children, but made no concessions for their increased domestic responsibilities, which effectively forced many of them out of a job. Finally, many firms were reluctant to hire women with children, even if the children were of school age, which meant that women found it difficult to return to factory work later in life.

Most of the managers interviewed viewed everything relating to domestic labour – and in particular to children – as a distraction from work. Production managers, above all, seemed to regard mothers as a constant source of problems, who would be continually drawn away from work by their domestic responsibilities:

> 'The married women are much more of a problem. They miss work and give more trouble. They have more worries and responsibilities. Children, husbands, sickness in the family etc. All of this gets in the way.'
>
> (foreman, E3)

A similar reluctance to employ married women was expressed by a production manager in the same plant:

> 'I've already done tests. At first, I preferred married women because the rate of pregnancy among single women is higher. Later, I saw that married women caused the same problems, and had some others as well. They start to miss work a lot to look after

> the child, or because they've no one to leave the child with, or because their minder doesn't turn up and they have to stay at home etc. And then there's taking children for vaccinations etc. You can't really count on married women.'

However, different firms put these prejudices into practice in different ways.

The clearest strategy on female employment, and the one most blatantly prejudicial to women, was found in factory F1. For women, just as for men, the plant paid wages substantially higher than in the automotive and electrical plants studied. The lowest-grade female production workers in F1 were paid more than the highest-grade female production worker in E3. Paying such relatively high wages, F1 was able to secure a stable, responsible, and well-qualified female labour force by employing relatively well-educated women in their late teens or early 20s and expecting them to remain in the plant until they married: 76.8 per cent of female production workers in the plant were aged between 18 (no under-18s were employed) and 25. Turnover was low by Brazilian standards – 30.8 per cent of the women had been employed for five years or more, and a further 54.7 per cent had been employed for between two and five years.

The management in the plant aimed to employ women until they married, but no longer. Marriage was associated with pregnancy, maternity leave, and childcare in a quite exaggerated way. The head of production in F1 responded immediately and unambiguously to a question about the employment of married women:

> 'They marry and then they become pregnant. They have three months off work. They are not at work, but the firm still has to pay out for them. Let's suppose we have 200 girls. If 10 per cent marry, we have twenty of them on maternity leave for three months. It's a very serious problem.'

Quite why he should assume that women who marry will immediately and regularly have children is not clear, but the resulting policy was designed to avoid any chance of this happening. Management refused to hire married women, sacked women upon marriage, and also dismissed women who had children as soon as they returned from maternity leave.[17] The firm's policy was open and well known:

> 'It is the Pharmaceutical Division's philosophy not to employ married women. The concern is not the marital status as such, but the dependants. We do not admit single mothers, although there are exceptions, when women hide the fact that they have children. They [the female employees] are not allowed to marry. If they inform their boss about it, they are dismissed automatically.'
>
> (recruitment manager, F1)

The personnel department described its policy as being designed to 'meet the mutual interests of the firm and the employee'. In fact the leaving interviews showed many women not to be convinced that their interests were being served by it. A number of women expressed a willingness to continue working in the factory, and even more stated that they would be looking for another job. Of 102 women leaving the plant in 1980–81, exactly half were explicitly dismissed because of marriage or having a child. They had been employed, on average, for three and a half years. Although one manager argued that after five years working in packaging anyone would be ready to leave anyway, the firm did not restrict the policy to unskilled workers. The management were perfectly willing to sack experienced and responsible women workers who had been in the plant a long time and not even supervisors were spared. Management clearly felt that it could obtain a perfectly adequate labour force while employing only single and childless women. While the firm's policy was not 100 per cent successful, it largely achieved its aims. In two years only seven women were sacked after taking maternity leave. Of the 172 women workers in the plant in July 1982, only 9 had children.[18]

F1's policy was not unique. The second automotive plant had pursued a similar practice up to the early 1980s, although it had discontinued it by 1983 after an internal struggle between production managers and the personnel department.[19] However, the policy seems to have been pursued more single-mindedly in F1 than elsewhere, and in other firms married women and women with children were more in evidence. Three reasons seem to account for this: (1) the selection of older women for certain specific jobs, (2) the labour market constraints faced by low-wage firms, and (3) management doubts about the practical advantages and disadvantages of not employing women with children. These will be discussed in turn.

In spite of a strong preference for employing single women in production jobs, managements did employ older women in certain specific areas, such as cleaning and canteen work. The young, single, and childless women so much in evidence in production and quality control jobs were reluctant to do cleaning and canteen work, which was considered either dirty, heavy, or demeaning. Hence, managements had to employ older women. Two personnel managers were quite clear on this point:

> 'For cleaners we give priority to married women: over 30 years old and married. A young girl on this kind of job would feel very inferior in relation to the girls on the line. They work in clean surroundings, while she works with dust and dirt. In the beginning we tried to use girls, but we had to change.'
>
> (personnel manager, E3)

> The older women in the kitchen are more stable. The work there is rather heavy and girls of 18 do not like to do it. In the case of the cleaning, only older women put up with it.'
>
> (personnel manager, A1)

Therefore managers hired workers who were older and more likely to have children than those employed in production and quality control. In E3 85 per cent of the cleaners were married, and 62 per cent had children under the age of 14. In E1 and A1, where there were very few women with children in production, 66 per cent and 90 per cent respectively of cleaners and canteen workers had children under the age of 14. A similar situation was found in the plastics firms, as was seen in *Table 14*: 80 per cent of the ancillary staff (mainly cleaners) were over 30, compared to only 20 per cent of the production workers. In fact 60 per cent of the female ancillary workers in the two plastics firms were over 40, compared to just 3 per cent of the production workers.

A second major factor opening up some chances of industrial jobs to older women was the labour market situation facing low-wage firms. In such firms the prejudices and preferences of managers were not necessarily different from those seen in F1 (with the exception of cleaning and other similar staff, as noted immediately above), as can be seen from this comment from the personnel manager in A1:

> 'Minors [under 18 years old] are inconvenient because they have to take their annual holiday in a single period. So, we hire them at 16 or 17, which means they are ready for full production at 18. The problem is marriage. This normally occurs between the ages of 20 and 25, and so a woman who works from 16 to 25 is reasonably stable. The employment of older women is a question of cost. A woman of 21 already earns more than a girl of 17, but she doesn't produce any more. Therefore, we prefer girls just out of school.'

The firm concentrated on hiring younger women: 68.1 per cent of all the production and quality control workers in the plant had been hired when aged 20 or under, and 93.7 per cent had no children on entry to the plant. The management saw such younger and inexperienced women as more likely to accept low wages and to be less resistant to routine and repetitive work than older women.

This policy was not without its costs. Because the firm paid much lower wages in F1, turnover in the plant was very high, for both men and women. In 1979, at a time of expansion and hiring of new workers, exits from the plant totalled 45 per cent of the average size of the labour force employed in the year. Very few workers, men or women, stayed in the plant five years, let alone the nine years from 16 to 25 mentioned above by the personnel manager.[20] Although the firm accepted the high turnover rate and refused to hire older women in order to reduce it, unlike one of the electrical firms studied by Paul (1983: 49–50), the turnover among women workers was reduced by taking a softer line than F1 on marriage and motherhood. Women who married were allowed to stay on at the plant if they indicated that they were not intending to have children immediately, and according to company records, 15 per cent of the production and quality control workers employed for more than a year in the plant had married while working there.

Another easing of policy in A1 arose as a result of labour shortages. Low-wage firms were more likely to have to relax hiring criteria at times of relative tightness in the labour market, and the personnel manager in A1 admitted to having to go to the extreme of employing single parents when labour market conditions were tight:

> 'When the economy was at its peak we ended up admitting single parents. We had no option. And we have women who put on their application forms, "I'm married, but I'm a person and I need to live." And then there are those who hide the fact and manage to get in. The firm does not take action against them, but it doesn't let it get out of hand.'

Even so, the numbers involved were very small. Well under 5 per cent of those hired by A1 both before and after the onset of the crisis were registered as having children on admission, and a policy of hiring single and childless women could be maintained for most of the time.

How then can one explain the larger numbers of mothers and married women working in E2 and E3? Labour market pressures may be part of the answer. Both plants were situated in areas of dense, industrial development in the city of São Paulo, while El and the two automotive plants were situated in more distant parts. However, there is evidence that some managers in the two São Paulo plants had reservations about the practical advantages of a policy of employing only single and childless women. Two factors seemed to lead to reservations about such a policy.

In the first place, it was recognized that avoiding the hiring of married women did not necessarily resolve the pregnancy and motherhood 'problem'. Single mothers, it was suggested by a manager in E2, became pregnant in such numbers that refusing to hire married women in no way resolved the problem of maternity leave and motherhood. Similarly the personnel manager in E3 remarked that:

> 'The married women are less likely to become pregnant, and they do it in a conscious way. If a single woman becomes pregnant it causes a lot of emotional problems.'

The problems of married women might not be considered to be worse than those of the unmarried:

> 'The married women . . . brings her problems from home into work, but there are lots of problems with the single women as

> well. They become pregnant, provoke abortions, and then faint while working on the line etc.'
>
> (production manager, E2)

A similar opinion was expressed by the manager of another major electrical company, interviewed in 1986. Employing single women could worsen the 'pregnancy problem' rather than alleviate it. According to Sarti, contraception was 'widespread' in the working-class district she studied in São Paulo (1985: 221), and the degree of control over fertility exercised by working mothers or wives may be better than that often achieved by single women.

In the second place, some managers considered that women who had difficulties in finding work were good employees because they were so dependent on the employment that they could obtain. Thus managers talked of the advantages of employing older, married women and single parents. Marianne Herzog has described how older women and women in difficult personal circumstances can be trapped in one job and dependent on that single employer for their livelihood (1980: 48–53), and a similar analysis was provided by a production manager in E2.

> 'The older woman is more responsible. She pays more attention. She tries to produce better quality so that she is not sacked when the cut-backs come. The younger girl has more options. She can fix up a job anywhere and has a mother and father to fall back on. She works to buy clothes and things. The older women need the wage packet.'

In E2 this kind of consideration appears to have been more than just talk: 18.3 per cent of the female production and quality control workers had been hired when over the age of 30, and 26.0 per cent had been hired when married. There was no indication that this policy had been reversed after the onset of the crisis in 1981. Of the 612 production and quality control workers hired in 1982, only 58 per cent were single and childless. Thirty per cent had children, and a further 12 per cent had entered the plant married, but without children.

Similar considerations could be advanced in the case of single parents. They would need the income, and they might be expected to arrange adequate and durable childcare:

> 'We have had good results with [female] single parents. . . . They are responsible. They want to give their child an education. They are excellent employees. They dedicate themselves to their work and do not cause any problems. When they really need to work, they have someone who they can trust to look after the children. Normally, they are no trouble, and when they have problems this has very little impact on their work.'

Clearly no concessions are being made here. Single parents have to prove themselves as good as, or better than, single, childless women who are generally in plentiful supply.[21] The full costs and advantages of such policies are impossible to quantify. Certainly some women in E2 had problems with children, as indicated by the leaving interviews. Similarly female absenteeism among direct production workers in E2 seemed to run at about 30 per cent above the male rate, and given that unjustified absenteeism was strictly controlled, women with children (and hence attendance problems) might have displayed higher rates than younger, childless women. However, there is no evidence that managements based their own policies on such exact calculations. Set beliefs and established practice seemed to be the main determining factors.

In the final analysis such management practices amounted only to limited exceptions to a well-defined general management preference for women workers: work up to marriage or the birth of children. Factories were mainly oriented to making maximum use of women in the period from their late teens through to the mid-20s, discarding them when they had, or might appear to be likely to have, children. Not surprisingly, many of the longer-service women workers in the plants studied had entered relatively young and either remained single or continued working after marriage and/or having children. A return to work with the youngest child of school age was restricted by widespread managerial reluctance to hire women in such circumstances. Firms were able to recruit the bulk of their female labour forces from younger, single, and childless women, and any core of more experienced and mature workers could be sifted out of this large group over a period of time. For the majority of women, the firms made it difficult to continue work after marriage or after having children, and household pressure also pushed strongly in this direction. By the time such household pressures had eased, women were considered 'too old' for industrial work.

CONCLUSIONS

The sexual division of labour in households and power relations between men and women are clearly of crucial importance for understanding the access that they have to work and the expectations they take into it. Women are obliged to take on domestic responsibilities which limit access to paid employment. Given the big difference between the activity rates of single and married women in Brazil, and also the strong pressure by men on women not to take paid employment outside the home if there are children to be looked after, the domestic situation of women is probably a more important determinant of women's employment possibilities in Brazil than in Europe. For many theories of women's employment, such domestic situations provide all that is required to account for women's disadvantage. Women's low pay and lack of access to better jobs would be accounted for by their intermittent participation in paid employment, or the domestic responsibilities which drew them away from an exclusive dedication to paid work, or the lack of training and education which arises from expectations of a domestic role.

It would be hard to underestimate the importance of either women's domestic responsibilities or men's assumption of the bread-winner role on their commitment to and availability for industrial work. However, it is quite clear that this alone does not account for the characteristics of female and male factory employment. The latter part of this chapter highlighted the importance of managerial policies in determining employment prospects, and these policies were based on very clear notions of gender. Managements treated men and women as two homogeneous and diammetrically opposed categories, forcing individuals to conform to one of the two stereotypes. Cockburn's comment about the 'malevolent effectivity' of patriarchy, cited in the introduction to this chapter, clearly does have relevance. 'Patriarchy' pursues women actively into the work-place. Women who engaged in factory work were treated as a single, inferior gender category, and their chances in the factory were largely determined by this, rather than by their personal characteristics. All single women were treated as potential wives and/or mothers who will present problems with childcare. Similarly all women were treated as temporary and uncommitted workers, while men were treated as stable, long-term employees. Managements forced individuals into these categories. In F1, for example, women who might have stayed on at the plant were forced to leave, while managements went out of their way to stabilize male workers by offering promotion opportunities and careful matching of workers to jobs.

Quite clearly this process of gender construction – the definition of two distinct categories, male workers and female workers – could not stop at the point of recruitment. Men's and women's expectations of employment and a working life are shaped by the experience of work over time and the opportunities available to people in similar circumstances. Thus, for example, women's 'dedication' to domestic tasks is reinforced by dead-end jobs and low pay. Men would find it hard to assume the bread-winner role if many men lacked relatively good pay and promotion prospects. However, male superiority has to be maintained in the factory in the face of the actual work performed by women and men and their experiences of factory life. The gender identities which are already clearly defined at the point of recruitment depend to some extent on the preservation of segregation and hierarchy in the everyday life of the factory itself, and Chapter 4 is concerned with this aspect of the construction of gender in the factory.

4

Factory hierarchy and gender

INTRODUCTION

Chapter 3 has shown that, even before entering a job, men and women were clearly distinguished from each other and regarded as two distinct groups. In terms of a hierarchy of work, the male group was clearly considered superior potential workers to the female group by managers, by male workers and, to a considerable extent, by the female workers. Women were seen as temporary and largely uncommitted workers, whose work was largely confined to the period prior to marriage (in the view of the male workers) or prior to parenthood (in the view of most of the women). Men, in contrast, saw themselves and were seen as life-time workers, seeking a working 'career' which would guarantee a family wage. Women were treated as 'girls', whether young or old, while men were treated as responsible adults. Women were held by the men to be earning useful, but supplementary, wages, while men regarded themselves as bread-winners. Women were expected to devote their main long-term energies to children and the family, while men's commitment to waged work was reinforced by marriage and parenthood.

Already, then, prior to entry into the labour market or factory, women and men were strongly differentiated by their domestic situations. This differentiation was not limited to availability for work. It concerned, too, status as potential workers, expectations of work, and clear notions of the general areas of work suitable for women and men. Such differentiations would have been increased by education and by the institutional arrangements which regulated men's and women's access to training and skilled work. In the latter area, for example, women in Brazil were generally denied access to both the informal areas of skill acquisition for many industrial trades, such as small workshops or garages, and also the formal training institutions. Women's access to SENAI (the National Industrial Apprenticeship Service) is largely confined to supervisor courses, and men outnumbered women by 200 to 1 on basic electrical, mechanical, and building courses in Rio de Janeiro in the 1970s (Ministério do Trabalho 1976: 190). In effect, women were socially denied the right to do or learn a broad range of jobs, and the conceptions of masculinity and femininity prevalent in society left them with little or no interest or desire to take up such work.

In non-capitalist societies the establishment of gender identities in the domestic sphere is often sufficient to determine the sexual division of labour in production. In pre-historical societies spheres of work (weaving or spinning, hunting or tilling, forest-clearing or weeding, and so on) are assigned to one sex or the other, and the division is closely regulated. Women and men have clearly defined and segregated areas of activity. In societies where the domestic unit is the primary productive unit, men usually head the household and control the allocation of work within it, as well as regulating the access of household members to work outside the immediate household sphere. In modern capitalist society, however, male control over the sexual division of labour in production is more problematic for three reasons. First, the capitalist organization of work and allocation of workers to it is undertaken in enterprises whose decisions are taken with some regard to questions of efficiency, profitability, and the rational use of resources. Second, decisions about the sexual division of labour are taken by people not linked to the families or directly affected by the impact of such decisions on families. Third, the nature of work is, itself, subject to constant changes as new industries and processes create new jobs and occupations and eliminate or transform old ones. In order to control the sexual division of labour in capitalist society, men have to influence day-to-day life in the factory as well as women's access to paid employment.

Without such control in the factory, the sexual division of labour would not take the form seen in Chapter 2. Rather, one might expect to see a sexual division where in horizontal terms there would be a tendency towards the concentration of the sexes into certain 'female' or 'male' areas, but few entirely single-sex occupations and some areas which would be well mixed. Vertically there might be a tendency for men to dominate the higher reaches of the job hierarchy if men's family situation encouraged greater dedication to work or a longer period of work experience, but many men would remain in the lower reaches and some women would rise up to the higher.

In this situation the division between men and women could quite easily be undermined. For example it might be perceived that the work men and women do is not all that different in many cases. The basis of male superiority might also be undermined by the fact that much of the work done by men requires little or no education and training. Further, it might become apparent that some women do not leave factories to devote their lives to rearing children. Similarly it might become obvious that while the average ability to perform certain types of work is different for the male and female populations, the distribution of such abilities between men and women will overlap. For example women might have, on average, a better socially acquired dress sense than men, but this does not disqualify all men from being fashion designers. Finally, in the course of work, it might be found that certain things done by women were more important or productive than those done by men.

Such a development would be unsatisfactory to male workers in industry. It would undermine not only their superiority at work, but also the superior status and power they enjoy in other spheres, particularly within families. The subordination of women at work facilitates the continued subordination of women in the domestic sphere by denying women both financial independence and an attractive alternative to motherhood. However, establishing male dominance at work is not straightforward. Although in exceptional circumstances men might defend their position by a simple reference to their masculinity – in the case where men demand that women are dismissed before men because they are not bread-winners, for example – this is a fragile basis on which to assert a durable position of dominance. Work hierarchies are organized around work categories, such as skill, competence, seniority, experience, training, and productivity. A hierarchy between different categories of male workers is partly constructed on such bases, and decisions concerning individual male workers are also made according to such criteria. At the same time, both managements and workers have an interest in establishing basic and generally applied rules of conduct within enterprises. Managements wish to run their enterprises with a certain degree of rationality and planning, while workers wish to protect against arbitrary managerial power by the use of such principles as seniority and equal pay for equal work. Within such a framework, men cannot simply oppose the work hierarchy by the application of a different set of principles, a gender hierarchy. This would lead to endless conflict. Rather, they have to incorporate gender into work hierarchies, devaluing, marginalizing, and segregating women *as workers*. This requires considerable attention to the internal organization of enterprises. Gender has to be incorporated into work categories themselves if men are to succeed in dominating women at work.[1] As a result, the sexual division of labour in factories should be seen as presupposing male domination, not causing it.

In order to turn work categories into categories which incorporate gender and turn the division of labour in industry into a pervasive and hierarchical sexual division of labour, three basic processes are required. First, male and female workers have to be defined as two opposed categories whose differences are far more important than their commonalities. Such a definition of two genders involves, as Rubin points out (1975: 179–80), a repression of 'feminine' traits among men and 'masculine' traits among women.[2] Second, masculine traits and work have to be given higher value than their female equivalents. This is done partly by denying women access to certain genuinely skilled jobs and partly by devaluing any work performed by women. In the latter case, there is pressure to value labour along the lines outlined by Margaret Mead with respect to pre-historical societies:

> 'One aspect of the social valuation of different types of labour is the differential prestige of men's activities and women's activities. Whatever men do – even if it is dressing dolls for religious ceremonies – is more prestigious than what women do and is treated as a higher achievement.'
>
> (quoted in Millett 1977: 224)

Translated into a modern context, the same problem was summed up by a woman worker in a Brazilian factory:

> 'Machismo is very difficult for us in Philips. Men think that since they are the ones that give the orders at home, they must also be

better than us at work. According to them, no woman can ever be better than a man.'

(TIE 1984: 36)

Third, a woman never being 'better than a man' involves the construction of job hierarchies in such a way that women neither have authority over men nor occupy comparable and superior positions to them within manual work.

In the first part of this chapter, attention will be focused on the construction of stereotypes of masculinity and femininity, and how the elements used vary from factory to factory. However, this alone is not a sufficient guarantee of male dominance. The incorporation of gender into work categories, which makes it appear that there is an objective basis for women's inferior position at work, is not achieved simply or once-and-for-all. In the day-to-day life of the factory, the actuality of male and female work might undermine the distinctions which are made. Men and women might perform similar work, or women might see the nature of men's work and realize that it is not so difficult as they had imagined. Work itself constantly changes, undermining old gender divisions and forcing the creation of new ones. In the second part, therefore, attention will be concentrated on how segregation is essential for the preservation of such stereotypes and the challenges posed to male dominance by lack of segregation and comparisons between men and women workers.

MASCULINITY AND FEMININITY ON THE SHOP FLOOR

It was seen in Chapter 2 that a considerable degree of segregation of male and female workers existed in the factories studied. Male and female work was differentiated along occupational, departmental, and functional lines. Sex-typing was pervasive in the factories studied – so much so that when production managers were asked whether or not jobs in their department done by one sex could, in fact, be done by the other, the evaluations they made were predominantly based upon sexual stereotypes. The managers merely considered whether or not the existing division of labour fitted the stereotype. The head of production in F1 provided a good example:

> 'I've worked with female machine operators, but not in . . . [F1]. It worked perfectly, but they don't do it here. It's a question of tradition. Here, the worker himself sets up the machine and lubricates it. In the other laboratory there was a mechanic. The women only controlled the weight and the time, feeding the machine and checking it. . . . Women can also prepare mixtures. I've already worked with women on this. Personally, I would prefer women on this work. They are more organized, and hygienic and meticulous. The work of preparation is not heavy. Only the material for the tablets comes in heavy cartons. . . . In my personal opinion, the chargehand on the automatic packaging line should be a man with mechanical ability. He would be trained to repair small defects in the machinery without the mechnanic having to be called.'
>
> (production manager, F1)

The striking feature of this analysis of the sexual division of labour in the plant is not the manager's belief that changes could be made in the distribution of jobs between male and female workers, but rather the pervasiveness of the sex stereotypes and the rigidity of the division between the sexes. It reaffirms the principle that men and women are naturally suited to different types of work. If machinists in the plant did not have to lubricate the machines, the job could be done by women. Preparation of chemicals is not really a heavy job, therefore women could do it rather than men. A man would be needed when mechanical ability was required. The list could be expanded by reference to other plants, but the principle is already clear. Not only are men and women supposed to be suited to different types of work, but also women and men are also reduced to two distinct and homogeneous groups. The option of finding a woman with mechanical ability was just not considered. While education, socialization, and work experience might make it more common for men to have mechanical aptitudes than women, the tendency is constructed as an absolute divide within the factory.

Certain stereotypes which characterize men and women's work are very widespread in industry. As Game and Pringle suggest in their study of the white goods industry in Australia, these stereotypes usually take the form of a series of polarities defining masculine and feminine: skilled/unskilled, heavy/light, dirty/clean, dangerous/less dangerous, interesting/boring, mobile/immobile.

In each case the first part of the couple is the more appropriately masculine characteristic, considered natural to men, while the second is more appropriately or naturally female (Game and Pringle 1983: 28–9). These categories could just as easily be drawn from Guilbert's study of the Parisian metal-working industries. One might add two more couples found in the latter's study: responsible/not responsible, which denotes the tendency for men to be employed on costly machinery or products, and machine ability/-lack of machine ability, to denote the belief of managers (and of male workers) that women lack mechanical sense (1966: 135).[3]

The pairings listed above form the lines along which distinct male and female identities are constructed in factories. They are not straightforward descriptions of the types of work women and men actually do, nor even ideal types (in the sociological sense) which define the general characteristics of female and male work, or female and male workers. First, they are designed to establish a difference, a divide, between men and women. They specifically discount the overlap in attributes and aptitudes between the female and male populations by suggesting that women and men are suited for very different types of work. As Rubin has put it, this 'requires repression: in men, of whatever is the local version of "feminine" traits; in women, of the local definition of "masculine" traits' (1975: 180). Second, the couples cited already incorporate male superiority, both by their selection of traits and the use of polarities which define a masculine attribute and leave the feminine as merely its negative. While a description of female work which includes such characteristics as 'continuous', 'requires concentration', 'requires dexterity', and so on, with the male equivalents being 'intermittent', 'requires less concentration', and 'not requiring dexterity' might be accepted by management (if not by male workers), such factors are not seen as giving value to the work. They are not seen as properly industrial attributes.[4] The couples offered by Game and Pringle, which reflect both manager and worker perceptions, merely select what men see as masculine attributes and define femininity by their absence. From the outset, then, the elements used to establish gender identities define women as inferior and inadequate – lacking in masculinity, in other words. Third, the pairings are used selectively in two senses. On the one hand, these attributes are given great importance in some circumstances and not in others. In one factory situation, emphasis might be placed upon the difference between heavy and light work, while in another this factor may be irrelevant and the line of cleavage between the masculine and the feminine constructed along the axis of, say, mechanical ability. On the other hand, the characterization of jobs as light or heavy, clean or dirty, can be selective, too. Dirt in a factory context means grease, oil, paint, and so on. The men who consider that women should not be exposed to dirt do not usually mind if women clean the toilets.

The remainder of this section will consider how these polarities are used in practice to construct labour forces which are divided on gender lines and give men a dominant position. The issue of strength and dexterity in the third electrical factory and workers' use of it will be considered first. This will be followed by a discussion of how the divide between men and women is increased by access to training and the nature of the divide itself.

Physical effort in the third electrical factory

The construction of masculine and feminine identities in a manner which devalues and subordinates women can be seen clearly in the treatment of the issue of strength and physical force in E3. In the factory there was a rigid sexual division of labour in production work. The women worked in five departments which made small electrical components and assembled them into tuners, radios, and radio-cassette players. The work was generally carried out sitting down, using the hands or the simplest of tools. It was typical of small electrical assembly, requiring patience and dexterity, and most women worked in clean, quiet, and well-lit surroundings. Only the radio department had poor conditions, including soldering fumes. The two largest male departments, from which workers were chosen for interviews, produced metal frames and cabinets for hi-fi systems and televisions. The work was heavy, particularly for the unskilled workers, involving cutting, sanding, and painting in the production of speaker boxes and television cabinets, and the stamping of metal parts for various product lines. Certain male jobs required a considerable degree of physical strength, as well as resistance to very poor working conditions. The work was often heavy, always noisy, and conducted in very poor working conditions. Many male workers had to put up with sawdust, paint and varnish, chemical

Male workers often work in very poor conditions. In this case the worker is sanding down a piece of wood by pressing a moving belt of sandpaper onto it. This raises a lot of fine dust, which can be seen on the machine and on the worker's arms, but no ventilation equipment is placed close to the machine. These are the conditions described by the worker who says 'it's thick dust from seven in the morning to six at night. A woman wouldn't last half an hour in there.'

fumes, and so on, as well as the noise and danger of presses, saws, and sanders.

How, then, would masculinity and femininity be constructed in such circumstances? On the shop floor one basic distinction between masculinity and femininity was constructed along the lines of strength and lightness. This became evident when the workers in E3 were asked whether male work was better than female work, or vice versa. The lines of demarcation drawn by workers drew heavily on the factor of strength and the associated features of dirt and danger.[5] Of the male workers 65 per cent said that women's work was better while only 7.5 per cent (three workers in forty) held the opposite opinion. The predominant view characterized women's work as better because it was either lighter, cleaner, or easier:

> 'Generally speaking, the women's work is better, because it is lighter. It isn't heavy work. It's better. They don't carry heavy loads and we do.'
>
> (male checker, quality control)

> 'Our work is a lot filthier. In the radio department [staffed mainly by women workers] it's cleaner. We have to have a complete wash, take a shower before we leave the plant. The machines and the timber throw off a lot of dust.'
>
> (carpenter, woodworking department)

The men also thought that their work was more dangerous than that done by women:

> 'It's very dangerous. I've seen a man chop off his arm. There are lighter machines and heavier machines. A woman could work on the light ones.'
>
> (male press operator)

Given the specific nature of the work in the plant performed by males, the men distinguished themselves from women in terms of their ability to face the dangers of presses and sharp cutting tools, the physical strength required to perform certain tasks, and their resistance to very bad working conditions (particularly the dust, varnish, and paint in the air in the woodworking department). When male workers were asked what types of work were appropriate for women, they generally ruled out heavy, dangerous, and dirty work, and in many cases felt that office and domestic work were more suitable for women than work in factories. In terms of women's capacity to do male work, the men felt that women might be able to do only the lighter jobs, which required less strength and involved less danger. The women interviewed held roughly similar views. They identified their own jobs as 'women's work', and saw them as lighter, easier, and better; 54 per cent of the women said that their work was better than the men's, while a mere 3 per cent (two cases among the sixty women interviewed) held the opposite opinion. Men's work, they thought, was dirty and heavy and they had no desire to do it. In some cases they felt physically unable to do it, and in others they were worried about the dangers involved.

Clearly the men's evaluations defined women, and women's work, negatively in relation to male work. Women's work was not considered to have any specific demands of its own. It was merely light (that is not heavy), easy (not hard), clean (not dirty), and safe (not dangerous). It was to be devalued in relation to male work which was an object of pride for the men:

> 'A man has to put up with staying on his feet for hours, like me. Women's work is lighter.'
>
> (carpenter, woodworking department)

> 'A woman couldn't do my job because men are much superior to women. The male body is stronger than the female's, and my kind of work could produce problems for a woman later on.'
>
> (painter, woodworking department)

> 'In woodworking it's thick dust from seven in the morning to six at night. A woman wouldn't last half an hour in there.'
>
> (machine operator, woodworking department)

The workers' (male and female) descriptions of the strength, dirt, and danger involved in men's work in the third electrical factory were, in themselves, fairly accurate, but the importance given to these factors and the neglect of the demands of women's work meant that men's work was given greater value. The heaviness and dirtiness of the work were seen as an object of pride, as well as unfortunate aspects of the job. While none of the men liked the conditions, they did establish a superiority over women workers. This superiority resided in the notion of masculinity itself, defined in the wider society and taken into the factory. Such work was definitely not suitable for women: they *should* not perform dirty, dangerous, or heavy work, even when they were physically capable of doing it:

> 'It's not a question of it being difficult. It depends. Women can do any type of work. But lifting up those heavy speaker boxes, and getting one's hands dirty with glue, and then the dust as well, being in the dust. There's all that working against her.'
>
> (carpenter, woodworking department)

In other words, women should be prohibited from doing such work because it was masculine/unfeminine, even if they were physically capable.

At the same time, men devalued women's work, regarding it as totally undemanding. One male worker described it as 'comfortable'. Of the forty male workers interviewed, only two referred to the close supervision and speed of activity required in many women's jobs, even though this is an important aspect of the work and a cause of male resistance to it (as will be seen in Chapter 5). Male workers gave no consideration to or credit for women's ability to work under pressure and the application needed for high output on repetitive tasks. They systematically ignored both the skills involved in the women's work and the intensity of their labour, giving no consideration to either dexterity or speed. Therefore the male workers tended to believe that they could do most or all of the women's jobs, while the women could not do their's. Thirty-five of the forty men interviewed felt that they would be able to do the job of an assembler. Although many of the male workers interviewed expressed a reluctance to perform such work, this was usually couched in terms of the possibility of lower wages or a disinclination to abandon their current occupation. The main obstacle for men doing 'female' work was its low status.

The stereotypes of masculinity and femininity held by managers in E3 did not in any way challenge these ideas. Stereotyped management beliefs about men and women can be found across the world. Beechey, for example, lists the following:

> '(a) women are better than men at doing boring, repetitive work; (b) men have an aptitude for mechanical skills; (c) women are not interested in career or promotion prospects; (d) women cannot lift heavy weights; (e) women are not capable of taking responsibility at work.'
>
> (Beechey 1984: 3)

Although these are based on the experience of Britain, they could easily be a summary of managerial attitudes in E3 particularly and in Brazil in general. The managers' own beliefs and prejudices were, of course, reinforced by the attitudes of male workers and by the state.[6]

The only view held by male workers which was challenged by the managers in E3 was the idea that men could perform assembly work. Management believed that men performed routine assembly jobs very poorly, both for 'natural' reasons and because of their frustration at being confined to low-wage, dead-end jobs, while other jobs requiring strength were more suited to them. Women, on the other hand, were considered to be highly suited for routine production work because of their dexterity and application, but not for work requiring strength or involving exposure to danger. The manager of a predominantly female department which also had four highly paid male technicians and four unskilled male labourers working alongside the women assemblers made the following distinction:

> 'In the radio cassette department I am using men on repair work, but they also do calibration if there's no other work to do. Men and women are about the same on calibration, but men do not have the patience to perform routine revision. At first, I only had women in the department, but it caused problems. When jobs required physical force they damaged the tools. With a man the tools last a lot longer.'
>
> (production manager, E3)

A similar point was made by a manager in the second electrical factory, who also stressed that women were satisfied with such a division of functions:

> 'Women do the more repetitive work, while men do other kinds of work, either heavier or less routine. The women complain less, they're more docile and they accept repetitive work more easily. In 1980 a study showed that few women complained of the type of work they did. They don't want more interesting or diversified work.'
>
> (personnel manager, E2)

This latter assertion will be contested in the next section.

The managers approved of the division between light and heavy work, and they devalued women's labour. Jobs requiring strength or involving exposure to danger were deemed to fall outside women's competence, and even when women might prove in practice that they could do certain 'male' jobs, managers were not convinced of women's capacities. They merely appealed to their notions of what was right and proper for women workers:

> 'The women in the firm where I worked even did the sanding down in the paint section. They choked with the dust. The only thing they didn't do was work with heavy machinery. I don't think women should do sanding work, because they have more delicate finger nails than men, and the chemical glueing processes are not advisable for women either. One would have to see that it did not endanger a subsequent pregnancy. One would need medical advice.'
>
> (manager, woodworking department)

Such concern might be legitimate, but it is important to see how it is used in the factory setting. Concern expressed about women's health (or, in many cases, the health of potential children) is used to construct a barrier to women's labour-force participation. In the case of men, such concerns are either not expressed – as with chemicals which might cause cancer or sterility, for example – or seen as problems to be overcome by technical measures. They are not used to exclude men from certain areas of work. In the case of women, medical problems are, once again, often used as a demonstration of women's unfitness for many types of industrial work. Similarly lifting heavy weights can be used to exclude women from certain types of work, even though ways to get around such lifting can be devised to help smaller or older men, as Cockburn notes (1983: 175).

THE NATURE OF THE GENDER DIVIDE

The third electrical factory provided an illustration of a situation in which the supposedly inherent aptitudes of men and women provide a basis for gender distinction. In other situations, the differences between women and men are developed or increased through training and experience. There are various ways this can be done. For example, as well as having their access to formal training barred, women can also find it difficult or impossible to exercise the skills they do acquire. A female metal-worker in São Paulo made the point quite unambiguously:

> 'In my own case, I took the SENAI course, and I never managed to get into a factory as a radio technician. But I did get in as a labourer and worked in quality control. It's just that before I'd never been turned down for a job. This only happened when I went to look for skilled work. . . . I don't know of any women employed as radio technicians. I know women who do the work, but they're employed as quality controllers. . . . Doing a professional course does a woman no good. Either we get a lot of women together to break through this barrier or it's no use.'
>
> (Leite 1982: 69)

Similarly the initial differences between men and women are often increased by differential access to on-the-job training. In the plants studied in Brazil, various instances were found of men being encouraged to exercise the mechanical abilities which women were either assumed not to have or positively discouraged from using. In the first pharmaceutical factory, for example, the recruitment office explained that a few men had been taken on as packaging workers to work with automatic machinery precisely because they would have the ability to make minor adjustments, whereas women would need to call the mechanics:

> 'The women did not have the mechanical aptitude to sort out the machinery. The mechanic had to be called. . . . The men find it easier.'
>
> (recruitment officer (female), F1)

In the second automotive plant women were actually discouraged from adjusting the machinery. As one machine operator said:

> 'I think I could adjust it, but I have never tried because I think that the foreman would object to it. He wouldn't accept it. . . . There's the problem of being responsible, or not doing it right, of me hurting the machine.'

Women are expected to ask for help, while men are encouraged to resolve problems themselves. As a result, men are trained on the

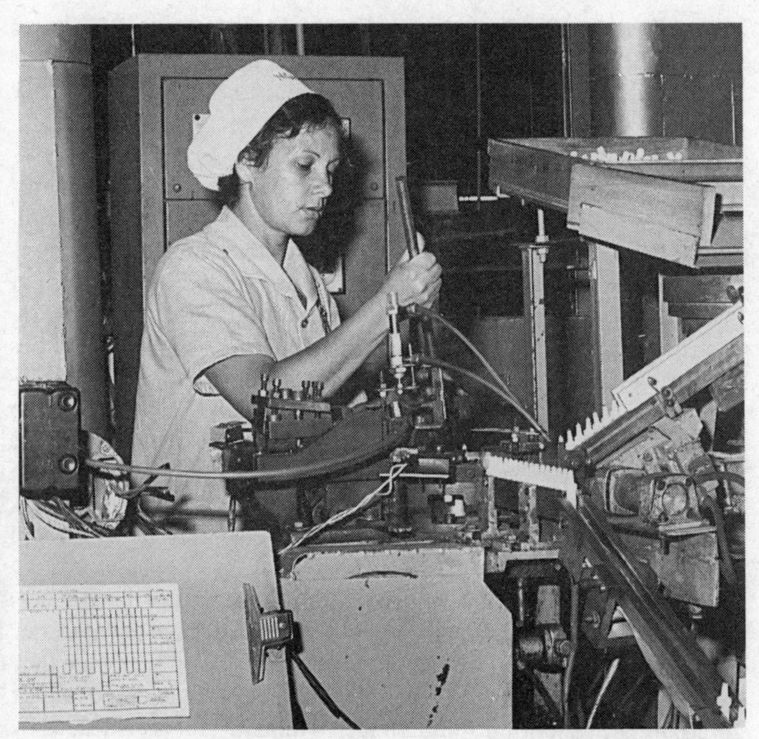

In many factories, particularly those in the electrical industry, 'women's work' is associated with sitting down or remaining in one place, a clear and quiet environment, and the use of hand tools. In this automotive parts factory a woman is tending a machine which assembles parts into a finished product. She is responsible for keeping the machine stocked with each of the components, checking on the quality of the product and keeping the machine running. She is using an iron bar to un-jam the flow of components. In spite of the noise involved, remaining on foot and moving around the machine, and getting dust, grease, and talcum powder on her arms, she is still considered to be doing 'women's work'. In this factory, 'men's work' means operating less automated machines, or setting and maintenance work. In different factories, different elements are used to create the division between male and female work and workers.

job, while women are discouraged (actively or passively) from acquiring mechanical ability.

However, the existence of differences in skills and aptitudes between women and men is not the cause of the sexual division of labour in industry. It does not account for differences in work and in wages, as the economists would have us believe. These differences are justifications for inequality between the sexes, not the causes of it. Godelier has made the point in relation to the Baruya of New Guinea

> 'However, among the Baruya as in our culture, sexuality, differences in form, substance and bodily function, the anatomical and physiological differences which arise from the different functions of the sexes in the reproduction of life, provide a permanent supply of material with which messages and discourses are constructed which interpret and justify all the social inequalities existing between men and women. Everything happens as if sexuality is constantly called upon to occupy all of social space, to serve as the language to express and the reason to legitimate realities whose bases are not derived, or principally derived, from it.'
>
> (1982: 13)

In our society women may be barred from (or have restricted access to) higher-status work, and the work they do may have low status or value, but this is not a result of their capacities or the work they perform. It is the result of the establishment of a gendered labour force and the superior position of men within it. This is evidenced by the treatment of women's work, as three examples can show.

First, women may be marginalized, generally speaking, from work which requires responsibility and crucial areas of production, as Guilbert suggests, but even doing such work does not ensure high status for women. Women were often treated as irresponsible, or as workers who were not properly suited to factory life precisely because they were women. One of the managers in the third electrical factory clearly expressed the feeling that he was controlling a group of irresponsible young girls:

> 'I have managed both women and men. Men are more responsible. The majority of men are married, and they are more responsible. A woman doesn't worry much about leaving what she's doing, and it's the same with all aspects of responsibility. If a [female] assembler sees that her production isn't right, she'll carry on assembling it. She doesn't care. A man would not normally do this.'

The assessment is based more on prejudice than observation, and it was directly contradicted by the manager of the (male) woodworking department, who praised women's attention and care. More importantly, even when women do have responsibility it is devalued. In the first electrical factory female production workers were responsible for the plant's output of silicon wafers, upon whose quality the whole of the plant's work depended. In spite of the care needed and the importance of wafer production, the women employed on it were still classified as unskilled workers. They earned the lowest wages in the plant. Had they been men, things would have been different.[7]

Second, presumed differences in aptitudes or training are often used to differentiate male and female work quite arbitrarily. Because they are generally believed not to have mechanical ability, women are discouraged from adjusting or maintaining machines, and this can provide the basis for differentiating between female and male operatives. As Guilbert points out, male workers might do the same basic production work as female workers, but at the end of the day they would do extra little tasks, such as lubrification and be paid higher wages as a result (1966: 135). This not only devalues women's general production work and abilities, but also leaves them powerless in the face of machinery which they are not allowed to control or understand.

Third, when women actually perform heavy, dirty, or dangerous work, such work is also devalued. Physical effort, dirt, and danger are used by (mainly) unskilled men as a means of giving value to their work relative to that done by skilled male workers and by women. However, men do not necessarily enjoy working in noisy, dangerous, and dirty conditions. Guilbert found, for example, that particularly unpleasant work, such as spray-painting by hand, was quite often done by either women or black males, usually immigrants (1966: 108–10). Similarly unpleasant work in Britain might be disproportionately performed by black workers (Willis 1977: 153), while in Sao Paulo many firms preferred to recruit migrants from the north-east for foundry work. In these circumstances the white or local-born male workers refuse such work because they can find better opportunities in the labour market.[8] Once such work is performed by blacks or women or migrants, the heaviness, dirt, or danger involved loses its value. While white male workers may, to a limited extent, secure a certain valuation of the

It is much more common for men to work in groups than women. In this case, three men are laminating wood. The wood is taken from the stack and then passed through the rollers from one man to the other. Once again, the poor working conditions should be noted. In particular, this type of operation gives off noxious fumes.

work they do by appealing to its danger, for example, other categories of worker cannot make the same appeal. Devalued workers cannot give status and value to the work they perform.

Guilbert's conclusions concerning the sexual division of labour are worth stating at length, as they confirm the extent to which the elements used to construct masculinity and femininity are justifications for inequality, not causes of it:

> 'The elements which intervene in the determination of masculine and feminine skills in relation to the work performed are, thus, very diverse. They have, however, a common feature: although they take different forms, they all converge to give female labour

a skill structure inferior to that of male. To justify this divergence, the idea of a difference in professional capacity between men and women has been seen to arise, as well as that of a necessary hierarchy of functions, even when they are of the same level of skill. It has also been seen that there is a tendency to value a natural quality of the male labour-force, physical strength, even though the greater speed of female labour does not intervene as a factor in skill. It is interesting to note that the extra skill frequently attributed to male labour by reason of greater physical strength does not play any part when that labour is North African. We catch hold of here an interrelation between the two elements capable of determining different skill structures, the sex distinction and the ethnic origin distinction.'

(Guilbert 1966: 139–40)

The divisions constructed along the lines of strength, skill, and responsibility have a considerable degree of flexibility. Whatever the importance strength might assume in the third electrical factory, a job requiring strength can still be devalued by the low status of the person doing it. In their different ways, women and black workers bring their low status to the work they perform.[9]

THE IMPORTANCE OF SEGREGATION

The establishment of male superiority in the factory is facilitated by the sexist ideology which encourages women to believe that they are valueless. It is further sustained by the familial ideology which assigns men the right to earn a family wage and devalues women's earning capacity and income needs. However, such ideologies cannot justify or hide direct and blatant inequalities at work. Women might devalue their skills, but they are much less inclined to accept lower wages than men for identical work, particularly if the men concerned are younger, less experienced, and unmarried. Precisely because higher wages and better promotion opportunities for men in factories are not based on superior skill, aptitudes, and productivity, a necessary part of male strategy rests on the enforcement of a high degree of segregation of female and male workers, as seen in Chapter 2. Segregation of women and men limits the contact between the sexes and reduces, in particular, the knowledge that women have of men's work. This enables the differential valuation of male and female work to be imposed with some ease, and it also provides symbolic and practical barriers to the performance of 'male' work by women. Collectively women are barred from such work, and individual women find it difficult or impossible to move out of female work and into male.[10]

As long as a high degree of segregation – occupational and physical – is maintained, it is possible to create significantly different male and female labour forces around minimal differences in the nature of the work performed. A case cited by Maruani (1985) makes this point with great clarity. She describes the introduction of women typesetters using advanced equipment into a French regional newspaper. The women were physically segregated from the male typesetters, who had negotiated a deal to protect their pay and conditions. As well as a physical segregation, the women were not allowed to justify and to correct text. This was the basis of a difference in professional status which gave women much lower wages, piece-rates, shorter rest periods, and more controlled hours of work. Over a decade, the women gradually came to do more of the tasks at first reserved for men but always within the capabilities of the women on the new machines. However, it was not until the men and women were finally moved into the same room, integrated into male work-teams, and allowed to do all the male tasks that the differences in wages and conditions became so intolerable that the women went on strike for equal conditions (Maruani 1985: 50–8). As Maruani states:

> 'The difference existed for a long time. But if the revolt breaks out now, it is because this difference, today, is perceived as a social construct, as a process which is produced, and produced daily, and not as the consequence of ineluctable technological or historical determinations.'
>
> (1985: 59)

The fact that male superiority in the factory rests upon social and symbolic barriers means that the sexual divison of labour has a certain degree of flexibility. In the case cited immediately above, the entry of women into work which had been previously done only by men (the earlier exclusion of women from printing having itself been a result of bitter struggles in the industry, as Cockburn – 1981; 1983 – has shown) was met by a strike of the male workers in 1969. They could not exclude the women altogether, but they were able to defend their own status and create a definite division between female and male workers. Less radical shifts in labour processes and labour markets can be accommodated, too. As work and the sexual division of labour shift, new lines of demarcation are defined – say, between 'light' and 'heavy' presses, or between semi-skilled press operators and skilled die-mounters and maintenance workers. This means that in practice a rapid feminization of limited areas of work can take place. Within a given factory, the work changes rapidly from male to female, even though this process may be very uneven in industry as a whole. As Cockburn has noted, men move away from women entering previously all-male areas of work, shifting either horizontally or vertically in order to re-establish the sexual division of labour (1985: 232–35).

A less dramatic transformation had taken place, but with certain consequences for the sexual division of labour, in the second automotive factory. The light machining and machine assembly part of the plant had been gradually feminized in the 1970s. This feminization took place alongside changes in the labour process and the local labour market. In terms of the labour process, the machinery used in the department was gradually modernized, becoming semi-automatic with improved component supply systems. At the same time, there were shortages of male labour in the region, and the firm had an incentive to substitute male workers by female. With industrial output rising at 20 per cent per annum in the early 1970s and little or no trade union organization at plant level, employers had some degree of flexibility in managing the margins of the sexual division of labour. As a result of the changes in A2, the women workers in the machining departments came to do jobs which were not typically female. They operated the machines, checking to see that they were ready before starting, keeping them supplied with components (rings, electrodes, talcum powder, and so on), making sure that they ran smoothly by unjamming the components when necessary, and keeping a check on the quality of the output. The machine operators worked in conditions which in many circumstances would be considered 'male'. They were on their feet all day, moving around from one part to another of machines which could be up to 5 or 6 metres in length. Very often their hands (or gloves) and forearms were covered in dirt, talcum powder, and cement. Some of the machines were noisy enough for workers to have to shout to make conversation.

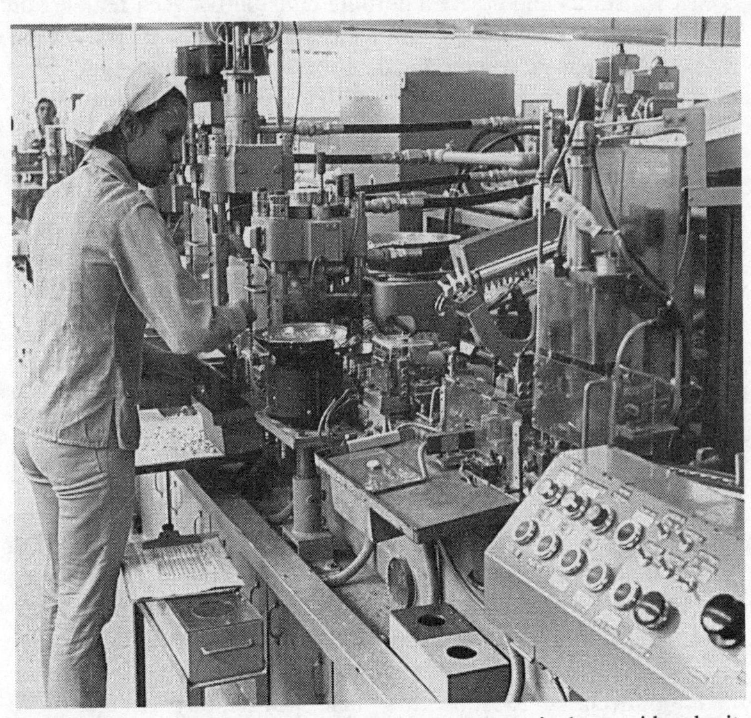

This woman is doing work which might in many factories be considered suitable for men. She is operating the machine by means of the control panel on the right, keeping the machine supplied, and checking the output. If the machine were operated by a man, some of the minor setting and maintenance work might be transferred to him, and the supervisors might also encourage him to resolve small problems as they arise – to experiment and to use his initiative. The women working these machines specifically stated that they were not supposed to fiddle with them. On some of the machines, the women were also dependent on men for the loading of one of the raw materials, concrete, because this was considered too heavy a job for women. The women were surrounded by a male hierarchy – supervisors, setters, and mechanics – who had claims to greater knowledge and skill than them.

This, by itself, was not enough to undermine the sexual division of labour. Although the women in the plant did work that might be considered suitable for men by workers in many factories, the line of cleavage between the masculine and the feminine had been reconstructed around skill, with strength playing a much lesser role than in E3. The male workers monopolized the machine-setters' jobs and

Table 15 *Distribution of workers by sex, occupation and department: factory A2, September 1982 (absolute numbers)*[1]

dept	*sex*	*occupation*[2]				
		machine-setter	*machine operator grades II–IV*	*machine operator grade I*	*assistant*	*charge-hand*
1	men	20	27	0	0	0
	women	0	0	0	0	0
2	men	7	10	0	0	0
	women	0	0	0	5	0
3	men	17	5	1	0	0
	women	0	0	0	12	1
4	men	12	13	0	0	0
	women	0	0	2	21	4
5	men	9	0	0	0	0
	women	0	0	8	27	4
total	men	65	55	1	0	0
	women	0	0	10	65	9

Source Company records.

Notes

1 Nine male apprentices are excluded from the calculations.

2 The occupations listed in the table are graded as follows:
Machine-setter – from grade 9 to grade 18 according to level of qualification.
Machiner operators grades II–IV, from grade 6 to grade 9.
Machine operator grade I, grade 3.
Assistant, grade 1 to grade 3.
Charge-hands are not graded. Their wages depend on the grade of the workers they are in charge of.

the high grades of machine operation, as can be seen in *Table 15*, which shows the distribution of men and women by occupation in each of the five machining and assembly departments. Four of the five departments were mixed in 1982, and in three of the five female and male workers were engaged on production work. Male superiority had been maintained, however. In each department the lowest-grade male occupation was higher than that of the highest-grade occupation held by a woman, and across the five departments only one man worked as a machine operator I, the highest-grade female occupation.

Although the women appeared to accept this division to some extent, particularly with regard to the requirements of the machine-setters' job, the bases of the sexual division of labour were partly undermined by the close contact between female and male workers. In four of the five departments it was patently obvious that only men would ever be allowed to do higher-grade work, and some of the women felt that the firm discriminated against them:

> 'It's very difficult [for women to obtain promotion]. You have to be exceptional. A man doesn't need very much, but for a woman it's difficult. It's because a man won't accept that a woman should earn more than him. So given that everything here is run by men, they're never going to accept it. A woman really has to be something special.'
>
> (female machine operator)

In this case a team leader was complaining that although she supervised the machine operators and took some responsibility for keeping the machines running, this work was not recognized, or paid, by the firm.

Such perceptions of discrimination become all the more important when on-the-job training is involved. In A2 even the job of machine-setter was not considered to be out of their reach by some women. Having seen the job done and being aware of some of the elements involved, they were not impressed with arguments about the difficulties of the work. They were on familiar territory because of their proximity to it. One woman described the situation in the following terms:

> ' "I do not adjust the machine. There's a setter for that."
> "Could you adjust it?"
> "I think I could but I've never tried because I think that the foreman would object to it. He wouldn't accept it. I'm not a setter, I'm just a plain operative. There's the problem of responsibility, of not doing it right, of me hurting the machine. The setter is not trained any differently. It's simply that he's a man. I think that there's a system of working which gives men a better chance of doing work that women are not supposed to be able to do. But I don't think women are unable to do it. On the contary, they can do it better than men. It's prejudice, I'm sure of it." '
>
> (female machine operator)

In part this statement may reflect the fact that skilled work poses less of a barrier to women in terms of brute strength than a lot of unskilled jobs. However, more importantly, it registers the fact that in mixed working groups, promotion and more skilled work are almost always reserved for men, and this male monopoly often lacks objective foundation. When men and women are segregated, the preference given to men is not normally questioned by women because they are unaware of the differential treatment or convinced that the men's jobs must be more demanding.[11] In E3, for example, it was common for women in the production departments to say that they had little or no idea of what went on in the male departments.

In mixed departments conflicts arise because of the contradiction between the principles of work and the principles of gender hierarchy. For example men strongly resist working alongside women who have equal or higher status, unless such equality is merely temporary.[12] Therefore they attempt to bar women from supervisory posts, monopolize promotion opportunities, and prevent equal pay for men and women being established. Within mixed departments the preservation of male superiority reveals itself as blatantly unjust because of the proximity of men and women, which de-mystifies the rationale for it.

It is very rare for women to supervise men. In the third electrical factory one instance of male labourers being under the charge of a female supervisor in a predominantly female department was found, but this appears to be extremely unusual.[13] Guilbert, for example, reports that among the 30,000 workers in the 130 firms she studied, no case of men being supervised by women was found (1966: 134). Male resistance to female supervision can be extremely strong, as Leite found in one of her interviews:

> 'I think that a woman can do the same job as a man. I think that she has the capacity. Only the men won't accept it. Like, for example, in my department. They won't accept a woman as a charge-hand. They think that she would be passing in front of them. They don't think that a woman has the authority to be a charge-hand in a department which has both men and women.'
>
> (1982: 60)

Hence women are barred from supervisory jobs, but the evidence is more than clear that women can be interested in promotion, responsibility, and career prospects, whatever managers and men might claim.

Promotion also creates conflict. Male workers naturally assume that they should be promoted first, and management often go along with this, asserting that suitably qualified women are hard to find, as a senior manager in E2 stated:

> 'When we look for people to promote, the men are better. They have more mechanical ability, so they can resolve problems, get round them. But it's not always like this. On one occasion the best technical person was a woman. But it's very rare. There have only been three in seventeen years.'
>
> (quality control manager, E2)

In other words, the exceptions merely underline the rule. In spite of these justifications the promotion patterns in mixed working groups in the factories studied were on occasions so blatantly discriminatory that the women concerned were fully aware of what was going on.

Evidence of conflict over promotion was seen above in the case of A2, and an even clearer example was seen in the third electrical factory. Quality control work in E3 was open to men and women workers, through both internal promotion and external recruitment. Leaving aside the unskilled labourers within the department, the quality control workers were divided into two basic functions: materials checkers and inspectors (the latter also divided into two grades). Inspectors were paid between 90 and 150 per cent more than checkers. All of the women, without exception, were employed as checkers, while three in five of the men were employed as inspectors. The male workers regarded this as natural. All eight male workers interviewed in quality control (materials checkers as well as inspectors) said that equal pay was given for equal work, and only one felt that women had a poorer chance for promotion than men. Although only two of the eight workers thought that women were unable to do their job, they expressed no surprise that women never gained promotion, and took as quite natural the fact that higher-grade jobs were held only by men. In contrast, the three female materials checkers interviewed were all convinced that they did the same job as the men for less money. They expressed the problem quite clearly:

> 'The men earn more. In quality control there are checkers, inspector 1 and inspector 2. The men are mostly on inspector 1 grade,

while the women are all checkers. I think that I do the same work as they do. There are lads who came in here after me earning a lot more. We talk about this. We're angry about it because they come in earning more than we do.'

'In quality control the men work less and earn more. The women do the same job and the only difference is that they are technicians. Even when the work's the same, the men earn more. . . . Sometimes the man's work is heavier, but in quality control it's the same.'

'For example, there are only [male] inspectors here. There are no women inspectors. In the other firm I worked in we had women inspectors. I don't see why women cannot do the same job.'

One of the junior foremen, too, expressed puzzlement at the fact that women did not seem to be promoted, even though they had the necessary experience and no formal qualifications were required.[14] Precisely because the women were able to compare their work, experience, and qualifications with those of the men, they could see blatant discrimination in action. They resented their own lack of promotion, partly because they did see their jobs as long term and wanted promotion, partly because they saw the preference for men as an injustice, and partly because their need for an income made promotion attractive. Had men and women been segregated, the same reservation of higher-paid jobs for men would not have been so noticeable or resented. In A2, for example, quality control was segregated. Even though men did the higher-grade work and women the lower-grade (see *Table 6*), the segregation prevented direct comparisons, and the women did not complain when interviewed.

In mixed-sex departments male superiority can also be threatened by equal pay for women and men for two reasons. First, men generally believe that they earn, or have a right to earn, a wage sufficient to support their family, while they consider women's wages to be merely supplementary to those earned by the male bread-winner. This was seen clearly in Chapter 3. They approve of wage differentials and the reservation of higher-wage jobs for themselves. Second, equal pay undermines the basic belief that men are superior to female. Even if it involves a levelling up of female pay to male levels, it devalues male work in the eyes of men by acknowledging that women are doing work of similar or of equal value to them. In practice, equal pay struggles can unmask the artificial distinctions that are used to distinguish and rank male and female jobs, revealing male and female work to be identical. The sole female executive member of a metal-workers' union in the Greater São Paulo area, who worked in a factory where a strike in 1978 had obtained equal pay, explained some of the male opposition to it:

> 'You can see that some of the brothers begin to question the fact that they are earning the same money as the women. Even here [at the factory], injection moulders say, "Well, here women are earning as much as I am . . .", and I say, "Look, brother, you don't have to worry about women earning the same as you. Don't they start work at the same time as you? Aren't they working in the same conditions as you in the plant? So, if they're producing the same as you, they should earn the same. So what you have to do is struggle together, women and men, to improve your working conditions, to see that you earn a decent wage. You shouldn't be fighting to ensure that the women earn less. You should be struggling for everyone to fight together for better pay, better health and safety." '[15]

The struggle for equal pay in the plant had taken the form of a regrading which recognized that women employed as labourers were doing the same work as the male injection moulders. But from the difficulties expressed by the union official, the men were not happy with the consequent diminution of their status and superiority.

The recognition that women workers do similar or identical work to them places male workers in a real quandary. The dilemma is not just that the entry of women appears to threaten male wage-levels and raises the prospect of the substitution of men by women. More importantly the one strategy which might prevent women undercutting male wages (and possible price the women out of jobs), equal pay, is also problematic for men, since it would recognize women's ability and rank them equally with men. It would devalue men in their own eyes by undermining their superiority (in work terms, as well as in the pay packet) in relation to women. Equal pay may be a good trade union tactic, but it undermines male superiority on the shop floor. As a result, male workers fear women because they are reluctant to adopt the kinds of trade union practices which might improve women's position, and diminish the threat they pose to male pay and conditions.

The entry of women in previously male spheres of work is strongly associated with reductions in pay, as evidenced by one of Leite's interviews with a woman metal-worker in São Paulo:

> 'A lot of men generally say that such-and-such a firm is good because no women work in it. But it's a fact. If a firm starts admitting women when it never has done before, to the extent that it starts to admit them, the wage rate is on the way down.'
>
> (Leite 1982: 64)

There is some evidence to support this impression. Guilbert found that within different skill groups in the Parisian metal-working industry, the wages paid for occupations in which both sexes were employed within industry as a whole varied between factories and departments according to whether work groups were entirely male, mixed, or entirely female. The highest wage rate was earned by men in men-only groups, followed by men in mixed groups and women in mixed groups. The lowest average hourly wage was earned by women in all female groups (1966: 142). Less precise information has been found for the Brazilian plastics industry, confirming the same point. As can be seen in *Table 16*, in five plastics firms the average hourly wage rate for men in mixed occupations was lower

Table 16 *Average hourly wage rate by function, sex, and sex compostion of occupation: five plastics firms, March 1981 (in cruzeiros per hour)*

function[1]	*occupational type*			
	all women[2]	*mixed*		*all men*
		women	*men*	
quality control	54	66	85	98
packaging	45	46	54	56
unskilled production[3]	45	46	49	52
semi-skilled production	50	59	69	87

Source See Appendix 1.

Notes

1 The functions selected are the only non-manual areas in which women had significant representation.

2 Included in this category are all occupational titles which in a given factory had only women filling them.

3 Unskilled production jobs were all those with a generic title, such as 'production assistant' or 'production labourer'.

than for men in all-male occupations, while women in mixed occupations earned more than women in all-female occupations. This is hardly surprising given the way men try to isolate and devalue women.

Men could try to protect their own position by trying to raise women's wages, but they prefer to reduce competition from women by segregation, which prevents comparisons of male and female wages and work and maintains differentials, but does not encourage the substitution of higher-paid men by lower-paid women. Hence male workers shun firms which employ a lot of women workers and they hanker after jobs in high-wage 'male' industries such as motor vehicles and mechanical engineering. In factories where there are women workers, the men try to segregate women from male work, reserve the best jobs for themselves, and disqualify women from competing with them by creating as large a gap as possible between the masculine and the feminine. The reservation of promotion opportunities for men, as described above in the case of the third electrical factory, is one aspect of this.

Male workers are in a strong position to enforce a strategy which excludes women from certain types of work, marginalizes them within the factory, and protects their superior position at work. Any attempt to place male workers in jobs generally considered to be for women, or vice versa, would have to overcome the resistance of the displaced male workers, or the reluctance of the new workers to assume the jobs, and also a possible lack of suitably qualified workers of the replacement sex. It is not surprising, then, that Joekes reports that in Morocco managements sometimes shift from employing male workers to employing female workers in the clothing industry by closing the factory completely and then reopening a short time later (Joekes 1982: 12). Even this strategy is only possible because in Morocco clothing work is not clearly sex-typed. When such dramatic options are not available, male workers are in a strong position, and they are unlikely to be subject to major challenges unless the 'masculine' aspect of their work is completely undermined by technical change. As was seen in the case of E3, stereotypes of male and female work are shared to a large extent by managements and there is usually little pressure from this quarter. Much more likely than the frontal assault on male privilege is the adjustment of the boundary between male and female work, without desegregation and without any challenge to stereotypes. Given the existence of the discrimination against women workers and the wage differentials established in labour markets, managements would lose by desegregating female and male workers and by paying women workers equal wages to men. Similarly driving down male wages by equalizing them to the rates paid to women is also unattractive. Management would either face considerable male resistance, or a decline in the quality of male labour (less experience or lower educational qualifications) as male workers prefer to seek other work. Equal pay, therefore, is rarely as attractive as a policy of maintaining segregation and discrimination. At most, managers might consider widening the areas in which low-paid women are employed.

CONCLUSIONS

The pattern of gender relations seen in society as a whole is reproduced within the factory. Men and women are divided into two stereotyped categories and segregated, and men dominate women. Women, mothers or carers outside the factory, become women workers destined for unskilled, boring, routine, dead-end, and temporary work. Men, supposedly heads of families and breadwinners, become lifetime workers, skilled or strong, anxious for challenges and worthy of reward. Male superiority as workers is secured by privileged access to higher-status jobs and the devaluation of women as workers. Both of these processes require segregation of the labour force if they are to be fully effective. Irrespective of women's supposed lack of qualifications and experience, and without reference to their supposedly greater instability of employment, there are strong forces which place women in an inferior position in the factory. In this and the preceding chapter, some of these forces have been outlined, and this having been done it is possible to explain and analyse the differences between male and female experiences of work and employment in the factory. In Chapter 5 attention will be focused on the labour process, the types of work performed by women and men, and the forms of control exercised over them by management. In Chapter 6 labour market issues – the patterns of wages, promotion, and skill recognition for male and female workers – will be discussed.

5
Gender and the labour process

INTRODUCTION

In the light of the arguments presented in the previous chapter, a discussion of the labour process might appear superfluous. After all, it was argued that women are placed firmly at the bottom of the job hierarchy and denied access to more skilled work. Thus one would expect to see quite different work and working conditions for men and women. One would not be surprised to enter a factory and see women subjected to the grinding monotony of the assembly line, while men moved around setting machines and maintaining them where necessary. Such a division of labour was described for the second automotive factory. However, to leave things at this point would be to assume that working practices and conditions are determined without reference to the types of people performing the work. When this is done, the organization and control of work is left unanalysed. The capitalist (or, indeed, socialist) organization of work would be seen as being determined independently of both class and gender.

As Phillips and Taylor have pointed out, Braverman's work on the labour process created the space for a discussion of class and sex in the organization of work, even though most labour process writings in the 1970s were not 'notable for their feminist content' [Phillips and Taylor 1980: 82]. Prior to the resurgence of interest in the labour process following the publication of *Labor and Monopoly Captial* (Braverman 1975), both Marxist and neo-classical analyses of capitalist development had shared the same preoccupations – price and value – which precluded a consideration of the capitalist organization of work. The labour process debate problematized the organization of work, emphasizing its class nature. Even so, in the first instance, the class struggle at the point of production still tended to be characterized as a confrontation between 'capital' in the abstract and an equally abstract and general 'labour'. When such capital and labour was given body in the flow of historical accounts of the development of capitalist organization of work, most analyses concentrated on the de-skilling of men and the introduction of Taylorist and Fordist methods into male industries.[1]

This absence of gender is a little surprising given that many of the characteristic features of modern capitalist organization of industrial work, such as de-skilling, fragmentation of work, external pacing of production, the assembly line, and extensive management surveillance are applied to a much greater degree to the work done by women than to that done by men. While Henry Ford's use of the assembly line is well known, assembly lines are to be found to a much greater degree in industries with high proportions of women workers than in 'male' industries. The detailed division of labour, too, is more characteristic of women's work.

It will be argued in this chapter that gender reaches right into the heart of capitalist production. Rather than merely being relevant to the allocation of workers to pre-defined jobs, gender influences the definition of the work to be performed and the manner in which performance is controlled. It also influences employment policies – wage levels and forms, promotion, training, and so on – adopted by managements, and the discussion of these will be taken up in Chapter 6. In the first part of the current chapter, attention will be concentrated on how jobs are defined, and the differences in the forms of control imposed on women and men workers. The second part will attempt to account for the differences observed in the patterns of control exercised over the two sexes and to use this to explain why managements have such strong preferences for using women in certain types of jobs.

WORK AND CONTROL

There are a number of enduring images of people in manual work. The worker on the car assembly line endlessly tightening wheel nuts is one powerful representation of male manual work. For women, an increasingly common image is that of the electronics worker, seated in front of the assembly line or peering into a microscope. Such images are doubly misleading. First, in terms of the kinds of work actually performed by the sexes, the assembly line is the exception for men, while being relatively common for women. Second, the focus on assembly lines can exaggerate the extent to which forms of control are built into machinery and the organization of work. These points will be taken up in turn.

Control embodied in work organization

The image of the electronics worker encapsulates a number of factors which characterize much of 'women's work' in contrast to that normally done by men: highly developed detailed division of labour involving short job cycles and repetitive work, work pace dictated by integrated working (the line) or automatic job cycles, and being tied to one spot. Given that women are found on assembly lines more frequently than men, they appear to be more controlled than men by the very nature of the work they do. The extent of such differences in control is not easy to quantify. Statistics on such questions are not as easily collectable as those on wages and hours of work, and they are rarely available. However, a general survey of the working conditions of waged workers was carried out in France in 1978, and some of the results have been analysed by Molinie and Volkoff (1981). They examined the degree to which the work of male and female employees had its rhythm determined by technical forces. They classified as work having a 'strong time constraint' all those jobs which involved assembly lines, or the regulation of work by the automatic movement of a product, part, or machine (1981: 53). In such jobs the worker would be constrained to work at the rhythm determined by the movement of machines or products. The survey found that women workers, and above all young women workers, were more likely to be working under a strong time constraint than men. While 15 per cent of all non-salaried (that is manual) male workers were subject to such a constraint, the figure for women varied from a peak rate of 40 per cent for the youngest groups of women to under 20 per cent for women over 50 years of age (1981: 53–4). These differences were not the result merely of differences in skill.

Female semi-skilled workers were twice as likely to work under strong time constraint as the equivalent group of males, and as Kergoat has pointed out, even skilled female workers were more likely to work under a strong time constraint than male semi-skilled workers (1982: 43).

Clearly the degree of control imposed by such external pacing can vary considerably. The time constraint involved in assembling part of an electricity meter once every ten seconds is different from that required by the supervision of an automatic machine with a long cycle. However, other studies of women's and men's work have shown that women are more subject than men to short-cycle external constraints. Guilbert's study of the Parisian metal-working industry, for example, found that jobs done by women were characterized by short job cycles (almost one-third of the jobs having cycle times of under ten seconds), few planned or accidental stoppages of work, confinement to one position, and repetition of the same movement for each operation [Guilbert 1966: 162–70]. The image of the rapid, relentless, and unchanging assembly line does correspond to the working conditions of women workers in many parts of the world. In the seven factories studied in Brazil, women were found to be much more subject to the constraint of the time imposed by the work process itself than men. Women were, of course, excluded from the maintenance and machine-setting jobs which give much greater freedom, and within production work it was very rare to find men, but usual to find women, working on assembly lines. Women were also found in large numbers on jobs where the speed of work was controlled by the machine. These included packaging machines which had to be fed or unloaded at a certain rate (A2 and F1) and semi-automatic machines for assembling products and filling phials and tubes (A2, F1, and F2).

In the factory studied in greatest depth, E3, assembly lines were used in various female departments. In mixed departments the women worked on the line, while the men did other jobs, and in some all-women departments assembly lines were in use.[2] In the tuners department a moving belt carried units in front of seated workers at a rate of approximately one per minute. In the radio department the radios (large, traditional, table-top non-portable models) were passed from worker to worker along benches. The pace of the lines was dictated, to a large extent, by the workers at the front, very often the more experienced and quicker women. A reserve worker described the pace on one of the lines.

> 'I put materials there for the girls, take materials from them and I take their place when they have a break. If a soldering iron burns out, I replace it. I fetch and carry the flux. . . . I fetch water for the girls, because they don't have time to go and have a drink of water. If they went for a drink there would be three or four radios piled up on the PT line, which is the quickest. I've gotten used to it, but it's a rush. The new girls find it very rushed indeed.'
>
> (reserve, radio department)

In this case the pressure of work and the fixing of workers to a single position was determined by the organization of work itself. The flow of radios was maintained by the workers at the front of the line, and this ensured that workers had no free time, needed to be replaced when they had a break, and had to have equipment and materials brought to them.

When assembly lines are used, operatives have to be serviced by other workers in order that continuity of throughput be maintained, but in the case of E3 it was noticeable that where assembly lines were *not* in use, women were still serviced by other workers (and hence captive), whereas men tended to service themselves. This was evident in a comparison between the largest female department and the two largest male departments. In all three departments there were individual or small group work stations, where the rhythm of work was determined by the worker's speed of movement, whether in conjunction with simple machines or using hands and hand tools. In the two male departments, woodworking and metal-stamping, the routine production of items was interrupted by stoppages for the collection of materials, adjustment of machinery, fetching of tools, and consignment of batches of the finished products. Although there were unskilled workers in these departments, the fetching and carrying jobs were not devolved on to them. Thus the stamping of thousands of metal pieces in the course of a day would be interrupted by attention to dies, fetching new coils of metal, moving bins full of parts, and so on. In the (female) components department these ancillary jobs were largely performed by the charge-hands, which meant that there were no specified breaks for the women winding, assembling, or calibrating coils through the day. Production varied from 650 per day for the largest coils up to 5,000 per day for the smallest and simplest, and in principle the women were expected to carry on through the nine-and-a-half-hour day. There were no breaks to be had for collecting equipment or materials, and thus the work was open to stricter specification and surveillance. It was more parcellized and quantifiable.

Determination of output and control of 'free' time

The incorporation of rhythm and control into the organization of work and division of labour is much more commonly found in jobs done by women than in those done by men. However, it would be misleading to regard such work organization as the sole instance of greater managerial control over women. The differences between management control strategies for women and men is seen even more clearly when work speeds are *not* determined by the organization of work itself. The 1978 French study, for example, found that women were more likely than men to have regular checks on their output and have strict instructions not to talk while working (Molinie and Volkoff 1981: 56). Once again the contrast between the same three departments in the third electrical factory as mentioned above provided a clear indication that management were prepared to use direct supervision to impose a thorough-going control over female effort, space, and time which they did not apply to men.

In terms of effort, the difference between male and female working can be summarized in the notion of the men being left to 'get on with it', subject to overall constraints on production, while the women were subjected to a much greater degree of vigilance and continual control. The workers themselves distinguished between working 'a vontade' (at ease) and having the supervisor 'ficar no pé' (to stand over, or literally to stay on one's feet). The difference is not one of working hard or not. Workers on assembly lines in the motor industry often referred to working 'at ease', in spite of the rigours and intensity of their job (Humphrey 1982: 82–4). 'At ease' means that as long as the job is done, the foremen leaves workers to get on with it. The auto workers interviewed contrasted their being allowed to work 'at ease' with the situations in other plants, where the foremen constantly demanded more work and interfered in the job. Thus working 'at ease' refers to two things: being given a fixed quota to attain and not being subject to constant harassment. These two closely linked aspects will be analysed together, taking the situation in the male departments in E3 first.

In the male departments there were clear production norms, and time-and-motion studies were used by management. Managers had output and labour-force targets to reach, and workers were expected to put in a 'proper' day's work. However, within these constraints, management generally (but by no means always) treated workers with a certain degree of respect and care. The workers were allowed to get on with the job without continual interference. The managers of the two largest male departments in E3 did not regard intense pressure as very productive. As the head of the woodworking department expressed it: 'It's no use demanding too much of them. When you are looking they do eighty and when you aren't they do sixty.'[3] In part, too, management considered that too much pressure on output might adversely affect quality. The very layout of the two male departments encouraged this form of supervision. Both were laid out without clear lines of sight. The managers' rooms had no direct access to the working areas, and the workers were often 'sheltered' behind machines and walls. Finally, as was noted above, the division of labour in the departments meant that workers had legitimate reasons to interrupt work and move around, and possibly also to talk with materials suppliers, setters and maintenance workers.

The general view of the workers in the two male departments was that they were not forced into producing more than was reasonable:

> 'There has never been any trouble about output. I've never had a warning about production. . . . They never demand a certain amount and then force us to do it. The work is always coming, there's plenty of it. When there's a lot of work, the foreman says, "Let's see if we can get that done today." But he never insists.'
> (painter, woodworking department)

At the time of the survey the woodworking department was operating flat out to keep up with orders, and so management would request special efforts and extra overtime, but there appeared to be few overt threats. Workers were asked to 'co-operate', or to 'help out', or to make a special effort:

> 'There's never a lot of pressure. Everyone has work to do, but . . . [Is there pressure to increase production?] Only when a request

for a certain quantity of components comes in. They ask for more production, and we make a special effort.'

(press operator, metal-working department)

Behind this facade of friendliness and co-operation, of course, lay the threat of dismissal at a later date, for the possibility of being passed over for promotion. Workers knew they had to co-operate. With high unemployment at the time of the survey and the fear of further cut-backs, the manager of the metal-working department referred to his workers as working 'half-oppressed, with fear' because of insecurity. In spite of this, the style was distinctive, being not so much paternalistic as respectful. The male managers were conscious of having to 'manage' their labour forces, particularly the more skilled elements, and they felt that overt pressure was the not best way to secure maximum performance.

Needless to say, there were exceptions to this veneer of friendliness and co-operation. Among the forty male workers interviewed there was at least one complaint about overt and oppressive supervision:

'Sometimes you are tired and you just can't do that amount of work. He [the foreman] gets annoyed, says that we're just pretending to work. . . . The more you do, the more they want you to do. The foreman checks the score. We do 800 up to lunch, every day. A total of 1,600 in a day. . . . I work on the basis of pills really, to stop my body from aching. It's heavy work.'

(laminator, woodworking department)

This type of managerial imposition seems to have been exceptional. None of the other thirty-nine male workers interviewed mentioned such pressure. Although the workers were asked about their foreman's job, discipline, their own work, what happened if the workers were unwilling or unable to do a particular job, and how understanding of their problems the foremen were, the above statement was the only clear expression among the forty workers that they worked under severe pressure. While the workers made it clear that not doing one's job properly could lead to warnings, suspension, or the sack (as could playing about, drinking, and fighting), fulfilling one's quota was generally enough to keep out of trouble. This is working 'a vontade'.

In the female departments production norms were imposed in a rather different way. Control over female workers was facilitated by both the division of labour referred to above, which tied production workers to one point, being serviced by charge-hands and supervisors who also had a disciplinary and control function, and by the lay-out of the female departments themselves. Either by accident or design, the female departments had clear lines of sight, and in all three departments studied the workers were directly in the view of the manager's office. When workers were asked about the jobs of the supervisors and managers, they often talked in terms of 'looking' and 'keeping watch'.

The use of surveillance and control was particularly evident in the largest female department, components, precisely because it did not have assembly line production. The manager of this department had a general contempt for the women workers he could see while sitting at his desk. He regarded them as inherently unreliable and in need of strict discipline. He expected them to work through the day and to produce as much as possible:

> 'A certain level of production can be enforced. For each item there is a given output, determined through time-and-motion study. After a certain period the timing is checked again. With practice, the timing is always lowered. There are no bonuses for production. The directors believe that the more workers produce, the more they are fulfilling their obligation.'

This rather open-ended commitment to increase production was enforced in his department by pressure for workers to keep up with each other. Workers were expected to emulate the achievements of the fastest workers:

> 'If you do not produce the right amount, what they ask for, you're called to the desk. Any little thing and they keep getting at you until you manage to do it. . . . Pascoal [the foreman] says that we have to reach the target at any cost. And if you can produce even more, then you have to do it. On my machine I'm not able to produce what they ask for [after having been on coil-winding for only two months]. I just can't manage it. You have to make 3,000. But Geralda [the charge-hand] wants even more, and

for me to get to 3,000 without any practice. If you do more than 3,000, they want even more than that.'

(coil winder, components department)

'Most of the time there's no fixed quantity that you have to produce. If someone manages a certain output, then the others have to do it as well. If you don't, then you get a warning.'

(assembler, components department)

Not all workers succumbed to this pressure, but the interesting point is that there appeared to be no truce on the issue. Those who did not

The women assembling coils work at benches or tables in full view of the manager, foreman, and charge-hands. Although the women are working side-by-side, they are not passing work along to each other. The coils are assembled in large batches, and each type has an hourly production quota. The nearest woman is using her right hand to press a counter. She does this after each coil has been assembled. Since there is no counting of the exact numbers in each of the boxes, the women can register more on the counter than they actually assemble.

accept the pressure to emulate other workers were forced to fight against it, as the second of the two workers quoted above explained at some length:

> 'Most of us manage to do 2,000, but we put down 1,800 because the parts change and it is difficult to maintain that level of output. There are a lot of different parts, and a lot to produce each day. Sometimes, they suspect that something is going on, but they understand. The basic, then, is 1,800 a day, and if you manage that it's ok. . . . I've had three warnings – one verbal and two written – because of my level of output. I just couldn't manage it. . . . I still can't manage, so I put down more on the sheet than I actually do. I put 1,800. When it's an easier part, I manage to do 1,800. . . . It's not only me that does it. The quantities they send to us are never right, and they don't have any chance to keep control. Because some of the others can't keep up, they already come from the coil-winders with a quantity written down that doesn't match what's actually there.'
>
> (assembler, components department)

The women could resist the pressure put upon them, but the pressure was there. They could be verbally warned in front of other workers, suspended, or even sacked if they failed to meet the supervisor's demands. Managers and supervisors treated the women like children – with a mixture of paternalism and oppression. In the male departments, workers were handled more carefully and the pressure applied in more subtle ways.

It is not being claimed that such a contrast between the determination of male and female production norms exists universally in industry. In particular, the pressure for emulation of production targets can vary significantly. Hirata reports a case of a factory where an 'internal olympic production games' was organized among the women workers (not the men). A competition was held to see who could perform certain work tasks the fastest, with the 'finals' being viewed by workers and managers. The competition was an effective way of bringing down timings and establishing new production norms (Hirata 1984: 204). In contrast, in a factory adjacent to E1 a production worker reported that as long as she assembled seventy television tubes per hour and did not flaunt that she might be able to do more, she was left alone by the supervisors. This treatment is similar to that experienced by the men in E3. Conditions do vary considerably from factory to factory, and even from department to department and foreman to foreman, as Cavendish describes (1982: 87–9). However, within such variations, women are subject to greater control than men. This is made clear by the widespread differential regulation of breaks, 'free' time, and rests for women and men.

The difference between the control of female and male time was summed up in a comment by one of the few male workers to note the restrictions placed on women:

> 'For us down below [in the woodworking department] things are fine. They treat you like a friend. But for the women it's quite different. They have to take a disk if they want to go to the bathroom. They're forbidden to walk around or talk etc. There are a whole series of things that they are not allowed to do.'
>
> (machine operator, woodworking department)

In E3, the male workers were allowed, within the overall context of doing a proper day's work, to take short breaks. There were smoking areas designated for male workers, and there were no overt restrictions on going to the bathroom. Both of these activities are forms of taking a rest, and as Game and Pringle have noted in Australia, men are generally allowed to walk away from production and take breaks (1983: 32). But the women workers in E3 were not allowed to take such breaks. Although the formal prohibition on talking was widely ignored in most departments – women whispered, or talked a certain amount without appearing to be chatting away – they were not expected to allow this to interrupt their work. As a calibrator in the components department expressed it, 'Working and talking that's ok. But some girls stop their hands moving. They [the management] like you to work straight through, without slacking.' Similarly a checker in the radio department said:

> 'You're not supposed to stop work, but we always stop a little bit if no one is watching. But today I've got so much work I don't even have time to talk.'

Even when workers fulfilled their production targets, they were not allowed to rest, as this would be 'giving an example to the others', according to one worker in the components department.

The demand for continuity of work was expressed through a series of prohibitions. Women workers interviewed at an electrical factory in São Bernardo do Campo, for example, made the point that men could stop and drink their coffee as they pleased, while the women in the plant were obliged to drink their's seated at their work-bench. Peijnenberg reports the same situation at Philips in Guarulhos.[4] Smoking restrictions applying to women, but not to men, were also reported at several factories. Wherever restrictions were applied, they fell more heavily on women than on men.

Perhaps the clearest, most resented, and most uniform of all the restrictions placed on women workers relates to controls over going to the bathroom. Going to the bathroom is only partially about going to the lavatory. Women (and men) have a rest there, have a smoke, a proper chat without fear of the supervisors watching, even eat snacks and have drinks. Given that while they remain in the production area, they are expected to work, the bathroom provides an avenue of escape for women workers. It is an avenue that managements try to narrow as much as possible. In extreme cases it provides no privacy at all. In one factory in São Bernardo, the women workers reported that the foreman used to march into the bathroom and bang on the lavatory doors if he thought women had been in there too long, while one of Leite's interviewees reported the use of women monitors controlling access to the bathroom (1982: 83). More generally, though, access to the bathroom was controlled by use of the 'chapinha', or disk. This was found very frequently in female departments, but no instance of men having to use a disk was discovered in any of the factories studied.

The disk system regulates the number of women who can go to the bathroom at any one time, and it is normally used in conjunction with restrictions on the length of time and the number of times women are allowed to go to the bathroom during a day. Commonly women are not supposed to go more than once in the morning and once in the afternoon, and for a maximum of five to ten minutes. A disk is provided for a given group of workers, whose size can vary from as few as six or seven to as many as fifteen. A worker going to the bathroom has to take the disk with her, thus preventing more than one worker from the group going to the bathroom at the same time. Its effect is the same as that of the reserve system for women working on the line. If there is only one reserve worker, only one assembly line worker can be absent at any one time. The disk prevents women from going to the bathroom together, so that they cannot chat, and it is also the symbol of the time restrictions placed on such visits. The disk is widely used in Brazilian industry, and resentment of it is a common theme among women workers:

> 'Men have their time to drink coffee, and more time to go to the toilet. Women do not. They can only go to the toilet when there is someone to replace them. They are not allowed to interrupt their work. We have demanded many times that this situation be changed, but without success.'
>
> (TIE 1984: 36)

Leite, too, cites statements about the use and abuse of the disk system to control access to the bathroom, taken from workers from various factories in the city of São Paulo (1982: 82–3).

In E3, the battle over the disk was a barometer of the degree of intervention in workers' lives. The freedom to go to the bathroom and the time to be spent there was a source of constant skirmishing betwen workers and supervisors. As the workers made clear, the aim was to have a rest, not go to the toilet:

> 'There are two disks for ten people, five for each one. I, myself, go to the bathroom every hour because I get tired. I go to have a chat and a little rest. I stay for ten minutes.'
>
> (assembler, components department)

The time spent is a constant source of friction:

> 'You are allowed seven minutes, but we stay for ten or fifteen, until they find out. If she [the charge-hand] is already suspicious she notes the time and keeps an eye on the clock. But she doesn't take too much notice. Only if she hasn't much to do.'
>
> (coil-winder, components department)

Management see the issue in much the same light. The battle is a constant one:

> 'There's a moving assembly line, so only one woman can go to the bathroom at a time. There's no need for a disk, because there's only one reserve for each section of the line. Saying "not more

> than two girls can go at the same time'' is no use. If you go to the bathroom, there will be five or six of them there. . . . They eat snacks, chat. They always go in little groups. That's ok, I'm not strict. But they mustn't abuse it. If we start to lose control, then we do become very strict.'
>
> (manager, tuners department)

Once again, it is not being claimed that men are given a wide area of freedom to do as they like, compared to the restrictions placed on women. Nor is it being suggested that women are defenceless against management pressure. A woman in one section of the radio department, for example, merely said that when a disk was provided, they 'made it disappear'. However, with respect to control over space and time, management seem to be prepared to be more intrusive and demanding with women than with men. Within the overall constraints of productivity, management appear to be significantly more flexible with men and to arrive at an established working relationship.

GENDER AND CONTROL

The first section of this chapter has shown that there were systematic differences between the types of controls exerted over male and female workers in the factories studied. Although such differences can be the direct result of the kind of work done by men and women (which are not, themselves, constructed gender-blind), it was seen in the previous section that even when control was not incorporated into the organization of work, women were subjected to a greater degree of supervision, control, and pressure to increase production than men. A typical effect of this was the imposition of fewer constraints on men's space and time with respect to coffee breaks, going to the bathroom, and breaks for smoking. The evidence provided so far in this chapter seems to indicate that while women workers do not accept a high degree of surveillance and control without some resistance, managements are able to impose quite significantly tougher conditions on women than on men and this needs to be explained.

The explanations of such differences proferred by managements usually appeal to the 'natural docility' of women. As Elson and Pearson have noted:

> 'Women are considered [by companies] not only to have naturally nimble fingers, but also to be naturally more docile and willing to accept tough work discipline, and naturally less inclined to join trade unions than men; and to be naturally more suited to tedious, repetitious, monotonous work.'
>
> (1981: 93)

Women's supposed lack of ambition and willingness to spend day after day doing the same routine and repetitive tasks have been reported in many other accounts of management attitudes.[5] Such managerial statements cannot be taken as accurate assessments of women's attitudes and outlooks. Quite rightly Elson and Pearson have argued that the naturality and unproblematic nature of women's supposed docility is belied by both the considerable effort and trouble taken to impose strict control over women and the resentment and resistance that women display towards such control, particularly when managements are not at hand. Similarly one could challenge the term itself. 'Docility' is not a term which is normally applied to men, however acquiescent they might be. However, the managers who impose close supervision are the same men who talk of docility. They must mean something by the term, and it is important to establish what it might be.

Discussions of the opposite side of this question, women's militancy and trade union participation, have given considerable emphasis to situational factors.[6] These suggest that the patterns of militancy and trade union participation displayed by women are explained by reference to the low-wage, unskilled, and unstable jobs they generally occupy. It is not femaleness which determines women's attitudes, but rather their experience of work. The same logic can be applied to the issue of docility. Some of the differences observed between women and men can be attributed to differences in skill, labour market conditions, and work experience. Skilled workers are inherently less subject to control and supervision than unskilled workers because of the degree of unpredictability and variability in skilled work. One of the elements of skill is the requirement to assess situations and make decisions on action, and this gives the work some degree of control. Given that men monopolize access to the major part of skilled work, they are less subject to intrusive control than women. The labour market, too, leaves men in a stronger position than women. There is a much wider range of industrial work open to men than to women, and a typical male reaction to intrusive control is to search for another job. For women alternative employment is harder to find and not likely to avoid intrusive control. In the case of the third electrical factory, the labour market was a particularly important factor. The firm paid relatively low wages to men and the reaction to increased discipline would have been higher turnover. For women such a response was not really possible, given that conditions for women in other firms paying low wages were not going to be any better than in E3. Finally, it is noticeable that older and more experienced workers are more resistant to management power than younger ones. In so far as firms have strong preferences for the recruitment of relatively young and inexperienced women workers, women would be less resistant as a whole to managerial pressure. The resistance of the older workers might be swamped by weight of numbers of the younger female workers.

While there is some truth in these arguments, and they certainly provide a welcome counter to notions of innate passivity and docility, they can provide only a partial explanation. In the first place, even when situational factors are allowed for, there still remains a difference between men and women with regard to control incorporated in work and to supervision. Among unskilled workers, for example, it has been shown that women are more likely to have a strong time constraint built into their work than men. Studies in France have shown that while skilled women workers are less subject to strong time constraints than their unskilled colleagues, they are still more likely to work under such a constraint than any category of male worker, including the unskilled (Kergoat 1982: 43). The previous section also showed that even among unskilled production workers in the same industry who were not working under time constraint, significant differences in control between men and women could be seen. In the second place, the situational arguments outlined above are, to some extent, circular. It will be argued below that men have greater access to skilled work and are less likely to be found on routine assembly jobs precisely because they are very resistant to close control. Or, conversely, women's greater concentration in assembly work is a reflection, in part, of generalized management success in the imposition of close supervision and control. It is the result of managerial success in controlling women, not the cause.

What accounts for this success? To a large extent, the degree of close supervision exercised over workers by managements, and the effectiveness of controls embodied in the organization of work itself are determined by constant skirmishing between workers and managements which define the boundaries of what is acceptable and unacceptable. As was seen in the previous section, women workers in a section of the radio department in E3 made the disk system unacceptable by just refusing to operate it. Similarly patterns of work can be challenged by worker resistance in the form of low quality, unplanned stoppages, passive resistance, informal collusion between workers, and even outright hostility or violence to management. In the previous section it was shown that women seem to have had less success in resisting the imposition of constraints over their time and space, being subjected to a much greater degree of harassment and intimidation over output, rest periods, and physical movement than was the case for men. This has to be related not only to situational factors, but also to gender identities and the exercise of power between men and women.

This issue has been taken up in the literature largely in terms of the general character of male–female relations outside the home. Basically men exert power over women in society as a whole, and particularly within families. Therefore an order given by a male supervisor to a female worker has the authority of both a supervisor and a man behind it. Bullying, humiliation, sexual harassment, or patronizing superiority might be used by foremen to control women. Women are not defenceless, and in some situations they can gain the upper hand, as Cavendish (1982: 89–90) has shown, but the odds are against them. When foremen are in charge of men, the legitimacy of an order depends to a much greater extent on the foreman's authority within the hierarchy of work, and the personal authority of the foreman is much more open to question. The men, supervisors and supervised, will struggle for dominance. While unemployment and instability of labour may give the foremen the upper hand, workers will try to demoralize and undermine them if they can. These considerations apply generally, and they result from the general nature of gender relations in western societies. However, a fuller appreciation of the issues involved requires consideration of the ways in which masculine and feminine worker identities are constructed in factories. The boundaries of managerial control are also influenced by the characteristics that men and women acquire as workers through their employment.

The identities that male workers assume or construct in their work provide a series of defences against management power. In part, these defences relate to the knowledge, skill, and experience which are required for certain jobs. As was seen in Chapter 4, men are expected and encouraged to relate positively to the machinery they use – adjusting it, understanding it, and making it work. This gives them a certain degree of control and knowledge, which may in some practical respects make them better informed than their immediate superiors about the production process. This is a basis from which workers can challenge the authority of their supervisors. The appropriation of such practical knowledge is, of course, one (but only one) of the objectives of quality control circles. Such knowledge provides both a material point of resistance to managerial power and a degree of self-respect and self-valuation which is an important psychological resource.

Even unskilled manual workers whose access to, or control of, machinery is limited, can still find some basis for pride and self-esteem in what Willis has termed their 'robust masculinity' (1977: 150), and such pride is reinforced by managerial acknowledgement of strength as a factor in pay. The pride of the British working class in physical resistance to hard work described by Willis (1979: 188–89) can also be found in Brazil. In Chapter 4 men in the third electrical factory were quoted expressing pride that they had greater physical resistance than women, and a senior motor industry manager once expressed a certain despair that the response to intolerable conditions in the company's foundry was pride in resisting them rather than revolt at having to suffer them.[7] Even unskilled male workers, who are at the bottom of the official factory hierarchy for men (which is based on authority, skill, and pay), can judge themselves to be superior to managers, skilled workers, and women who lack their masculinity. As Willis suggests (1977: 150), they derive self-esteem from physical sacrifice and strength, and this can be used to view their 'superiors' with disdain and protect themselves from overbearing exertions of authority.

This masculinity is also in evidence in men's use of aggression to establish or subvert hierarchy and authority. Aggression, the implied threat of violence, and outright violence itself are characteristic of male behaviour to women and are also involved in the establishment of male hierarchies. Even though physical violence is relatively rare in factories, intimidation and the threat of trouble are not. When male managers and supervisors attempt to demean or degrade male workers, and particularly when they do this in the presence of other men, they are posing a direct challenge to the masculininty of the worker concerned. The response to this is two-fold. On the hand, the insult is diminished by a greater or lesser degree of insubordination. On the other, insubordination in the form of swearing, surliness or lack of co-operation is used to make it clear that the exercise of authority in this way is intolerable and will lead to trouble. The workers will tend to react as 'men', not as subordinates, to commands given in the wrong way. As a result, supervisors and managers often find it is easier to adopt the strategy of 'matiness' mentioned in the previous section, making suggestions to workers which they cannot refuse. Masculine pride responds to challenges rather than obligations. Men know they are obliged to work and obey orders, but they like to salvage their pride.

Women are denied many of the defences available to men. As was seen in Chapters 3 and 4, they are denied any status in the factory. Upon arrival they are classed as temporary and uncommitted workers. The work they do and the abilities they have are regarded as inferior to male work and male abilities by both managers and male workers. For this reason they are also denied the chance to acquire technical competence and skill, even when male workers in similar work situations might be encouraged to acquire such competences, as was seen in Chapter 4. Women are always surrounded by men – managers, supervisors, technicians, or machine-setters – who claim to know much more about their jobs than they do. Women are left without the material defences of skill and knowledge. At the same time their ideological and collective defences are undermined. The competences, abilities, and skills they possess are denied or ignored. It is hardly surprising that women very often lack the self-confidence needed to resist management pressure on a day-to-day basis.

At the same time, women are oppressed by the use of male power by supervisors and managers. Sexual harassment, which can take various forms, is just one part of this. The women in the third electrical factory reported things such as demands for sexual favours, usually starting by an invitation to go out for a drink, by supervisors and managers in return for promotion or a favourable probationary period report. Managers may also hire or promote women on the basis of their attractiveness. Even though some women may, in certain circumstances turn this weapon to their own advantage, the cards are stacked against them. They can be sacked by foremen and managers for rejecting advances, sacked if a relationship comes to an end, and in many cases sacked if they denounce the offender. However, direct sexual harassment appeared to be limited. Possibly more persuasive and generalized are the public humiliations and demeaning of women through bullying, shouting, abuse, and disciplinary warnings. Although, once again, by no means universal, such practices seemed quite common in Brazilian factories, and some of them were described in the earlier part of this chapter. It seems fairly clear than neither the content of such admonitions nor the tone in which they were administered would have been in any way acceptable to men.

This kind of intimidation is particularly effective against younger women, who constitute the majority of the labour forces in the various factories studied (see Chapters 2 and 3). Older women tend to be more assured and more comfortable in the factory situation because they have generally had a longer period of time in it. Cavendish, for example, noted an instance of aggressive female sexual behaviour to a foreman by older women (1982: 89–90), and Cunnison has described older women making fun of younger men and being assertive towards them in a work environment (1983: 83). Although Cunnison argues that such behaviour does not improve the economic situation of women workers, it can be suggested that it is a sign of their greater powers of resistance to management. In some Brazilian factories, too, management were aware of the greater ease of control afforded by younger workers, and it is interesting to note that the only sign of overt resistance to the disk registered in the previous section came in the radio department, which had a distinctly older and long-serving labour force than the other departments.

For some male trade union activists, the only way for women to resist such pressure would be to adopt the 'male' style. The comment of a male unionist who had played a crucial role in a struggle for equal pay in a motor components factory in São Bernardo was illustrative:

> 'We used to say, "Look, sister, when some bloke wants to put one over on you, to give you a suspension, you have to do like a man would. It's no use crying about it. You have to answer back in the

same way. Tell him – or if it's a women, tell her – where he can go''.'[8]

Even when such a statement is sincere, and not merely used to indicate that women are unfit for the rough-and-tumble of industrial work (Cockburn 1983: 177–78), it is hardly of much use. For women workers, male violence is both threatening and real. Women are much more subject to the violence and intimidation of men than are other men. At the same time, responding in kind to male aggression is likely to be considered outrageous not only by men, but also by many women, too. Swearing back at a foreman is considered a male preserve.

Women, men, and assembly work

These differences in resistance to managerial control by men and women provide a starting-point for a discussion of why management so strongly prefer to employ women for certain kinds of routine assembly work. The fact that the work is unskilled does not explain why women are found performing it to such a disproportionate extent. Men perform unskilled work, but of a rather different kind. Managements clearly believed that women are more productive than men in routine, assembly line work, and work of a similar nature in general, and once again this was often attributed to natural factors, as was noted in Chapter 4. Women were considered to be both 'naturally' more dexterous than men and 'naturally' more adaptable to routine and monotonous work.[9] It is the second of these two attributes which deserves the most attention.

Lim reports that in some Singapore factories comparative trials showed that women workers were considered to be better than men on assembly lines, not because they worked faster, but because the work they produced was of a higher quality. She suggests that this might not be the result of dexterity as such – the ability to perform certain physical tasks – but rather the product of the greater care, patience, and attention shown by women workers, as well as their training in needlework (1978: 23). However, one might turn the question around and ask why men do not display care, patience, and attention, and relate the issue to the perceptions that men (and women) have of particular jobs and the careers they entail. A quality control manager with long experience of managing both male and female workers in the second electrical factory made a clear distinction between the outlooks of male and female workers and the impact of such outlooks on job performance:

> ' "Why are women preferred for routine inspection work?"
> "It's because the work is very repetitive. A man will get fed up and start to let through defective radios. On the male lines they used to let a lot of defective radios through. A man wants to get ahead more. He's going to be looking to do that little bit extra. He wants to escape from a set pattern. A woman – give her the ten commandments and she follows them. With ten boys, eight will be looking for promotion. But not with women. The women will stay for ten or fifteen years in the same job. . . . Men work more as radio technicians, which is trouble-shooting. . . . It's less repetitive. For example there are no men inserting components [into radios]. They would do it all wrong." '

The manager is suggesting that male workers lack patience and care, not because they are innately incapable of possessing or using such characteristics, but because they are frustrated by work which appears to offer no scope for initiative. In part, this is due to the promotion and 'family wage' question discussed in Chapter 3. Care and attention depend on the work and how it measures up to self-perceptions. Men can be careful and responsible working at a lathe and irresponsible and careless when performing assembly work.

Male irresponsibility in relation to assembly line work, and their resistance to doing it appears to be based partly on the nature of the work and partly on the definition of such work as 'female'. The latter involves not only low status, but also low wages and lack of promotion opportunities, as will be seen in Chapter 6. The first problem for male workers is that assembly line depends on continuous working for high productivity.[10] If men are to be employed in such work and match female productivity levels, then they would have to be subjected to the same degree of control as imposed upon women workers. Male workers are normally very resistant to such controls, and in industries where such controls are applied, such as the motor industry, wages have to be high in order to attract and retain men willing to accept such discipline (Humphrey 1982). Even with high wages, such industries are often characterized by poor labour relations. Given women's greater susceptibility to managerial close supervision strategies, they are easier to manage when put to assembly line work. Furthermore, male workers also resist assembly line work because of the terms and conditions of service usually associated with it. The low wages and lack of promotion opportunities which mark many production jobs performed by women (as indicated in Chapter 2) make such jobs very unattractive to men, for the reasons outlined in Chapter 3. In a country like Brazil, where wages for unskilled workers (male and female) are not only low in absolute terms, but also very low in relation to wage rates for even marginally more skilled workers, lack of promotion is a serious threat to long-term income, as was seen in Chapter 3. Just as the manager of the woodworking department said that it was necessary to select male workers for dead-end jobs with great care, so putting men on to dead-end assembly line jobs causes problems.

As a result of these factors, male workers present a number of problems for management when performing certain kinds of routine work. The quality of production would be relatively low, there would be resistance to close supervision, and turnover rates would be high, because workers would leave in search of better jobs. This would be the case even if the work was not identified as 'female', although this severely compounds the problem for men. It is the absence of such problems that lead managements to talk of women's 'docility', even when they control closely the movement and work of women workers. Women accept and prefer the lightness of the work (as was seen in Chapter 4), and they may accept the monotony of routine work and continue doing it for a long time because they are consistently led to believe that more complex work is beyond their possible reach, in terms of both ability to perform it and the chance of men allowing them access to it. At the same time, they do not push for promotion because their right to be in paid employment at all is only grudgingly conceded by management, by male workers, and by males who claim authority over them in the domestic situation (see Chapter 3). Although management may interpret the results of these factors as a 'preference' for monotonous work, as was noted in Chapter 4, it might more accurately be considered as women's only realistic alternative. To this extent, therefore 'docility' in management eyes is compatible with a considerable degree of resistance by women, and the 'preference' for monotonous work can be combined with a great degree of job dissatisfaction and resentment.

Therefore managements preferred to employ women for certain types of work. At the same time, managements attempt to make certain kinds of job more acceptable to men. This was seen in the third electrical factory, where peripheral aspects of jobs, such as materials supply, were incorporated into the job definition, thus allowing greater freedom of movement to the male workers. Jobs can also be made more acceptable by relatively high wages and promotion opportunities. The use of such strategies to control male labour forces in the Brazilian motor industry has been described in detail elsewhere (Humphrey 1982). The use of such employment policies – stabilization of labour, wage levels, promotion, and so on – can be combined with work organization practices and tailored to meet management requirements with respect to male and female labour forces. The construction of gender-specific employment policies is the subject of the next chapter.

6
Gender hierarchies and the structure of industrial labour markets

INTRODUCTION

The discussion undertaken in the previous three chapters now provides the basis upon which to reconsider the occupational structures outlined in Chapter 2. That chapter showed that women workers in the plants studied were generally concentrated in a small number of quality control and production occupations at the bottom of the job hierarchy, earning low wages relative to the male workers in the same plants. The male workers, in contrast, were distributed across a much broader range of occupations, skill classifications, and wage rates. It was argued in the introduction that theories of dual and segmented labour markets have provided one major and influential attempt to explain such differences in the occupational fortunes of different classes of workers, who might be distinguished by race, gender or some other factor.[1] Originally brought into prominence in the early 1970s by Doeringer and Piore's analysis of patterns of racial disadvantage in industrial labour markets in North America (Doeringer and Piore 1971), such theories have been applied by many writers to the analysis of sex discrimination and the sexual division of labour in industry. They have also been widely used in discussions of differentiation within the working classes of Latin American countries, although these analyses have tended to treat the industrial labour force as wholly or predominantly male.

It was suggested in the introduction that dual labour market theories could not account for the sexual division of labour because they treated labour as non-gendered, and in Chapter 4 the construction of gender identities within plants was discussed in some detail. In the light of this, the theoretical foundations of both the so-called 'orthodox' school of dual labour market theory, best represented by Peter Doeringer and Michael Piore, and the 'radical' school, whose main exponents have been Richard Edwards, David Gordon, and Michael Reich, have to be examined and criticized. This will be followed by a re-examination of differences in job grading, promotion, skill, and stability of employment for women and men. These differences will be reassessed in the light of the notion that they express and reinforce gender hierarchies rather than provide the causes of them.

THEORIES OF LABOUR MARKET SEGMENTATION

Segmented labour market theory developed as a critique of the theory of wage determination provided by neo-classical economics, which assumes that the price of labour, the wage rate, is determined by the forces of supply and demand, as is the case with the price of any other goods. The equilibrium price of any particular type of labour should equal the extra value produced by the last worker to be hired.[2] The wages of different categories of worker are directly related to their productiveness for employers. If all workers have a chance to compete for all jobs, then wages should reflect productivity. Any differences in pay rates for groups of workers of equal productivity would lead to a substitution of the higher-paid workers by the lower-paid. As a result, differences in wages should reflect real differences in productivity, and the causes of women's low pay should be sought in labour supply factors, such as education and training. The problem lies outside the market.

This link between wages and productivity is not, crucially, questioned by dual labour market theories. However, it is suggested that workers' productivity can be increased by the experience of work itself, with the result that once workers gain access to certain kinds of jobs, their advantages relative to other workers are reinforced by the very fact of having gained access. This acts as a restriction on open competition for jobs, as workers within a particular enterprise have privileged access to other jobs within it. Greatest attention has been given by dual labour market theorists to internal promotion systems within large enterprises and their impact upon industrial labour markets.[3] Such promotion systems create a 'primary' labour market, formed by clusters of jobs which offer workers relatively high wages, opportunities for training and promotion, and stability of employment. Outside of this primary labour market lies the 'secondary' sector, composed mainly of low-wage, dead-end, and unstable jobs. Barron and Norris have summarized the characteristics (but not the causes) of a dual labour market structure:

> '1. There is a more or less pronounced division into higher paying and lower paying sectors; 2. Mobility across the boundaries of these sectors is restricted; 3. Higher paying jobs are tied into promotional and career ladders, while lower paying jobs offer few opportunities for vertical movement; 4. Higher paying jobs are relatively stable, while lower paying jobs are unstable.'
>
> (1976: 49)

The labour market, then, is divided into good and bad jobs, the former being associated with internal promotion and career ladders. Once a worker finds her- or himself in one segment of the market, it is difficult to move across to the other. The theories of segmented labour markets, as applied to the explanation of women's disadvantage in work and the sexual division of labour, have to address the issue of why women are largely confined to the bad, low-wage jobs, while men have much better chances of moving up occupational hierarchies, along the so-called 'mobility chains' which link together groups of jobs, each being better paid than the one lower in the chain. The issue is why women do not have opportunities to raise their productivity. As Lloyd and Niemi so unambiguously put it:

> 'Productivity-enhancing job experience and differential access to such experience are the keys to the vicious circle of constrained opportunities in which the woman worker is still trapped.'
>
> (1979: 12)

Women, it is argued, are not given a chance to increase their productivity and thus their wages remain low and promotion opportunities limited.

The two main versions of segmented labour market theory purport to explain both the causes of the segmentation of jobs into two or more distinct groups and the principles upon which particular categories of workers are selected for, or allocated to, each segment of the market. It has been argued that neither version of the theory is really a theory at all, but rather little more than a description of labour market structures in the USA in the 1970s. Rubery suggests that successive developments of segmented labour market theory without any clear statement of principles has resulted in 'more a rationalisation of the present structure of the American labour market than an explanation of how this was arrived at' (1980: 243). However, both lines of argument must be taken as theoretical accounts of the development and operation of the labour markets they describe. If they are not, the segmented labour market notion loses all its analytical value. Perhaps more importantly, it is only by treating such notions as theories and criticizing them theoretically that their widespread use as explanations of the positions of women and men in employment can be challenged directly.

The orthodox version of segmented labour market theory developed by Doeringer and Piore attributed the development of the divide between primary and secondary labour markets to three factors: the specificity of skills, the importance of on-the-job training, and custom and practice (1971: 13–26). The authors give greater emphasis to the first two factors than to the third, arguing that in modern manufacturing enterprises there is an increased demand for job-specific knowledge which can best be acquired through training on the job. This, it is claimed, provides firms with an incentive to recruit workers at the lower levels of the job hierarchy and fill vacancies at higher levels through internal promotion, because workers can acquire the attributes necessary for performance of higher-ranked jobs while being employed to do lower-ranked tasks. Thus access to good jobs is restricted to workers already hired.[4]

Doeringer and Piore argue further that the acquisition of such job-specific knowledge by workers leads firms to concern themselves with the stability of their labour forces. Labour force stability will maximize the return on investments in training, and this leads to the payment of relatively high wages as a strategy to reduce turnover. Therefore skill specificity and on-the-job training create an occupational structure characterized by relatively high wages, stability of employment, internal training, and advancement along lines of promotion (or mobility chains) within enterprises. These conditions are most likely to be found in large enterprises, which have both sophisticated technology and the financial and organizational power to develop internal labour markets. Outside of these large enterprises, however, non-craft, blue-collar occupations will remain largely low-wage, unskilled, and unstable. Workers in the secondary sector are denied the chance to compete for better jobs because they fail to gain access to the lower parts of the mobility chains leading to them, and because over time they acquire the characteristics of the secondary sector jobs which they occupy, such as instability and lack of skill.

The determinant factor in the formation of labour markets is said to be the technologies employed by modern, large-scale industries. The upper- and lower-tier mobility chains which constitute two parts of the primary labour market arise as a result of the use of large-scale technology, while small-scale production tends not to produce them (Piore 1975: 141). The number and characteristics of jobs in the two segments of the labour market, primary and secondary, are thus determined to a large extent by the technologies being used in industries, with only minor adjustments to be made at the margin by the lengthening or shortening of the bottom end of the mobility chains:

> 'The basic hypothesis is essentially that the underlying determinant of mobility chains is the structure of technology. This dictates a core of jobs that lend themselves to the building of lower-tier mobility chains. . . . The technology which generates these core jobs also has a much smaller complement of work which lends itself to upper-tier mobility chains.'
>
> (Piore 1975: 147)

While the dual labour market structure might be reinforced by the activities of trade unions, it pre-dates unions and is a product of modern technology.[5]

The radical theory of labour market segmentation shares much of this analysis. Developed in a number of jointly authored and individual publications by Edwards, Gordon, and Reich, the radical theory accepts that industrial labour markets are segmented and that the main features of the primary labour market are stability of employment and opportunities for advancement (see Edwards 1979: 170–71). However, they suggest that the segmentation of industrial labour markets arose as a reaction by North American employers to the struggles of workers in the early years of the twentieth century. They locate the emergence of segmented labour markets within the specific historical context of the rise of what they call 'monopoly capitalism' (that is, a capitalist industrial and economic system dominated by large firms who face limited competition at the sectoral level), and the changes in the organization of work associated with it – particularly the decline of the skilled worker and the gang system following the development of mass production techniques. These techniques not only undermined the position of the skilled worker, but also concentrated and homogenized the labour force, creating a rising tide of labour opposition (Reich, Gordon, and Edwards 1980: 234). The employers tried various means of containing this protest, including welfare capitalism and company unions (Edwards 1979). One particularly successful and long-lasting strategy was the creation of divisions within the labour force along the lines of skill and experience, dividing workers into an unstable peripheral group and a stable core labour force. Such segmentation of the labour market was made possible by the growth of the large corporation, whose size and market power made long-term manpower planning feasible. Alongside such large firms, the small continued to exist, but their susceptibility to cyclical fluctuations of the economy denied them any chance of offering employment terms comparable to those in large firms.

In both versions of dual labour market theory the definition of a particular job (that is type of work performed) immediately defines a given set of employment policies. Wage levels and forms, skill classifications, stability, promotion opportunities, and so on, are largely or entirely determined by the nature of the work required. Specification of a job is seen to determine the worker's productivity, his/her skill, the training opportunities which might arise, and the chances of access to higher occupations. Hence the structure and importance of primary and secondary labour markets appears to be determined by technology and work content.

The radical theory is less an alternative to the orthodox theory than an extention and modification of it. As Rubery argues, the capitalists' need for a control strategy has merely been added to the technically based labour force stabilization arguments of Doeringer and Piore [Rubery 1980: 247]. The radical perspective retains the ideas that productivity-enhancing experience is central and that occupations are defined without reference to the gender of those who will fill them. At some points the direction of the causal relation between technology and labour market structures seems to be inverted. Reich, Gordon, and Edwards, for example, suggest that technologies will evolve on the basis of existing labour market structures (1980: 239), and Edwards argues that firms will choose between existing technologies according to the type of control strategy they wish to adopt or maintain (1979: 179). Even so, the strong causal connection is maintained. If a certain group of workers is at the bottom of the job hierarchy, then they must have been denied access to the productivity-enhancing job experience mentioned by Lloyd and Niemi (1979). Thus the low-wage, dead-end jobs occupied by women are defined as such independently of the fact that women occupy them. Places in the labour market are defined before gender is considered.

The effect of this is to leave the labour market itself largely outside the discussion of women's oppression. The factors which determine the characteristics of jobs and the allocation of individuals to them are not, themselves, gendered. Even when dual labour market theory specifically addresses the issue of the sexual division of labour, it is forced to explain why women have certain attributes (or lack others) which would, if they were possessed by men, also deny them access to the primary labour market. Walby has put the point with admirable clarity in her critique of Barron and Norris:

> 'They describe the structuring of the labour market into two sectors in non gender-specific terms. They do not see the structure of the market as being determined or even shaped in any way by sexual divisions. It is seen as a consequence of the employers' needs both to retain skilled labour and to buy off the better organized workers (who are referred to in a non gender-specific manner). Sexual differentiation is seen as largely determined outside of the labour market in the sexual division of labour in the household.'
>
> (Walby 1983: 155)

A further effect of this conception of places in the labour market is that neither the orthodox nor the radical versions of the theory need to pay attention to the actual characteristics of the workers found in the various segments of the market. It is assumed that workers in the secondary sector must be there because they have secondary characteristics which dispose employers to locate them in that segment. The same applies for primary sector workers. Workers in primary sector jobs must have the objective economic characteristics which led employers to select them for such jobs. By and large, workers are placed in the jobs for which they are suited. Even if critics argue that the specific reasons advanced by dual labour market theorists to account for women's disadvantage are 'stereotyped assumptions' offered with 'little evidence . . . that these attributes actually are significant in concrete situations' (Beechey 1978: 176), the theorists can respond by saying that these or other similar factors must be operating, otherwise women (or any other social group which tends to end up in secondary sector jobs) would have greater access to better jobs.

In this way dual labour market theorists manage to assume exactly what they need to prove. For example Chiplin and Sloane state that 'in the industrial case one must recognise that natural endowments differ between the sexes' (1980: 291).[6] This is not the issue. Of more concern is whether or not employers concern themselves only with endowments which translate into higher productivity. The evidence presented in Chapters 3 and 4 shows that this is not the case. Irrespective of productivity considerations, some endowments seem to matter much more than others.

A similar problem can be seen with regard to turnover. If any doubt is cast on the assumption that women's turnover is higher and more problematic for employers than men's, the dual labour market theorists would argue that female turnover must be higher, given that equal turnover would tend to lead to men and women having similar training and promotion opportunities, which they manifestly do not. This line of argument allows empirical evidence which might question the general line of approach to be deflected. For example Chiplin and Sloane cite evidence from a study which showed that 75 per cent of the return on a training scheme for women in a clothing firm was derived from increased stability of employment, and only 25 per cent from higher productivity. The conclusion they draw from this is that female turnover is an important factor in management preferences for training men (1980: 247). This conclusion makes sense only on the assumption that firms are rational profit-maximizing institutions whose preference for training men is cost-efficient. If this assumption is not made, the same data can be taken to show that women's turnover is greatly increased by the reservation of training opportunities for men, and that female turnover (and male) is largely a result, not a cause, of management policy.

For dual labour market theory, then, the labour market operates in an objective manner. Differences between categories of workers are, to a large extent, seen to be the result of differences in the productivity of their labour, even if the labour market operates in such a way as to widen initial differences in qualities of labour. Gender is either left as a pre-market phenomenon or introduced as a distortion of the correct market functioning. There are two versions of such distortions. The first suggests that employers might choose or prefer to discriminate against women, paying men higher wages for work of equal value or employing men when women might be more available or better qualified. Such discrimination is seen as irrational, and the employer would suffer a loss in profit in return for some presumed benefit from pure discrimination against women. This notion is clearly unsatisfactory as an explanation of the sexual division of labour and women's disadvantaged position. Its perspective views labour power as a commodity like any other and defines the issue solely in terms of price and the point of purchase. Discrimination is confined to an arbitrary and irrational preference by some employers. It has no systemic quality and workers are not involved.

The second attempt to introduce gender into labour market models is altogether more satisfactory. Hartmann has argued that capitalism creates places in the labour market, while gender and racial hierarchies determine who will fill them:

> 'Capitalist development creates the places for a hierarchy of workers, but traditional marxist categories cannot tell us who will fill which places. *Patriarchy is not simply hierarchical organisation*, but hierarchy in which *particular* people fill *particular* places.'
>
> (1981: 18, stress in original)

Male power bars women from good jobs. Hartmann stresses worker-led segregation and criticizes radical dual labour market theory for seeing labour markets structured solely by capitalists and not by male workers. Hartmann's approach has the merit of putting patriarchy and male workers at the centre of the analysis, but it is still unsatisfactory because it views the factory from the outside and maintains the link between wages and productivity. Captitalism is characterized as an objective hierarchy of work and occupations which is then changed by the action of patriarchy (Phillips and Taylor 1980: 81–2).

This characterization of the relationship between the principles of capitalism and the principles of patriarchy has three weaknesses. First, the conception of the secondary labour market remains too abstract. It comprises all the bad jobs which are left to those workers who are excluded from the primary labour market. As a result, there is no basis for considering how divisions may be constructed differently along racial and gender lines, and the considerable degree of sex segregation within secondary labour markets is left unexplained. Second, Hartmann does not provide an account of how labour markets can adapt to the nature of the available labour force. In other words she cannot theorize how occupations can be constructed around the characteristics (gender or race) of those occupying them, and this means that the flexibility with which types of workers can be matched to types of jobs is seriously underestimated. Third, Hartmann's conception does not provide sufficient analysis of how gender identities for masculine and feminine workers are constructed within work situations. Partiarchy is seen to challenge capitalist principles, rather than subvert them, as was suggested in Chapter 4.

In order to create space for gender to operate as a factor within the labour market, two fundamental aspects of dual labour market theory have to be questioned. The first concerns the concept of occupation, which in the theory conflates, on the one hand, the work performed by a worker, and, on the other, the wages, promotion prospects, skill classifications, and so on, associated with performance of that work. These need to be distinguished and their relation problematized. This then allows a second aspect of the theory to be questioned – the link between wages and productiveness or, in other words, the assumption that promotion and higher wages are dependent upon increased productivity. Once this has been done, the structure of labour markets can be considered in a fresh light.

Comparisons of labour market structures developed around similar or identical technologies have shown a considerable variability in the division of labour and employment policies. The same jobs can be combined with a variety of employment policies, as can be seen in international comparisons. Coriat's study of French and Brazilian cement factories, for example, reveals that identical plant could be combined with the use of polyvalent work teams in the parent company and specialized workers in the subsidiary (Coriat 1981). Similarly Hirata's analysis of factories in Japan and Brazil highlighted the ways in which different labour systems in the two countries were combined with the same technology in the petrochemical industry (Hirata 1984: 205–06). Rubery's arguments concerning the role of the trade unions in the emergence of labour markets in Britain points in the same direction. Well-organized workers can impose skill classifications and pay scales which are not defined by the work performed alone (Rubery 1980: 261–65).

The importance of these cases is that they show how different employment policies can be combined with the same work being done. This implies that labour market structures depend very much on labour supply and that if, therefore, there are well-established expectations about the statuses of male and female workers and the segregation of work along gender lines, and if these are backed up by male workers and managements alike and rarely challenged by women workers (as was seen in Chapter 4), there is no reason why different employment policies might not be developed for female and male workers. When managements consider how to resolve the difficult and often contradictory problems posed by the needs of recruiting, keeping, training, and controlling a labour force, they could find different solutions for the male and female labour forces, as was seen in the discussion of management strategies for men and women in Chapter 3. In certain circumstances the same work (or similar work) might be ranked differently, or divided up differently, or linked into mobility chains differently according to the sex of the workers concerned. In other words, far from the jobs being defined independently of sex and the discrimination against women consisting of their allocation to the worst jobs, as Hartmann has argued (1979: 207), the employment policies might themselves depend on the gender of those filling them. Skill classifications or promotion opportunities would be adapted according to whether women or men are occupying the jobs concerned.

In a situation where managements make decisions in a context characterized by such factors as male pressure for a family wage, the pervasive devaluation of female attributes and capabilities, and the resistance of men to being given an equal or lower status to women workers (seen in Chapters 3 and 4), it is likely that managements will structure employment policies so as to down-grade women and up-grade men. Such up-grading of men and down-grading of women (relative to the work they actually perform or could perform) can take two distinct forms. First, access to those jobs which do require a certain degree of training, or command a wage premium irrespective of the sex of those employed in them, is reserved almost entirely for men. Second, even when men and women perform work of roughly equal value, or work which requires a similar degree of training and experience, managements will construct different employment policies for each sex, paying male workers higher wages than female. To the extent that this takes place, pay will not reflect productivity, with women workers being paid less than men quite systematically, even when productivity levels are comparable. The substitution of high-cost male workers by lower-cost-women in these circumstances is prevented by job segregation, the gender identities which allocate women and men to different sorts of work, male resistance, and the complicity of managements.

In these circumstances labour market structures incorporate gender hierarchies but do not cause them. Promotion chains, skill categories, and job evaluation can be used to maintain male privilege. In some cases this is seen quite clearly. Snell cites the case of the United Kingdom following equal pay legislation, where job evaluation procedures were modified in order to give greater and disproportionate emphasis to lifting, which was performed mainly by men. This resulted in the overvaluation of male work and the maintenance of pay differentials in spite of the new legislation (Snell 1979: 45). She also notes that segregation by department and occupational title, confidentiality about wage rates, and the exclusion of most women from wage bargaining and trade union activities meant that employers' non-compliance with the Equal Pay Act could pass by unnoticed (1979: 43–4).

These forms of discrimination are much more common than the simple case of men and women being paid unequal pay for equal work. Such cases do exist – as was seen in the plastics factory cited in Chapter 4, where a struggle for equal pay did take place – but a lot of discrimination against women is incorporated into the division of labour and segregation of male and female workers. Direct comparisons between male and female workers are largely avoided, and separate spheres of male and female work with non-comparable employment policies are constituted. Seen from this perspective, the labour market structures analysed by dual labour market theorists acquire new meanings, and their functions and causes have to be reinterpreted.

A CASE STUDY OF MOBILITY CHAINS

A case study from the first of the electrical factories clearly illustrates some of the mechanisms that allocate women to low-paid jobs, reserve promotion for men, and grade women's work as unskilled. The plant produced a range of silicon chips, which involved all the stages of production, from initial coating of the silicon wafers, through testing, mounting, and sealing for final use. Women workers constituted 76 per cent of all the hourly-paid labour force, and over 90 per cent of production workers. The women employed were concentrated at the bottom of the job hierarchy, with 90 per cent of the 374 women in production and quality control jobs classified as 'production assistants', the lowest-paid job in the plant. They earned less even than the unskilled workers in the canteens and kitchens, and their wages were close to the minimum payable in the industry.

Some of the female production workers did simple but exacting jobs, such as cutting and breaking wafers into single chips, sorting chips into approved and rejected groups, and wiring small numbers of connections. Such work certainly required a degree of manual dexterity, good eyesight, and considerable concentration over the course of the working day, but it would be classified as unskilled, as were the few production jobs done by men, which mainly involved standing, lifting, and exposure to heat. However, there were other jobs which required a good deal more training and experience, chief among which were those related to the production of the wafers themselves. These were made in a special sterile area, sealed off from the rest of the plant. The wafer department's output was the foundation of the work in the rest of the plant, and the success of the plant as a whole depended on acceptably low levels of wastage being achieved there. All the non-supervisory staff in this department were women, and they had to use sophisticated machinery with great care in order to achieve the successful cycles of photo-engraving, etching, and particle depostion which produce chips of the required standard. Each woman in the department was expected to be capable of carrying out all the functions within it, and although the machinery was highly automated and set up by male technicians, the women were obliged to work with extreme care and attention and to have experience and responsibility. In the photo-engraving stage, for example, the workers had to take a batch of wafers, check that they were the ones specified on the instruction card, check the kind of chip being made and the layer being applied, and then select the correct mask and align it correctly over the first wafer in the batch, using a microscope to check the alignment at a certain number of points.

The inspection of wafers which followed required even greater experience and attention. This consisted of a visual inspection by microscope at nine reference points in order to check for approximately twenty basic defects. The male supervisor in the department explained that if badly engraved wafers were allowed to pass the inspection, they would have to be scrapped at a later point. In his opinion, the best young, female workers, chosen from the assembly lines, would require between four and six months' intensive training and constant supervision in order to be able to spot the main defects that arose. The women working in the department represented a considerable expenditure in terms of training for the company and also an asset in terms of their experience and knowledge. However, in spite of this and in spite of the need for high standards of care, cleanliness, attention to detail, and discipline, *all* the female workers in the wafer department were classifed as unskilled 'production assistants'. Without exception they were being paid the lowest wage rate in the plant.

Let us consider what might happen if the supply of female labour were to disappear for some reason. Had male workers been employed in the plant, the occupational structure would have looked very different. The plant's manager revealed that prior to the construction of the new factory and the introduction of more advanced technology, both men and women had been employed on the basic production processes. In his opinion, while the quality and productivity of the male workers had been equal to the female, the relatively high rate of turnover among men had been a problem. Male workers, he said, had tended to leave in search of better job opportunities, and this he attributed to dissatisfaction with the low wages and poor promotion prospects. Women workers, in contrast, did not present these problems: they remained in the firm for relatively long periods in spite of being confined to low-wage and dead-end jobs. As Brazilian managers so often remark, women workers seem to be more stable within a given occupational category, while male workers either push for promotion or leave in search of opportunities elsewhere.

It is not hard to imagine how management would tackle the 'problem' of male turnover. Even if the organization of work and specification of occupations were to remain unaltered (and in view of Chapter 5 this is unlikely), there would be drastic changes in employment policies. The firm could increase wage rates across the board as a means of reducing the male turnover, but a more cost-efficient means of stabilizing the male labour force would be to recognize that certain jobs require more training, responsibility, experience, and dexterity, and to pay these jobs more highly than the others. Mobility chains would be constructed to link the less skilled occupations to the more skilled. This would have a number of advantages for the company. The more experienced workers would be offered higher wages and be encouraged to stay in the job. At the same time, the unskilled workers would be given an incentive to put up with relatively low rates of pay, because they would have the hope of promotion to something better. The company could also use the offering or withholding of such promotion to stabilize some workers and encourage others to leave, in accordance with its preferences, given that no seniority system was found to exist in this or any other of the plants studied.[7] Wage costs would be kept down, and managerial control increased.

The changes outlined in the previous paragraph could be achieved without any substantive changes in the work actually carried out in the plant, or even in the specification of tasks to be allocated to individual workers. Under the new arrangements occupations would appear to correspond to the skill and experience involved in the work, just as the female occupational structure described above would appear, at first sight, to reflect skill and productivity. However, in practice, the two patterns of employment – one for women, one for men – incorporate male domination and the systematic devaluation and subordination of women. Women suffer from being excluded from more skilled jobs, from the refusal of managements to recognize the skilled work they quite often do, and from being denied the artificial progress along jobs lines often afforded to male workers. Once this is recognized, the structure and significance of occupational hierarchies take on a new aspect. They are organized around gender and incorporate the subordination and devaluation of women.

LABOUR MARKET STRUCTURES

Recognition of the ways in which labour markets incorporate the subordination of women does not imply that labour market structures are mere ideological fictions. In Chapter 3 it was shown that men and women differed in such matters as expectations of work and training. At the same time, as Hartmann suggests, men really do monopolize the best jobs. Real differences exist in the work performed by men and women. However, after all of these factors have been taken into account, there is the further issue of the differential evaluation of female and male labour in plants. Managements can construct segregated labour forces and apply quite different employment policies within each gender category. The criteria used to regulate each category objectify the subordination of women already described in Chapters 3 and 4. Three particular aspects of the construction of job hierarchies will be discussed in this section: (1) wages and job grading, (2) skill, promotion, and training, and (3) turnover and stability of labour.

Wages and job grading

Chapter 4 showed that the evaluation of the attributes and aptitudes of female and male workers played a significant role in justifying a given division of labour and in establishing the higher status of male workers in relation to female. Such evaluations can be distorted in two ways. On the one hand, the same attributes and aptitudes can be evaluated differently according to whether they are possessed by women or by men. Thus, for example, educational achievement or the responsibility required in doing a certain job might be a significant factor in the determination of male status, but would not confer equal status on women. On the other, attributes which vary between the sexes can be evaluated in a non-comparable fashion. Thus the importance given to the strength required for a particular job is not evaluated in the same way as the dexterity required for other jobs, because strength is considered a masculine attribute and dexterity a feminine one.

The differential evaluation of similar attributes among female and male workers was seen in all the factories studied. Without exception, the female 'virtues' of punctuality, discipline, and a readiness to follow orders were taken for granted and not paid by managements. Whereas dual labour market theory might lead us to believe that among male workers, such attributes would command a wage premium, it was clear that among women workers such attributes were not deemed to merit more than the lowest wage levels. They were taken to be common attributes of all workers in the relevant category, women workers, and no comparison was made with men workers. The same contrast between management policies for men and women was seen in the area of educational qualifications. In the third electrical factory, management raised its educational requirements for women workers, and managers reported themselves to be satisfied with the resulting increase in productivity, but wages for women were not increased, nor were pay differentials between female and male workers reduced, even though the male workers remained as ill-educated as before (and with lower educational qualifications than the female workers). The factors which might explain why some men are paid more than others, or some women more than other women, do not explain the wage differentials between workers of the two sexes. Once again, unless it is realized and accepted that the labour market institutionalizes and solidifies the differential treatment of women and men, it is difficult to explain such practices.

Inequality in the valuation of aptitudes was not limited to dexterity as opposed to strength, although this was the most commonly found example. In the second pharmaceuticals/toiletries factory, the industrial relations manager pointed out in the course of a visit to the production area of the plant that on the high-price eau-de-Cologne packaging lines it was essential for the labels to be applied with extreme care. Creases and stains had to be avoided because of the product's status, and this work required what the manager called the 'feminine touch'. In spite of this, women workers were always paid less than men on production jobs. The starting rate for women was 10 per cent lower than the male starting wage, and after three months, both male and female workers received a 10 per cent rise. This led to the posing of the obvious question of why, in a factory which employed both male and female workers on packaging, the most important jobs were paid at the lower, 'female' rate. The manager replied that male workers were required to work a third shift at night in periods of peak demand, while the women were legally allowed to work only the two normal shifts (6 am to 2 pm and 2 pm to 10 pm). One might wonder, however, why men should be paid higher wages throughout the year because one-third of them might have to work nights at periods of peak demand. Further, it is not hard to imagine that had male workers been the only bearers of the special dexterity and care required for the packaging of high-price products, then this would have been used as the basis of a wage and occupational differentiation. An occupational category such as 'specialized packer' would have been created.

In this case, as in many others, it is hard to avoid the conclusion that the wage differential was established first and the justification for it came afterwards. Male workers were simply paid more than women, and in this factory this was revealed directly in the pay scales – there being one scale for women and another for men. This example merely shows clearly, however, what is often hidden by the occupational classifications used in industry. The evaluation of workers' attributes seem, in many cases, just a way of institutionalizing lower wages for women within occupational structures.

Skill, promotion, and training

Differences in the valuation of male and female work were also revealed by a close examination of skill, skill recognition, promotion (or advancement along mobility chains in the terminology of dual labour market theorists), and training. These factors are linked together in dual labour market theory, given that the advancement of workers within enterprises takes the form of supposedly acquiring certain experiences or skills (through training off- or on-the-job), which are then recognized and rewarded by promotion to higher occupational categories. The higher wages of male workers are assumed to depend upon their access to productivity-enhancing experience, without there being a great need to verify in practice whether or not promotion for men and lack of promotion for women is really linked to training and skill. The fact that men tend to rise up job hierarchies both within factories and as they move from one factory to another, whereas women remain firmly tied to the bottom rungs of the ladder, is taken as proof that men are trained and skilled and women are not.

Once the link between wages and productivity has been questioned, and once employment structures are seen to incorporate a systematic devaluation of women, then skill, training, and promotion can be viewed in a different light. In the first place, genuine opportunities for training and promotion tend to be reserved for men because of the pressure they apply to management for higher status. In the second place, there is a considerable undervaluation and non-recognition of female skills, and quite different job hierarchies are constructed for male and for female workers. Differential access to promotion in mixed departments has already been discussed in Chapter 4. Evidence from the factories studied also shows that different practices and rules for promotion are applied in segregated female and male departments.

For male workers some form of promotion in the course of their industrial employment is the norm in Brazil. As was noted in Chapter 3, the head of the woodworking department in E3 said that he had to choose male workers for dead-end jobs with great care, hiring only those workers whose ambitions for promotion had been crushed by experience. Managements regarded pressure for promotion from male workers as normal, and to some extent justified by their family responsibilities, and they took this into consideration when planning personnel policies. If some realistic chance of promotion was not provided, turnover would rise as frustrated workers left in search of better opportunities. The prevalence of very large wage differentials in underdeveloped countries like Brazil makes the possibility of promotion very attractive to them. Promotion from a job classified as unskilled to one classified as semi-skilled can mean a substantial rise in pay, even when there is little difference in the nature of the work being required. In the motor industry, for example, it was a common complaint among the all-male work force that unskilled workers on the assembly line did the same jobs as the longer-service workers classified as assemblers. The latter could earn an hourly wage rate up to 80 per cent higher than the former (Humphrey 1982: 79–80).

The desire for promotion was reinforced by the fact that it was a very common occurence. As was shown in *Tables 6* and *7*, the proportion of male workers in low-grade jobs in the factories studied was relatively small. This meant that workers had a good chance of obtaining promotion within one or two years of being hired at the bottom of the job hierarchy. Even in factory E3, which had the highest proportion of male workers on the (lowest) labourer grade of all the factories studied (32 per cent of all hourly-paid male workers were classified as labourers in December 1980), 70 per cent

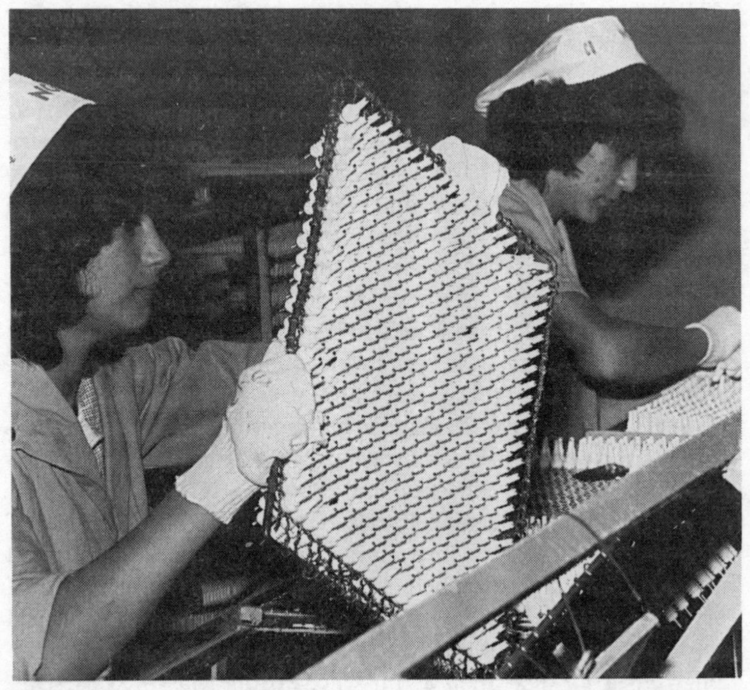

These quality control workers are visually inspecting racks of 500 components. They work in an area separate from male quality control workers. Although they share a job title, 'quality control assistant', with male workers, they are locked within a purely female promotion structure. Female quality control workers are promoted from assembly jobs and regard their future promotion prospects as being restricted to the team leader job. In contrast, the male quality control workers have a hierarchy of inspection jobs to which they can aspire. 'Quality control assistant' is only the bottom rung of the male mobility chain.

of the labourers had been employed for less than one year, and among workers with more than one year's experience in the plant, there were six higher-grade workers for each labourer. Promotion opportunities really did exist. Twenty-eight of the forty male workers interviewed in E3 had been employed for more than two years, and of these, nineteen had been promoted during their time in the factory to a job paying higher wages than their initial starting occupation. Of the nine *not* promoted, only one had been hired as a labourer, while five had entered the plant employed as higher-wage workers whose further promotion opportunities were limited.

To a considerable extent, promotion possibilities were written into the male job titles. In the second electrical factory, for example, a line of advancement was mapped out by the job titles of 'press assistant', 'press operator', and 'specialized press operator', and there were similar clusters of jobs seen in the other plants. In A2, for example, they took the form of machine operator, grades I, II, III, and IV. While one should not overestimate the real chances of promotion available to male workers – they tended to leave jobs rather than stay at the bottom of the occupational hierarchy for a long period – the hope of promotion was clearly fostered by management.

The importance of promotion for male workers was reinforced by the fact that it often led to a permanent increase in status. Occupational titles are registered on workers' employment documents in Brazil, and a male worker would reasonably expect to move between firms without losing status gained in previous employments. In E3 there was no evidence of male workers being hired at lower job classifications than they had enjoyed in previous employments. Men who had worked as press operators in another firm were hired as press operators, not as press assistants, and so on. Similarly when E3 dismissed male workers in 1981 and then rehired them at the end of the year, most were taken back at roughly the same occupational level, with only minor demotions and promotions being registered. The manager of the woodworking department said that care had been taken not to reduce the status of the rehired workers.

The policies applied in the selection and recruitment of women workers were quite different. As was seen in *Tables 6, 7,* and *8*, a very large proportion of women workers were employed in one occupation at the bottom of the job hierarchy. Inevitably the chances of promotion to higher-grade occupations were very restricted. In E3,

75 per cent of all female production workers employed in December 1980 were classified as assemblers, the lowest-grade occupation in the plant, and even among those workers with more than one year's employment, assemblers outnumbered higher-grade workers by two to one. Promotion opportunities for women were limited, and managements neither provided clear lines of promotion nor expected women workers to demand it. An experienced senior personnel manager in A1 expressed a common managerial view:

> 'Women are more stable within a given funtion. . . . They are capable of staying in the same job for much longer [than men], as long as it is well paid. . . . Women are more stable from a job point of view.'

This factory paid the lowest wage rates among those studied, but in spite of this, management could still rely on women to show acceptable (to management) rates of turnover, even while working in dead-end jobs. Another manager in the same plant described the firm's lack of interest in promoting women:

> 'There's a certain undervaluation, complacency [in relation to women's work]. After four years a woman can still be doing the same job. There might be a certain difficult job, which needs a certain dexterity. So the foreman prefers to keep her in that job. That's what tends to happen in production. And the women put up with it. They are educated to be like that.'

Managements were not under pressure to promote women because they did not present the problems seen with the men.

In fact women were not only denied promotion opportunities (real or artificial), but also often refused recognition of the skills and experiences acquired in the course of their work. Four forms of non-recognition of female on-the-job training were found in the factories studied. First, it was quite common for women to be grouped together in a catch-all occupational title, such as labourer or assembler, even though this did not reflect the variety of the work they performed. In the second electrical factory, for example, most of the female production workers were classified as assemblers, even though many of them did not do assembly work. In August 1980 at least eight women were dismissed for signing a petition in support of their regrading. The personnel department employee who conducted the normal leaving interviews with the workers concerned recorded the following account of what had happened:

> 'Seventeen people signed a petition demanding to be regraded from assembler to machine operator, given that they worked with machines. The interviewee does not know who organized the movement. They would like to be machine operators given that it pays better wages.'

The same situation was seen quite clearly in the case of factory E1, which was cited at length above. The women producing wafers were given the same occupational category as those assembling them. In such situations managements down-grade certain female jobs, refusing to recognize or take advantage of the elements in them which are often used to up-grade similar work when performed by men.[8]

Second, managements imposed extensive probationary periods on women before promoting them to higher occupations. Although by law workers were not supposed to work for more than a three-month trial period in a higher-grade job before being formally promoted to it, it was quite common in E3 to find women workers being subjected to so-called probationary periods of six months or even a year. In the meantime they worked at the new, higher-grade job and were paid for lower-grade work. There was no evidence of male workers in the plant experiencing this problem to anything like the same extent. Third, in the same factory, E3, the abilities and previous experience of women were not recognized when they were hired. While over half the male production workers interviewed had been taken on as semi-skilled or skilled workers, only one out of the sixty female workers in the plant had been hired at other than the bottom grade, even though many of the women had had previous industrial experience. The one exception had been hired as a checker in the quality control department, and this constituted a demotion relative to the woman's nine years' experience in inspection in the electrical industry and her previous employment. In many cases firms prefer to hire inexperienced women workers, but when women do have prior experience, firms do not recognize or reward it.

Finally, an extreme example of the non-recognition of women's skills was revealed in 1981, when a large number of workers in E3 were dismissed and a small proportion selectively rehired later in the year. While the male workers were rehired at more or less the same grade as they had worked at previously, all the women workers were rehired as assemblers, irrespective of the occupation they had previously attained. According to the head of the tuners department, this was done 'precisely to generate some interest among them – competition for promotion'. Some of the women rehired as assemblers had previously worked in the plant as coil winders and calibrators, and this fact, combined with the policy of extended periods of probation, led to an extraordinary situation in the components department

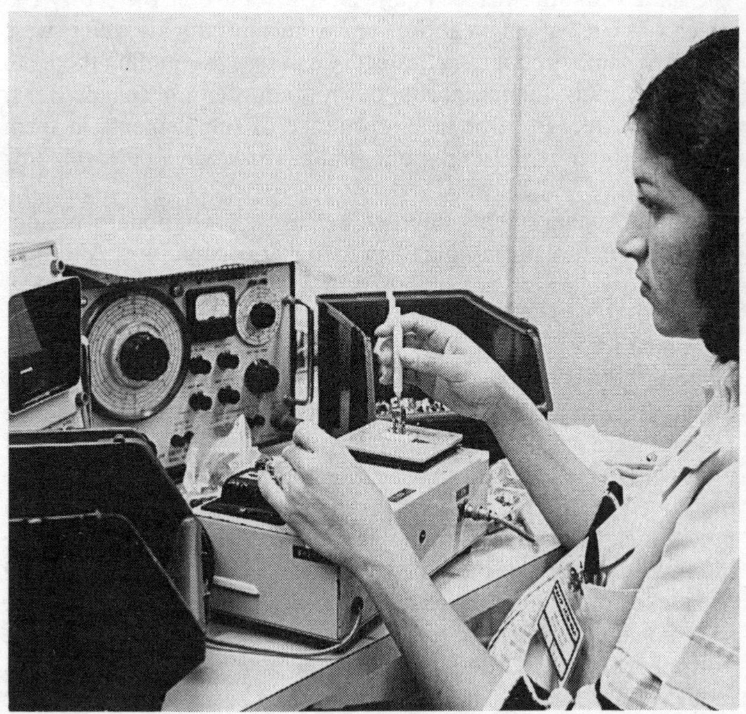

This woman is calibrating a coil by adjusting it with the screwdriver in her right hand until the oscilloscope shows the correct pattern. The occupation of calibrator is paid considerably more than assembler or coil-winder, and it requires speed and accuracy rather than technical skill. In the summer of 1982, women working on calibration were being paid as assemblers or coil-winders. Some of them had been employed up to 1980 as calibrators, then rehired at the end of 1981 as assemblers. They were back doing calibration for an assembler's pay.

mid-way through 1982. Only two of the ten women doing calibration work were being paid as calibrators, and three of them were working for an assembler's pay even though they had already worked in the department in higher-grade occupations. In other words, nine months after having been rehired, a former calibrator could be found doing a calibrator's work and yet being paid the assembler wage rate. The difference in income was significant. The wage rate for an assembler was cr$113 per hour, compared to cr$160 for a coil winder and cr$180 for a calibrator.[9] The women had skills which had once been recognized by the firm, but they were unmarketable even in the same firm. This unmarketability of female skills is not a technical issue. It arises directly as a result of the differential treatment of male and female workers by firms.

The contrast between promotion and skill recognition patterns for male and female workers indicates the extent to which the categories used in managing labour forces are saturated with gender. Phillips and Taylor's conclusion on this point seems amply justified on the evidence from Brazilian industry:

> 'What all of these examples illustrate is the extent to which skill has become saturated with sex. It is not that skill categories have been totally subjectified: in all cases *some* basis was found in the content of work to justify the distinctions between men's and women's work. But the equations – men/skilled and women/unskilled – are so powerful that the identification of a particular job with women ensured that the skill content of the work would be downgraded. It is the sex of those who do the work, rather than its content, which leads to its identification as skilled or unskilled.'
>
> (1980: 85)

Similarly it is the sex of workers which, to a large extent, determines whether or not mobility chains are constructed.

Turnover and stability of employment

Labour turnover and the supposedly greater instability of women workers play a central role in dual labour market accounts of why women end up in low-paid, dead-end jobs. For dual labour market theorists the relatively greater instability of women workers is almost axiomatic, and it is based upon two assumptions which need little or no empirical verification. First, anecdotal evidence about the impact of child-rearing and moving home when husbands move jobs appears to imply that women tend to be less stable than men in any given job. Second, this anecdotal evidence is linked to female participation rates. The fact that participation rates for women have, up until the recent period, tended to fall for the period in which they have young children is taken to indicate that over a cycle of working life women will tend to have an intermittent participation in the labour force. In addition, as was noted earlier, women's low pay and poor promotion prospects are themselves taken to be indicators of higher turnover.

However, the situation is much more complex than this. First, even though evidence from life-cycle studies of women workers indicates the importance of intermittent paid employment for women (see, for example, Labourie-Racapé, Letablier, and Vasseur 1977: 33–4), participation rate data alone cannot prove that female workers are less stable than male workers. A participation rate of, say, 50 per cent does not indicate that each potential worker is employed for half of the available time,[10] and figures on participation do not tell us about age, or cohort differences, how many interruptions women have, or what proportion of job changes occur for this reason.

Second, and more fundamentally, management policies themselves have an impact on stability. This is particularly true in Brazil, where turnover rates in general are rather high, and labour legislation and the weakness of trade unions give employers a relatively free hand. Overall, rates of turnover for both men and women in industry have been very high in Brazil. For example, in general unskilled automotive jobs in the city of São Paulo in 1980 there were 196 occupants for each 100 jobs in the course of the year,[11] and even for skilled male jobs such as turner and grinder there were 150 occupants for each 100 jobs. Both female and male workers change jobs more as a result of dismissal by their employers than upon their own initiative. Intra-firm mobility is more likely to be a much greater source of turnover for women than movements out of the labour force altogether. At the same time, many firms do not seem to attach great importance to labour-force stability, compared to discipline and control of wage costs, as was seen in Chapter 3.

The discussion in Chapter 3 provided ample evidence of both a complexity of employee-initiated turnover and the different policies applied to men and women with respect to stability of employment. In relation to the impact of domestic factors on employment, these were seen to be quite different for men and women. Domestic responsibilities associated with marriage and motherhood tended to make continued paid employment difficult for women, partly because of the opposition of husbands and partly because of the incompatibility between domestic work and the extensive demands of employers. However, significant numbers of mothers did work in some of the factories studied. For men, on the other hand, domestic responsibility in the form of an expectation of a 'family wage' led to turnover as men sought good jobs and promotion prospects. Significant differences in patterns of female and male turnover are shown in *Table 17* which summarizes information on workers leaving the second electrical plant in 1980.[12]

The results from the leaving interviews provide only a rough guide to patterns of turnover and their causes, but a clear and important result emerges. In the case of women workers a significant proportion of exits from the plant were the result of factors linked to the domestic situation: 45.3 per cent of the women explicitly cited factors relating to their domestic situation as the cause of their exit. Marriage, the birth of children, and difficulties with childcare accounted for over 25 per cent of exits, with the rest arising from such problems as moving house, being dismissed for lateness and absenteeism resulting from childcare responsibilities, the care of other relatives, and pregnancy-related illnesses.[13] Only 13.1 per cent left of their own accord because of dissatisfaction with wages or were sacked for not showing interest in their work.

The factors influencing male turnover were quite different. Domestic factors accounted for only a very small amount of male turnover, just four cases in seventy-eight. The most important factors cited by the men related to dissatisfaction with work; 25.6 per cent of the men explicitly stated that they were leaving because of discontent over their wages or because they had found a better job. A further 28.2 per cent were dismissed on the grounds of 'lack of interest', which is the term commonly used in Brazilian industry when workers force their dismissal by lowering their output and refusing to co-operate with management. Workers do this in order to leave on the initiative of the company and qualify for compensation for

Table 17 *Exits by reason and by sex: factory E2, 1980*

reason	*women*	*men*
	%	%
reasons linked to domestic situation		
marriage	7.8	0
care of children	18.4	0
lateness and absenteeism	4.9	2.6
care of other relatives	3.0	0
other domestic reasons[1]	11.2	2.6
total	45.3	5.1
other reasons		
seeking higher wages or better opportunities	5.6	25.6
'lack of interest'[2]	7.5	28.2
lateness and absenteeism	4.9	9.0
working conditions	7.9	5.1
problems with supervisors or workmates	8.2	10.3
others[3]	20.2	16.7
total	54.7	94.9
all cases	100 (n = 267)	100 (n = 78)

Source Company records.

Notes

1 Includes moving house, bereavements, pregnancy-related sickness, etc.
2 This is the term used to describe workers' behaviour when they deliberately reduce their output in order to force dismissal.
3 Includes hours of work, workers sacked for asking for regrading, etc.

dismissal. Of all the male workers leaving the plant 53.8 per cent did so for reasons relating to work dissatisfaction and alternative employment. These figures are not exceptional. In factory A2 a similar pattern was found. In 1980 over half the women leaving did so because of marriage or pregnancy (in this case being dismissed by the firm), while half the men left because of dissatisfaction (expressed by low output, leading to dismissal) or a change of employment. Clearly the domestic situation of female and male workers, as outlined in Chapter 3, had an impact on turnover, but in quite different ways for the two sexes. The caring responsibilities placed exclusively on women, which entail spending time in the home or arranging suitable alternative arrangements, and the subordination of women's needs to other household members created a significant amount of instability. The male need, or desire, to earn a 'family wage' or something approaching it, led to increased job searching and turnover among male workers.

These figures do not indicate that women's turnover is an intractable problem for management. Nor do they indicate that women must inevitably have a higher turnover rate than men because of their domestic situation. Rates of turnover for both men and women could be influenced by management policies. In the case of male workers turnover could be diminished by management reducing its use of dismissal as a disciplinary procedure, and by giving greater opportunities for advancement to men. For women turnover might be reduced by a combination of less discrimination against older and married women, greater access to better-paid jobs, and better provision of facilities for women with children. Turnover needs to be seen more as an effect of conscious management policy than an unavoidable management problem.

Therefore the actual turnover rates displayed by men and women should be considered the result of management policies with respect to the generation of male and female labour. In particular a number of factors were noted in Chapter 3 which would tend to increase female turnover rates relative to male. First, some firms were quite willing to employ young and inexperienced women workers, even though they tend to display higher turnover rates than older women workers. A1 was the most clear example of a firm willing to do this. It tried to employ younger, inexperienced women because they would work for lower wages, and presumably the lower wage costs and greater degree of control over such young workers more than offset the turnover costs. Paul's study of the Brazilian electrical industry noted differences between factories in this respect, with some employing older, more stable women, and others content to see high turnover rates (1983: 49–50). Second, it has been seen that some firms deliberately sacked women workers when they married or had children, and more generally, very few firms provided the facilities for women with children which might have reduced turnover. Third, it has been suggested that managements deliberately did not provide incentives to greater stability for women workers, precisely because they were relatively stable even in dead-end jobs. Conversely the training and promotion opportunities which would have encouraged greater stability were reserved for male workers.

In spite of these policies, female turnover was not noticeably higher than male. Large-scale dismissals of male workers have been very common in Brazilian industry, and male turnover is also raised by male searches for better jobs and promotion prospects.[14] The RAIS statistics provided by the Ministry of Labour give a general indication of turnover by sex, and in 1976, for example, they showed that for every 100 jobs in manufacturing industry occupied by women, there were 163 contracts of employment in the course of the year. For male workers the comparable figure was 157, indicating a lower rate of turnover. If one controls for age, the differences disappear completely, and skill also has an influence. Older workers were more stable than younger, for both sexes, and the more skilled workers were more stable than the unskilled. Controlling for age, female and male workers were equally stable, which is the same result as that found by Rubery and Tarling for Britain in the early 1970s (1982: 59–62). However, it should be borne in mind that the number of older women in manual work is relatively small, and in Chapter 3 it was suggested that older women in industrial jobs would tend to be those who remained at work through their 20s. They would either be childless or have continued to work while their children were very young. Therefore these figures on turnover cannot be extrapolated to a situation where much larger numbers of older women are employed, even though it should not be assumed that older women will be unstable.

CONCLUSIONS

It has been argued that dual and segmented labour market theories have a conception of occupations and sex segregation which defines women's disadvantage in terms of a lack of access to high productivity employment. The link between wages and productivity is maintained. Wage differences between men and women are based on the allocation of workers to positions which are not themselves defined in relation to gender. In criticism of this perspective it has been suggested that labour market structures can be adjusted to take into account the characteristics of the available labour force, including gender, race, age, and so on. This implies that labour market structures are potentially quite flexible, in so far as the same technology can be combined with a variety of patterns of employment.

As a result, women's disadvantaged position arises from two processes. On the one hand, women are marginalized from more productive and prestigious work and the training opportunities which lead to it. On the other, employment policies are constructed differently by employers for the male and female labour forces. Even when women have skills or require training, their occupations are often not classed as skilled, and their stability in low-paid employment works against them, since employers do not need to adopt the kinds of stability policies applied to men. Both these processes which work to women's disadvantage arise from the construction of gender identities in factories which devalue women's work. In this way the male and female labour forces are differentially rewarded. The commensuration of female and male labour, which would in principle undermine this differential reward is prevented by job segregation by sex, rules which regulate and maintain sexual hierarchies, and the prevalence of notions of work suitable for men and for women – as was seen in Chapter 4.

This implies that the sexual division of labour is much more adaptable to changing economic and technological circumstances than dual labour market theories might suppose. The matching of people to places within an economic structure is facilitated by the malleability of the places being filled. As a result, women's subordination is much more flexible and resistant to attack than the dual labour market theory would suggest. Access to higher-productivity work alone will not guarantee a better deal for women. The problems lie in the area of the sexual division of labour itself and the ways in which different types of work are evaluated. If women enter new areas of work, or take over old ones, these can be devalued and acquire 'female' characteristics – low pay and lack of promotion opportunities, for instance. This can be overcome only by either a much greater degree of integration of male and female work, or a much greater degree of comparison of work and establishment of equal value principles. In both cases the problem is one of social relations between the sexes, not merely one of training or productivity-enhancing experience.

7
Economic crisis and the sexual division of labour

INTRODUCTION

In Chapter 1 the evolution of male and female employment in industry was analysed in the context of the growth and transformation of Brazil's manufacturing base in the post-war period. In particular, emphasis was given to the strong rise in female employment in the 1960s and 1970s. It was argued that a combination of underlying feminization of the labour force and shortages of male labour led to a significant jump in female manufacturing employment in the 1970s. This rise in female employment was significantly higher than the rise in male employment in manufacturing, which at 5.7 per cent was higher in the 1970s than in the previous decades. This reflected a booming economy. In the 1970s the Brazilian economy as a whole grew at an average rate of over 7 per cent per annum, and even at the end of the decade industrial production was still rising at this rate.[1]

Rapid growth came to an abrupt end in 1981, when mounting balance of payments and debt problems forced a reversal of economic policy and a credit squeeze which cut industrial production. In 1981 industrial output fell by 10 per cent compared to the previous year. In the São Paulo region, the focus of this study, the impact of recession was even greater, and manufacturing employment in Greater São Paulo fell sharply in 1981 and again in 1983. By December 1983 employment in manufacturing industry was 25 per cent below the peak level registered in October 1980.[2] This raises the issue of what would happen to female and male employment and the sexual division of labour in a period of crisis. An analysis of industry and firm employment trends will allow consideration of the general questions concerning women's employment and economic recession in the light of the findings concerning the sexual division of labour in the earlier chapters. These findings should indicate how the economic crisis would affect female and male labour. To a certain extent, the general arguments on the sexual division of labour can be examined by reference to the data available at industry and enterprise level for the crisis period after 1980, and this chapter will demonstrate how the impact of the crisis was mediated through the gender categories described in the earlier chapters.

CRISIS AND JOB LOSS

The possibility of a differential impact on the male and female labour forces of an economic crisis has been viewed from two diametrically opposed standpoints. On the one hand, the reserve army of labour hypothesis views job loss in a recession as an expulsion of people, and it suggests that women are more likely to lose their jobs than men because they form a labour reserve, which can be mobilized when the economy needs labour and demobilized when labour demand falls. On the other hand, the occupational segregation model suggests that job loss involves the suppression of particular posts or positions largely occupied by workers of one sex. The sex of workers losing jobs is determined solely by the types of jobs being eliminated. The original version of the reserve army of labour hypothesis, advanced by Beechey (1977), among others, is clearly untenable. Women cannot be seen as a labour reserve which can be shifted in and out of the economy as the level of employment rises and falls. The theoretical basis of Beechey's argument has been challenged by such writers as Anthias (1980), and empirically trends of male and female employment in the early 1970s in Britain did not support a simple labour reserve thesis. Female employment rose while male employment fell.

This experience appeared to give credence to the occupational segregation model. However, Bruegel (1979) reformulated the reserve army thesis, offering it in a weaker form. She showed empirically that women in industry suffered from a greater disposability than men, and suggested that this was not because they were dismissed and substituted by men, but because for a variety of reasons they performed jobs which were more vulnerable to elimination. Bruegel suggests that as well as suffering from the differential impact of the application of such rules as seniority (last in, first out) and priority for full-time over part-time workers, which might imply some substitution of work done by women by work done by men, women were disproportionately located in the jobs which were most vulnerable to elimination in times of recession (1979: 13–18). Women were deliberately selected for less stable jobs so that their disproportionate expulsion did not require substitution of women by men. As Rubery and Tarling argue (1982: 49), Bruegel's revision of the reserve army thesis provides a degree of complementarity with the segregation hypothesis. Women's greater vulnerability to job loss is seen to derive in part from their disproportionate allocation to jobs which are unduly affected by economic fluctuations, and partly from such factors as lack of seniority, a greater degree of part-time work, higher turnover, and ease of replacement in the up-turn, which makes them easier to fire and rehire than men. Bruegel's argument is similar to that presented by Barron and Norris (see Chapter 6). It is being suggested that unstable jobs are matched to potentially unstable workers, which makes women more vulnerable to job loss than men without the need for direct substitution of one sex by the other. Bruegel points to part-time work as the key mechanism which enables employers to do this (1979: 18–19). However, little empirical evidence is offered to substantiate the claim about the matching of vulnerable workers to vulnerable jobs other than the reference to part-time work. This presents problems, since the increased vulnerability of women is also seen in countries such as Brazil where part-time work is rare. At the same time a degree of ambiguity remains. Are women selected by employers for unstable jobs precisely because they are easier to dispose of, as Barron and Norris suggest (1976: 54–7)? Or do women obtain inferior jobs, which are generally the more unstable ones, which seems to be Rubery and Tarling's notion? The latter is a significantly weaker version of the labour reserve model.

Bruegel's concentration on the macro-level analysis provides a chance to throw light on to the general performance of women's employment in the British economy and to make a valuable restatement of the reserve army concept. However, a study at the level of the plant or enterprise can attempt to answer some other important questions. First, to what extent is the operation of the labour market during a period of crisis 'non-gendered'? Are women merely disproportionately affected by such supposedly non-gendered factors as hoarding of skilled labour, or is there a direct selection of women for dismissal because of their sex? Second, in so far as men exert power to maintain their employment, is this at the expense of women (as the reserve army model might imply), or at the expense of the employers, who are forced to retain more male workers than they would otherwise wish to (as the occupational segregation model might imply)? Third, to what extent is the disposability of male labour in a crisis limited by the use of artificial skill recogntion, demarcation of occupations, and a technically unnecessary differentiation of male occupations? Conversely, does the non-recognition of female skills and the use of general occupational titles increase their vulnerability? In other words, closer examination is required of the determinations of degrees of vulnerability of men and women workers and the jobs they do, which requires greater attention to the factors structuring the male and female labour forces outside the crisis period.

A consideration of these questions in the Brazilian context will allow further examination of the arguments presented in earlier chapters. On the basis of the findings of these chapters, a series of expectations concerning the short-term impact of economic crisis on male and female labour in Brazilian manufacturing industry can be drawn up. At the same time, the different institutional and labour market conditions prevailing in Brazil should cast light on the relative importance of the different factors which might contribute to women's possible greater disposability. The results of earlier chapters provide the following indications about the impact of the 1981 crisis on male and female employment.

1 Given that female and male employment is very unevenly distributed between major sectors of employment, it is likely that the impact of a recession on women and men will be different. In particular, a crisis centred on industry would hit men disproportionately.
2 Male and female manufacturing employment is concentrated in different industries. Therefore the impact of crisis on women and men in manufacturing will depend very much on the sectors of manufacturing affected. In the state of São Paulo 50 per cent of male manufacturing employment was concentrated in the four metal-working industries, while 45 per cent of women

worked in the three traditional industries, and a further 23 per cent in metal products, electrical goods, and plastics.[3]

3 The high degree of segregation of men and women workers in industry should prevent any significant degree of substitution of female by male workers or vice versa during a recession. There seems little reason for management to promote such a substitution, and if it were to involve a transfer of workers to jobs normally done by the other sex, the workers might also oppose it. At the most, one might expect a slowing down or stopping of the underlying trend to feminization seen in the 1960s and 1970s. It is possible that in a few marginal, non-segregated areas, such a tendency might be reversed.

4 There is little reason to expect that women workers in Brazilian manufacturing might be adversely affected by some of the factors noted by Bruegel. Seniority was not a principle followed by Brazilian managements, and no evidence of part-time working was seen. Similarly female turnover was not significantly higher than male – particularly among unskilled and semi-skilled workers – and more generally, managements had considerable freedom to dismiss any workers they chose. Therefore there would be no need to find alternatives to sackings, or find principles for sacking acceptable to the unions. In the few industries where unions were relatively well organized – such as the motor vehicle industry – there were very few women workers. Union pressure should be insufficient either to protect men to any significant degree or to force managements to favour men at the expense of women.

5 A possible source of differential treatment of men and women might lie in managerial concern with parental status. Firms might be concerned to protect the positions of male bread-winners, or shed female parents. However, in the light of the sexual division of labour noted in (3) above, such preferences might affect only other workers of the same sex. Even so, there might be some substitution in mixed areas such as quality control, and firms might even hoard male bread-winners.

6 Given that men monopolize work classified as skilled, they should benefit from any hoarding of skilled labour.

7 Given the greater occupational differentiation of the male labour force, firms may be less able to substitute one man for another, and the preservation of a full range of occupations

might require a larger male labour force than would be the case for the undifferentiated and polyvalent women workers.

8 Women workers are concentrated in production and quality control work, which tend to be more immediately and directly affected by falls in output. This could have a major impact. This impact might well be more than one would expect as a result of (6) above.

THE SECTORAL IMPACT OF THE CRISIS

The measures taken by the Brazilian government at the end of 1980, which were designed to restore the confidence of foreign banks and tackle balance of payments and inflation problems, had a severe and uneven impact on the economy. Manufacturing industry, and within it the consumer durables and capital goods sectors, were hit particularly hard. As can be seen in *Table 18*, total manufacturing output fell by 10.1 per cent in 1981, but the falls in consumer durables and capital goods were much greater. In 1982 there was some stabilization, and in 1983 output fell again, although this time the fall was more evenly distributed. Over the three years there was a catastrophic decline in capital goods production, a sharp decline in consumer durable goods output concentrated in 1981, and lesser declines in production of intermediate goods and non-durables. In terms of the twenty-one industrial sectors used in the census and RAIS figures, this meant steep falls in production in the four metal-working industries (19 per cent in 1981, and an average of 10 per

Table 18 *Manufacturing production by category of use: annual rates of real growth, Brazil 1980–83*

use category	*1980* %	*1981* %	*1982* %	*1983* %
capital goods	+6.5	−19.0	−10.8	−20.2
intermediate goods	+8.3	−10.6	+0.4	−3.0
consumer durables	+10.7	−26.3	+8.0	−4.0
consumer non-durables	+5.2	−2.9	+1.8	−5.2
total	+7.6	−10.1	+0.1	−6.3

Source *Relatório do Banco Central do Brasil*, 1982 and 1983.

cent per annum over the three years), while textiles and clothing were much less severely affected, and production in the food industry registered rises in each year. Although the food industry was the only one to maintain positive growth rates in all three years, the only other sectors as badly hit as the metal-working industries were plastics and non-metallic minerals. This pattern of decline hit industry in the Sao Paulo region particularly hard because the metal-working and consumer durable industries were concentrated there. According to Employers Federation data, employment in Greater Sao Paulo fell by 13.5 per cent from December 1980 to December 1981, and by 24.4 per cent up to December 1983.[4] The heaviest falls were in metal-working, where employment fell by over 15 per cent in 1981 and by over 30 per cent from 1980 to the end of 1983.

Measuring the impact of this dramatic fall in employment on men and women is not easy. Neither the Employers Federation nor the 1981 Industrial Survey give any breakdowns by sex, and the RAIS data for 1980 and 1982 give few or no employment figures discriminated for women and men. The only figures available from the RAIS with industry-by-industry breakdowns of male and female employment are for 1979, 1981, and 1983, and given the varying coverage of the survey from year to year, they can be taken only as a rough guide to employment trends.[5] Data for eleven key industries are presented in *Table 19*. Overall, the female and male shares of manufacturing employment in Sao Paulo remained constant between 1979 and 1983, even though total employment fell by just over 15 per cent. However, the constancy of male and female shares was the result of two contrasting influences. On the one hand, the industries employing relatively large numbers of men were worse affected by the down-turn than those employing relatively large numbers of women. This was indicated by the figures in *Table 18* on the decline of production according to category of output. In particular, employment in the four metal-working industries fell by over 12 per cent between 1979 and 1981 and by a further 12 per cent from 1981 to 1983. In contrast, employment in the three traditional industries fell by only 2 per cent in the period 1979–81 and by 4 per cent between 1981 and 1983. On the other hand, in each of the four groupings selected for *Table 19*, female employment fell more than male over the four-year period as a whole. In the three large groupings the difference is about 5 per cent, and in plastics it is 16 per cent.

Table 19 *Changes in male and female employment by selected industrial grouping, state of São Paulo, 1979, 1981, and 1983*

industrial grouping[1] *(selected)*	*employment*					
	women			*men*		
	1979	*1981*	*1983*	*1979*	*1981*	*1983*
		(1979=100)			*(1979=100)*	
four metal-working industries	158,320	82.2	72.9	875,489	88.3	77.8
chemical-related industries	36,476	95.3	86.6	112,619	99.4	92.1
plastics	29,293	87.6	78.4	53,266	95.5	94.5
three traditional sectors	268,264	97.0	91.8	309,643	98.9	96.4
all manufacturing	598,727	91.6	84.5	1,752,260	92.2	84.5

Source Unpublished figures from the *Relãçao Anual de Informações Sociais*, 1979, 1981, and 1983.

Note

1 These eleven industries aggregated into four categories as in *Table 3*, account for 82 per cent of female manufacturing employment and 77 per cent of male.

Clearly women were more vulnerable to labour-force reductions than men (just as Bruegel found for Britain), and from 1979 to 1983 this was sufficient to offset the advantage of tending to work in the less-affected industries.

Across the twenty-one sectors of manufacturing, shifts in male and female employment over the four years can be divided into three categories: (1) those where the fall of female employment was at least 3 per cent greater than the fall of male employment (or, in the few industries where employment rose, female employment rose at least 3 per cent less than male), (2) those industries where the difference was less than 3 per cent, and (3) those where the reduction in male employment was at least 3 per cent greater than male. Four sectors of manufacturing fell into group (2) – no significant difference. Of the remaining seventeen sectors, fourteen fell into group (1) and just three into group (3). The fourteen industries in group (1) accounted for 77.6 per cent of female employment in 1979, and they included transport materials, electrical equipment, plastics, textiles, clothing, and food. The three industries in group

(3) were leather and hides, toiletries, and printing and publishing, which between them accounted for less than 5 per cent of female manufacturing employment in 1979. Clearly, then, women displayed a much greater vulnerability to job loss than men within most industries, and this vulnerability is all the more marked when compared to the broad advance of female employment shares in the 1970s (see Chapter 1).

FIRMS AND THE CRISIS

The data from the RAIS show a clear tendency for the female labour forces in the various sectors of manufacturing to be reduced more than the male. A similar pattern was seen in some of the seven firms. Among the plants studied it was possible to find detailed information from three of them on employment both prior to the 1981 crisis and at some point following it. The third electrical factory has been discussed in some detail elsewhere (Hirata and Humphrey 1984: 1985), and attention will be concentrated on the two other plants: the second electrical factory and the first automotive

Table 20 *Fall in male and female hourly-paid employment by category of work: factory E2, January 1981 to May 1982*

category[1]	*men*		*women*	
	employment in Jan. 1981	*reduction in employment (%)*	*employment in Jan. 1981*	*reduction in employment (%)*
ancillary workers	114	22.8	65	55.4
tool-room and maintenance[2]	232	24.1	—	—
machine-setters	12	50.0	—	—
stores and prod. control	233	32.6	39	30.8
packaging	30	16.7	13	53.8
quality control	197	35.0	128	21.9
production	1,073	43.4	3,959	47.8
total	1,891	37.2	4,204	47.0

Source Company records.

Notes
1 Excludes twenty-two hourly-paid workers in technical and office jobs.
2 Excludes apprentices.

Table 21 *Fall in male and female hourly-paid employment by category of work: factory A1, December 1980 to December 1981*

category[1]	*men*		*women*	
	employment in Dec. 1980	*reduction in employment (%)*	*employment in Dec. 1980*	*reduction in employment (%)*
ancillary workers	38	28.9	70	25.7
tool-room workers[2]	127	33.9	—	—
maintenance workers[2]	92	26.1	—	—
machine-setters[3]	65	21.5	13	23.1
stores and internal transport	61	22.0	3	(+)33.3
quality control	59	32.2	32	9.4
production	189	54.0	1,308	58.4
total	631	35.7	1,426	55.3

Source Company records.

Notes
1 Excludes ten women and nine men in technical occupations, and all supervisors.
2 Excludes apprentices.
3 As specified in *Table 22*, plus die-mounters.

factory. Both of these plants were severely affected by the economic crisis in 1981 because they produced consumer durable products – consumer electronics and parts for vehicles. *Tables 20* and *21* show that in both plants female hourly-paid employment fell considerably more than male. In E2, employment was 44 per cent lower in May 1982 than it had been in January 1981, and this was after some hundreds of production workers had been hired early in 1982.[6] Female employment in the plant fell by 47.0 per cent compared to 37.2 per cent for male. In the case of A1 the difference between men and women was even greater. Employment overall fell by almost half, 49.2 per cent, but this consisted of a drop in women's jobs of 55.3 per cent, compared to 'only' 35.7 per cent for men. A similar situation prevailed in E3: only 30 per cent of female hourly-paid workers employed in December 1980 were still employed a year later, compared to 47 per cent of the men.

Although women's employment fell by much more than men's, there was no evidence of substitution. The section-by-section declines of male and female employment were roughly comparable, which is the opposite of the prediction by the substitution hypothesis of a tendency for men to be less affected than women in each category of work. Production workers, both male and female, were more hit by labour-force reductions than other categories in both the plants, and women's overall vulnerability was to a significant degree the result of their concentration in production work. In A1, for example (*Table 21*), the fall in production jobs was 54.0 per cent for men and 58.4 per cent for women. Outside production, the reductions were more limited for both men and women, and women were no more vulnerable than men. With these figures, the only possible type of substitution would have been by non-production workers taking the places of production workers while continuing to keep their former job titles. There is absolutely no evidence of this happening. Even seen in the case of E3 (Hirata and Humphrey 1985: 55–7), where female production workers were cut back more than male, no substitution of women by men occurred.[7]

The lack of substitution was particularly significant in A1. This was a low-wage firm, and as an extension of its low-wage policy in the late 1970s (and partly in response to labour shortages, which meant that male workers would not stay in a low-wage firm) it had recruited some women into jobs more usually done by men, and still partly done by men in the plant. In December 1980 the firm employed women machine-setters in training, a lathe operator, machine lubricators, machine-cleaners, and stores workers. The numbers were not great, as can be seen in *Table 22*. Even when quality control workers and cooks are included in the figures, the total number of women involved is 51 out of a total hourly-paid female labour force of over 1,400. *Table 22* confirms that women were concentrated in lower-grade occupations than men – in quality control, for example, men were found predominantly on grades 9 and 11, and women on grades 5 and 6. In spite of this, no tendency for women to be expelled in greater numbers than men is revealed. In quality control it was men who were reduced in greater numbers than women. Similarly the female automatic lathe setter did not lose her job and nor did the female machine-setters, the lubricator, and the stores workers. The two groups of women most affected – the automatic lathe operators and machine-cleaners – had their fate shared by men. There is little indication of substitution here, even though on the basis of the limited evidence available it seems to have been an option open to management.[8] Even though the personnel

Table 22 *Employment in selected occupations: A1, December 1980 and December 1981*

category	*occupation*	*grade*	*men*		*women*	
			1980	*1981*	*1980*	*1981*
quality control	charge-hand quality control	13	11	10	—	—
	specialist qual. insp.	12	2	2	—	—
	qual. insp. A	11	14	10	1	1
	qual. insp. B	9	28	14	3	3
	qual. insp. C	8	1	1	—	—
	prod. insp.	6	3	3	21	21
	assistant insp.	5	—	—	7	4
setters	autom. lathe setters	12/11[1]	24	20	—	—
	autom. lathe setters (in training)[2]	8	1	0	1	1
	machine-setter (in training)[2]	6	—	—	5	5
	autom. lathe operator A	8	2	1	—	—
	autom. lathe operator B	6	17	0	5	1
	machine lubricator A	10	3	2	1	1
	machine lubricator B	9	1	1	—	—
	machine cleaner	5	5	3	6	3
other	stores assistant A	5	3	2	1	1
	stores assistant B	4	11	5	1	2
	cook A	8	3	1	1	1
	cook B	7	1	1	1	0

Source Company records.

Notes

1 There were two grades of setters.

2 'In training' denotes workers who have finished their SENAI courses but require further on-the-job experience before being paid the full rate for the job.

manager did state that the crisis and its impact on the availability of men for work had led the firm to abandon its plans to extend further the recruitment of women for 'male' jobs, *Table 22* shows little indication of the process being put into reverse. The only possible evidence for a reversal is in the suppression of the automatic lathe operator category. It is possible that this work was transferred to the machine-setters. Even here the impact is not clearly sex-specific.

Male and female operator jobs disappear, and male and female setter jobs remain. Taking the five setting and operator occupations together, the men are reduced from forty-four to twenty-one and the women from eleven to seven. Substitution, it seems, can be ruled out.

The data from *Tables 21* and *22* also indicate that the stronger version of the idea that women form an indirect labour reserve – that women are chosen for the jobs most vulnerable to suppression during a crisis precisely because they are easier to dispense with – is not applicable to Brazil. The considerable job cuts in areas of skilled male work such as tool-making, maintenance, and quality control show that management had no difficulty in dismissing male workers. Neither skilled male workers nor longer-service workers were protected. In tool-making in A1 one in three male jobs disappeared, and management was able to reduce the male production labour force by over a half. In other words, there was no need for management to seek to use women as a labour reserve – men were dispensable as well – and this notion is reinforced by the fact that even when substitution of female by male workers was possible, management in A1 did not take advantage of it. The data presented in the tables do not sustain the thesis that women are allocated to the jobs most vulnerable to recession precisely because management find it easier to dispose of women and hence adjust their labour force with greater ease to any decline in requirements for labour.

SEGREGATION AND DISPOSABILITY

To some extent, then, women are protected by the sexual division of labour, as Milkman (1976) argues. Jobs, not people of a certain sex, are lost in the crisis. However, as has been seen in earlier chapters, women's and men's occupations are constructed in different ways, and access to jobs is highly sex specific. The greater vulnerability of women to job loss in a period of economic crisis, notwithstanding the importance and durability of the sexual division of labour, has to be attributed to the general processes which establish the characteristics of jobs and the allocation of women and men to them. As has been argued in earlier chapters, the characteristics of male and female jobs are defined by a double movement. On the one hand, certain types of work are reserved for men and women. Men monopolize some jobs and are very reluctant to perform others. On the other, the occupations women and men fill acquire characteristics deemed suitable for the sex which fills them. This double movement has a decisive impact on stability during a crisis.

Production jobs are much more subject to elimination as part of the short-term management response to a crisis than non-production jobs, and a good part of the lesser dispensability of male workers resides in their near-monopoly of non-production work. Non-production work is significantly differentiated from production work in a number of ways. First, it tends to require greater training, both formal and informal. This is one of the reasons why men are attracted to it. The formal training in tool-room, maintenance, and setting, and the more on-the-job-based training in areas such as store-keeping give workers a bigger pay packet and a negotiable skill and scarcity value. Second, the work in non-production areas tends to be more fragmented and differentiated, and this makes wholesale dismissals more difficult. Substitutability (between workers of the same sex) is much more limited in non-production work. Third, the relation between output and the number of workers required is much more direct in production than in the non-production areas.

These differences are not merely technical and objective. Around the question of skill, for example, practices can arise which overemphasize the problem of skilled labour shortages and the need to stabilize, or hoard, skilled workers at all costs. Similarly management treatment of production workers could have been conditioned by the hire-and-fire mentality seen throughout the 1970s. Job differentiation and demarcation, too, is something which is constructed around the elements of the work performed, and it has been seen how much this differs for men and women. The number of occupations needed to fit a given range of work can be expanded or compressed quite considerably. Finally, the number of workers required for a given level of production can be the subject of considerable negotiation between workers and management and between departmental managers and the central (particularly financial) administration.

In non-production areas employment was clearly protected by these factors. First, managements hesitated to cut back skilled workers in large numbers. Hoarding of male labour, particularly tool-room workers, was evident in some plants. In E3, management also reported using skilled production workers in the woodworking department to do not strictly essential maintenance work such as re-fitting doors and painting walls in an effort to generate work. This was not merely an attempt to protect men as men. In the second largest department, metal-working, the male labour force was cut back as severely as the female labour force in other departments. The perceived need to maintain skilled labour seems to have been the main determinant in the woodworking department. However, it should be noted that such retention of labour was largely on the initiative of the department's manager, who juggled with his output and manning figures in order to avoid dismissals. In departments where labour is valued, attempts will be made in this direction. In departments where managers have contempt for their workers – seen in some of the female departments in E3 – no such efforts will be made.

Second, in the non-production departments it was evident that jobs were pared away rather than eliminated wholesale. In A1, for example, hundreds of general production jobs disappeared, while tool-room jobs were cut back one by one. Among the 127 tool-room workers, 43 job losses were achieved by reductions spread across many of the 40 or so job titles. In the case of the ten pattern-makers, a 30 per cent cut was achieved by the loss of one worker from each of three grades. In part this reflects a more differentiated occupational structure. It was argued in Chapter 2 that male occupational structures tended to be highly differentiated, while women were usually grouped into a few broad categories, which tends to overestimate the differences in male work and homogenize what are quite often distinct female production jobs (see Chapter 6). Differentiation can reduce the scope for dismissals. If there are many occupations, managements may be obliged to retain a full range of occupational titles, either because there are real skills which have to be available, or because the existence of different titles acts as a barrier to workers doing more than one job. Women might do a wide range of jobs under the title assembler, but a maintenance turner might be able to resist working on milling or grinding. At the same time, if there are hierarchies of skill and competence in given areas of work or within job titles (machine-setter A, B, and C, for example), management may wish to maintain the proportions of each. If too many of the more skilled are sacked, then necessary expertise could be lacking. If too many of the less skilled are sacked, management face three problems: (1) the danger of the long-term skill requirements being skewed upwards, (2) the skilled workers resenting being forced to take on less complicated work, and (3) the average wage rate rising, which may not be considered desirable at a time of sackings and difficulties. The result of these factors is a tendency for jobs to be cut back in broad swathes in production and to be pared away in some other areas.

Third, even unskilled workers in non-production jobs are protected by the fact that the link between their work and the plant's output is indirect. In production work managements tend to enforce much stricter and more immediate controls on wage costs per unit of output, and even in periods of expanding employment hiring and firing was common. The immediate response to a collapse in output is a cut in wage costs. In non-production areas the pressure is less intense. The need for non-production labour does not vary directly with production levels, and the measurement of need is less precise. All types of non-production workers can benefit from this. Women cleaners, for example, were cut back by much less than production workers (both female and male) in E3 and A1, and by less even than male toolroom and maintenance workers. Clearly skill is not the main or only determinant of non-production worker stability, as cleaners have a generally available female skill acquired outside the factory which managements do not recognize as a skill. Rather, the stability of women cleaners should be related to their small numbers, relative stability in times of boom (they tend to be older women), and the lack of a clear relation between levels of output and cleaning requirements.

Women in production jobs, in contrast, would suffer from the stringent control over wage costs in production areas, and this would be combined with management notions of dispensability. As was seen in Chapters 3 and 6, managers viewed women workers, particularly production workers, as highly dispensable, and they were willing to operate low-wage, high-turnover policies. It was noted in Chapter 6 that in E3 management even had the luxury of rehiring women workers at lower wages than they were earning previously.

In these circumstances direct discrimination against women appears to have been of relatively minor importance. Given management views on male bread-winners and the widespread lack of interest in providing long-term employment for women described in Chapter 3, one might expect the managerial response to the crisis to have favoured men. There were indications in some of the plants that managements certainly had thoughts in this direction. In the third electrical plant managers referred to the need to protect heads of households against the threat of unemployment, seeing only men as being in this position (Hirata and Humphrey 1985: 51), and in quality control one of the supervisors suggested that if faced with having to choose between a man and woman of equal ability, he would choose to sack the woman. In the second electrical factory, too, the personnel department talked of the need to ameliorate the worst effects of the crisis by retaining male heads of households wherever possible.

However, in practice these considerations do not seem to have had a great effect. It is possible that male workers were hoarded to a greater extent than female in an attempt to ride out the crisis, but the evidence points to the overwhelming influence of two opposing factors. First, the firms faced financial penalties if they favoured men over women, given the occupational structures outlined in Chapter 2. There was no clear incentive to dismiss women disproportionately. Second, the sexual division of labour prevented any significant degree of direct discrimination against women; this was seen clearly in E3. The management did seem to have tried to keep men with family responsibilities in a job, but this seems to have been at the expense of single men (Hirata and Humphrey 1985: 52). Similarly in A1, management claimed to have selected among women according to some criteria of need related to household situation, but not as between women and men. It was claimed that dismissals among women were made according to the following order of priority: (1) those wishing to leave (but waiting to be dismissed in order to receive compensation), (2) those displaying poor performance, (3) single women with relatives working in the plant, (4) married women whose husbands were in employment. Whatever the assumptions made by management about women and families, there is no evidence of them providing any basis for dismissing women rather than men. It is not even likely that such considerations changed the composition of the female labour force significantly. The third criterion favours married women over single, and the fourth single women over married, and the plant employed few married women even prior to the crisis, as was seen in Chapter 3.

CONCLUSIONS

The sexual division of labour protects women from direct substitution, but leaves them more vulnerable to dismissal because of the areas in which they work. Once again it is clear that women's disadvantage is mediated through work categories. Women do lose their jobs in the crisis to a greater degree than men, but not because they are deliberately chosen for dismissal, nor because they are specially selected for vulnerable jobs. Rather, women tend to be concentrated in production jobs, partly because they are less skilled and less well paid than many non-production jobs, and partly because many such jobs are tightly controlled and defined by management (see Chapter 5). The work is quantifiable, and the workers replaceable. The reaction of managements in the crisis are reinforced by the way in which work-forces are managed and controlled at other times. Women and production workers are devalued and considered unimportant, while more skilled (male) workers are handled cautiously. As a result, women's jobs in particular and production jobs in general are more vulnerable to suppression, and women suffer as a result. However, as the figures from the various factories show quite clearly, it is the type of work, not the sex of the workers which is the key factor. Female cleaners and quality control workers in the factories studied, for example, were much less likely to lose their jobs than male production workers, and management showed no inclination to substitute men for women in mixed areas of work.

This confirms one of the key arguments of earlier chapters. Women's subordination and disadvantage in industrial employment is achieved through the construction of work identities and allocation principles which devalue women *as workers*. Women are vulnerable in the crisis because of the type of work they do and the type of workers they are. Women are disadvantaged and men privileged by the construction of male and female worker identities. These disadvantage women both in times of expansion and at times of crisis. Such identities, as was shown in Chapter 4, involve much more than the supposedly objective factors outlined by dual labour market theorists. They concern the value placed on work, attitudes towards workers, and their needs and expectations about stability and family responsibilities. These factors devalue women's status and importance as workers and reinforce the disadvantage which arises from the male monoploy of skilled work and training opportunities. The fact that women's disadvantage is mediated through work identities and work categories means that men are not uniformly advantaged and women uniformly disadvantaged. Just as women cleaners tended to keep their jobs, so male production workers tended to lose their's along with the many women workers in production. Direct discrimination is relatively unimportant, but women's disadvantage is secured through the processes which define the identities of male and female workers from the moment they enter the factory.

8

Conclusions

The initial interest behind this book was a concern with the sexual division of labour in the modern sectors of Brazilian industry. The intention was to provide a systematic empirical investigation of female and male manual workers in the newer industries of one of the Third World's leading industrial nations. This did not confine the research and analysis to mere empiricism. Rather, the empirical investigation created a platform for empirically informed theoretical discussion. A detailed study of industrial workers was intended to refine and apply gender theory. Such an application is never without implications for theory. In the course of studying concrete situations, new light is thrown on theory and the consequences of adopting certain theoretical positions are teased out.

In the introduction the book's direction was outlined. It focused on a Third World country, and this in itself provided a wealth of information on a still little-studied area. Second, it was directed at both male and female workers, directly comparing the two. Third, it was concentrated on the factory and on the process of gender construction within the factory and how an understanding of the maleness and femaleness of industrial workers was a necessary precondition for the analysis of labour processes and labour markets in factories.

In spite of the focus on theoretical issues which could be examined as much in Britain or France as in Third World countries, the analysis inevitably cast light on the specificity of women's and men's employment in the Third World. Clearly the situation in Brazil, and above all the situation in its most developed region, Greater São Paulo, cannot be generalized to the Third World as a whole. The Third World is highly differentiated in terms of level of industrial development, form of insertion into the world economy, and patriarchal structures. However, the situation in Brazil casts light on to a number of questions which have been raised concerning women workers in the Third World. It was clearly established, for example, that women's massive entry into industrial employment was not dependent upon export-oriented development. It was also seen in Chapter 3 that the female labour force was extremely heterogeneous. While industry showed a preference for employing young, unmarried, and childless women in unskilled and semi-skilled work, this was far from a universal practice. Significant and growing minorities of women in industry were older, married, and had children.

The research also cast some interesting light on the situation of male workers in Brazilian industry. All too often, the youth and instability of the female labour force is implicitly contrasted with an image of male workers as more mature and stable. In Chapters 1 and 3 it was shown that male workers, particularly the unskilled, were also markedly unstable in their employment. While skilled male workers might expect to work in industry through their 30s and 40s at least (even though they could be sacked in times of crisis, as was shown in Chapter 7), the less skilled tended to be much younger. They either obtained promotion or were forced out of industry by low wages or competition from yet younger workers.

The analysis also outlined the importance of domestic situations for male as well as female workers. This was seen in Chapter 3. Managers were well aware of the importance of male domestic situations and the implications of the assumption of the bread-winner role for men's employment strategies. Male pressure for promotion was one effect of the assumption of this role, and a recent survey of male responses to unemployment during the economic crisis has shown a similar pressure on men with families.[1] In the case of women, Chapter 3 revealed nothing startling to anyone familiar with women's employment in the developed world, although it did show how both material and ideological factors influenced women's decisions about factory work.

From a theoretical point of view, the most important result of Chapter 3 was its discussion of management strategies in relation to the hiring of women and men. Domestic situations and ideologies might affect the supply of labour – both female and male – but the putting into practice of personal strategies clearly depended on the opportunities allowed by managements. Here it was shown that managements had clear views on employing men and women, seeing them as gendered employees within specific domestic and social situations – actual or future bread-winner, young girl, mature woman, elderly male with no prospects, and so on. However, it was evident that these management preferences could not be pursued in a vacuum. Gender preferences had consequences for policies in other areas. Management strategies might be heavily influenced by gender considerations, including outright prejudice against women in general or certain categories of women, but decisions made on the basis of such considerations had to be taken in the light of the factory as a capitalist enterprise. A preference for unmarried women, for example, would have implications for the stability of the female labour force. A low-wage strategy would oblige the firm to employ young women and men. If young male workers were employed, there would be pressure for the creation of lines of advancement and promotion. The logic of the factory and the logic of gender come face to face.

This issue is the central one: the relation between gender and work. In many discussions of the sexual division of labour and occupational segregation, gender and work are defined as two separate spheres. Gender is created in society (above all in the home) and its determinations arrive at the point of production ready formed. The experience of work is not held to alter gender identities. Similarly work (or more broadly the occupational structure) is held to be defined without reference to gender. Jobs are jobs and they are considered to be largely or entirely determined by technological factors. As a result, the interrelation of gender and work – or of workers and jobs – is limited to matching people and occupations. The issue is reduced to that of why certain people fill certain places in the occupational structure, and to a lesser extent how the number of places of different kinds comes to match the number of workers supposedly suitable for them. In this matching process either work or gender criteria are seen to dominate the allocation of women and men to specific jobs. In the dual labour market theory, people are allocated to jobs according to their characteristics as workers. Hartmann, in contrast, attributed allocation to gender factors – men wielding power determine access to jobs according to the sex of the person. In both cases the analysis of the relation between workers and jobs is impoverished by the assumption that gender and work are distinct and separate spheres of influence.

Both positions produce quite untenable conclusions. In the case of dual labour market theories, the disadvantage of women is held to be justified by the quality of labour they have to offer. Hartmann's position states that capitalists are forced by the power of trade unions into adopting policies which have no justification in terms of their own rational calculations. This is hard to swallow even in countries with strong trade unions, and in countries such as Brazil where unions are notoriously weak in the work-place, the explanation is even less convincing. In Chapter 4 the discussion on the relation between gender and work was raised through an examination of the creation and maintenance of gender identities in factories. These identities cannot be read off from pre-factory situations. Specific worker identities were seen to be constructed along gender lines within the factory itself. This involved creating two categories through the imposition of stereotypes, the stressing of opposition, and the establishment of hierarchy. The two categories, female workers and male workers, were assigned specific characteristics as workers. Women were devalued in relation to men in terms of their capabilities as workers. This was achieved through a double process of marginalization of women from prestigious jobs and the devaluation of the kind of work women carried out. In this way the gender hierarchy in the wider society was reproduced in terms of work categories within the factory.

As a result men could defend their superior status without having to appeal directly to the principles of gender in opposition to the principles of the organization of work and labour. Men could claim to be better, more capable, and more valuable workers and have this claim accepted by women workers and management. Even so, such success could not be established once and for all. While women may accept the notion that men need to earn higher wages because of their family obligations, and while managers recognized male pressure for the family wage, there was no sign that women accepted the idea that men should earn higher wages for work of equal or lesser value. This was seen clearly in the case of the quality control workers in E3. Further, women's experience within the factory had to be controlled in order to prevent them from realizing that they were capable of doing work done by men. Acceptance of lower status and a lesser claim for wages depends on both the maintenance of the illusion that male work is of greater value and the restriction of women's opportunities so that they doubt their own capacities and restrict their demands for and interest in advancement. Hence, Chapter 4 focused not only on elements used to create the gender identities of women and men in the factory, but also on the mechanisms necessary for the maintenance of such identities in everyday factory life. In particular, segregation was emphasized as a key mechanism which prevented male privilege from being undermined by a direct comparison of female and male work and capabilities.

This characterization of the relation between work and gender then threw new light on to both labour processes and labour markets in the industrial sector. In Chapter 5 the labour process was discussed. Detailed examination of male and female workers showed that men were much less subject to strong time constraints and close supervision than women. All too often, discussion of this subject is polarized around the question of whether differences in control are attributable to the work performed or the workers performing it. Chapter 5 argued that even if the greater control exercised over women did arise partly out of the nature of the work performed, the allocation of women to these jobs and the creation of the jobs themselves had to be problematized. People are matched to jobs and jobs to people in much more flexible ways than appear at first sight. The study also revealed differences in control which were clearly not reducible to technology or the organization of work. Such differences did not have to be attributed solely to the characteristics women and men bring ready formed to the factory. They are partially explained by the experience that the two sexes have of being workers. Women's experience of being devalued workers affected their powers of resistance to capitalist control.

Chapter 6 raised similar issues. It started with a discussion of dual labour market theorists, criticizing the assumption that women's disadvantage is the result of lack of access to high-productivity work. A case study from E1 argued that the same work could be incorporated into different occupational structures (division of labour, promotion and training prospects, wage levels and forms, and so on) according to the sex of the workers doing it. While women may be marginalized from certain important types of productivity-enhancing training, equally important within the factory is the devaluation of their work capabilities and the work they actually do. However, although critics are often content to show the failings of dual labour market theory, this does not explain away the fact that labour markets are quite highly stratified. Chapter 6 re-examined various elements of this stratification in the light of the discussion in Chapter 4. It was argued that labour market structures institutionalized and solidified male superiority in the factory but did not cause it. Certain aspects of industrial labour markets were means of institutionalizing the devaluation of female labour and controlling women's access to certain areas of work. Similarly it was argued that other features often stressed by labour market theorists, such as turnover, were effects of existing labour market structures rather than causes of them. Labour market structures are a consequence of women's subordination, but they also play a crucial role in controlling women's factory experience and justifying women's subordination in terms of work categories.

Finally, Chapter 7 attempted to show how the ideas developed in earlier chapters could throw fresh light on the issue of gender and economic crisis. Once again, the literature contained two opposing viewpoints: one stressing work and the other gender. The occupational segregation theory predicts that workers will be selected for dismissal during a recession according to the jobs they have. The reserve army thesis predicts that workers will be selected for dismissal according to their gender. Bruegel attempts to reconcile the two positions by suggesting that women are matched to unstable jobs prior to the crisis. The detailed examination of men's and women's employment in Brazil showed a more complex picture. Occupations, not people, seem to be eliminated during the crisis, and the unchanging sexual division of labour in several factories indicated this. However, women still suffered, on average, greater job losses than men in particular industries and firms. Given an occupational structure already saturated with gender, job loss according to occupation can still disproportionately affect women workers. Women are not necessarily selected for unstable occupations, but the way women's occupations were defined relative to men's increased their vulnerability. Women were grouped into catch-all occupational titles, while the male occupational structure was highly differentiated. Women were treated as dispensable at all times, while male labour was more carefully handled. Women's work was more tightly organized and quantified, making it easier to calculate adjustments of output and labour. Even so, it was striking that women in certain occupational categories, such as cleaning, were much less likely to lose their jobs than male workers in badly hit production jobs. This indicates yet again that women's disadvantage relative to men is achieved via the construction of gender categories within the place of work. Being a man was not, in itself, a means of avoiding dismissal, and in those cases where firms did try to avoid sacking male bread-winners, the losers appeared to be single men, not women.

Women's disadvantage is mediated through work categories. Processes which devalue women as workers are an essential element in women's subordination in the factory. For women workers (and for men), this means that women's situation can, in principle, be improved by struggles within the work-place. The experience of factory work is not solely determined by the world outside. Education and training, domestic responsibilities, and familial ideologies certainly place women at a great disadvantage, but within the work-place there is a potential terrain for struggle. Women can challenge occupational hierarchies in terms of work categories because the notion of equal pay for work of equal value is not directly challenged in industry. Men devalue women's work rather than claim a right to higher wages as men. However, it is also clear that the sexual division of labour and occupation segregation which underpin much of women's subordination are much more flexible than would be predicted by theories that see gender and work as two separately constituted spheres. It was argued that occupations can be redefined to make rapid adjustments to changing situations. Women's problem is not the types of work they do as much as the things which go with occupations – pay, status, promotion, and so on. Through segregation, marginalization, and devaluation, women are confined to subordinate positions, and entry to new areas of work may just change the position of the boundary line without changing the nature and effect of the boundary itself. Without a direct challenge to the construction of gender identities and the occupational segregation which sustains them, entry to new areas of work will not by itself undermine women's subordination. As long as the work women do acquires the status of women's work, the specific nature of the work performed will not entitle women to the privileges enjoyed by men. Therefore either a direct assault on occupational segregation or a vigorous implementation of the principle of equal pay for work of equal value (which undermines the devaluation of women's work) would be necessary if women are to get a better deal in the factory.

Appendix 1
The firms studied

In the course of field research in Brazil in 1982, attention was focused on seven factories, to which very differing degrees of access were obtained. Listed below are the seven factories, some basic information about them, and the types of data and access obtained from them. In addition, information is supplied about the data obtained on five plastics factories.

E1, THE FIRST ELECTRICAL FACTORY

Hourly-paid workers: total 520 (June 1982), female 400, male 120.
Ownership: multinational.
Location: Belo Horizonte, Minas Gerais.

Access: two plant visits, including interviews with personnel managers and some plant supervisors and managers. Personnel department records were made available.

Main data sources:

1 Tables on employment by grade, occupation, and sex for June 1982 constructed through consultations of listings of workers and the occupational structure for hourly-paid workers.
2 Personal information from a sample of women workers. The following information was supplied for a sample of 20 per cent of basic-grade women production workers and 100 per cent of all other female hourly-paid workers: date of birth, date of entry to the plant, date of marriage, marital status on entry to the plant and at the current time, number of children eligible for the family supplement, occupation at time of entry and in October 1982, when the interviews were carried out.

E2, THE SECOND ELECTRICAL FACTORY

Hourly-paid workers: total 3,400 (May 1982), female 2,200, male 1,200.
Ownership: multinational.
Location: city of São Paulo.

Access: extensive in the personnel department, recruitment, and wages, but limited elsewhere. Two production managers were interviewed, but after an initial visit to one part of the plant the production management refused to co-operate with the study.

Main data sources:

1 A list of hourly-paid employees giving occupation, grade, sex, and length of employment in the plant for May 1982 was made available for consultation, and from this tables were constructed. The same tables, less the information on length of employment, were constructed for December 1980 and August 1983. As in E1, information about the occupational structure of the plant was made available.
2 Personal information on a sample of women workers, stratified by occupation and length of employment. The sample was 7 per cent of assemblers and higher for workers on higher grades. The data collected were as for E1.
3 Leaving interviews. Written personnel department records of interviews with 330 women and 115 men who left the plant in 1980 were made available. This group of interviews was much smaller than the total number of people leaving the plant in the course of the year, but the selection staff could not explain why only these particular interviews could be found. They covered the whole year, both sexes, many departments, and workers leaving of their own accord and being dismissed on the initiative of the company. The interviews contained information on occupation, sex, date of hiring, date of termination, and wage rates, as well as the workers's own perception of why they were dismissed. Additional comments by both workers and the interviewer were also noted down.
4 Applications for jobs. A 20 per cent sample, 222 cases, of applications made by women in March–April 1982 for jobs in the plant was taken. The information which applicants provided included sex, age, marital status and date of marriage, number of children, previous employment, and previous employment in E2.

E3, THE THIRD ELECTRICAL FACTORY

Hourly-paid workers: total 540 (June 1982), female 250, male 290.
Ownership: joint venture between Brazilian and multinational capital.
Location: city of São Paulo.

Access: extensive access to the whole plant and a high degree of co-operation from management. Extensive data were made available and managers and workers were interviewed at length. Work in this plant was carried out jointly with Dr Helena Hirata.

Main data sources:

1 The company's pay roll print-out, giving for each worker, department, sex, works number, wage (and from this occupation), number of children. In 1980 the data also included marital status. These print-outs were available for December 1980, June 1982, and June 1983.
2 Interviews with sixty women and forty men in the production and quality control areas of the plant.
3 Information on date of birth, marital status, and number of children and dates of birth for a small sample of women workers. This information was cross-checked with interview data and found to be accurate. Together with (2) above, information on these items was available for half the women employed in production and quality control.
4 A list of persons leaving in 1981. This gave works number, department, name, date of entry and exit, and whether they were dismissed or left of their own accord. This could be cross-checked with one above for December 1980.
5 The occupational structure of the plant giving occupations, wage rates, and increments.

Al, THE FIRST AUTOMOTIVE FACTORY

Hourly-paid workers: total 1,150 (December 1981), female 650, male 500.
Ownership: Brazilian.
Location: periphery of Great São Paulo.

Access: to the personnel department, with one visit to the plant.

Main data sources:

1 Tables on employment by occupation, grade, and sex for December 1980 and December 1981.
2 Personal information on a sample of 10 per cent of female production workers and 20 per cent of all other women workers. The information collected was as for El and E2.

A2, THE SECOND AUTOMOTIVE FACTORY

Hourly-paid workers: total 550 (September 1982), female 150, male 400.
Ownership: multinational.
Location: periphery of Greater São Paulo.

Access: three lengthy visits to the plants and access to personnel department records. The first two visits were carried out jointly with Dr Helena Hirata.

Main data sources:

1 The company's personnel print-out, giving for each worker, department, occupation, sex, wage, and date of hiring, for September 1982.
2 Leaving interviews for 1982, giving sex, initial and final occupation, date of entry and exit, age, marital status, and reason for leaving for thirty-eight women and twenty-eight men.
3 Interviews with ten women machine operators and two male machine-setters in 1982. Interviews with six female quality control workers in 1983.
4 The occupational structure of the plant, giving occupations, wage rates, and increments.

F1, THE FIRST PHARMACEUTICAL FACTORY

Hourly-paid workers: total 210 (July 1982), female 172, male 28.
Ownership: multinational.
Location: Greater São Paulo.

Access: two visits to the plant, interviews with production and personnel managers, and access to company records.

Main data sources:

1 Access to workers' personal files, giving information on sex, grade, occupation, date of birth, date of entry to the plant, wages, marital status, and number of dependants. Information on all the workers in the plant was collected.
2 Leaving interviews in 1980 and 1981, for 102 women and 8 men. The records of these interviews gave the sex, date of entry and exit, age, marital status occupation and reason for leaving for each case. Additional comments by the personnel department interviewer were also included in the files.

F2, THE SECOND TOILETRIES FACTORY

Hourly-paid workers: total 400 (August 1982), female 150, male 250.
Ownership: multinational.
Location: fifty miles from the city of São Paulo.

Access: one visit to the plant and an interview with head of personnel.

Main data source:

1 Tables on length of employment, age, and number of dependants by sex.

THE PLASTICS FACTORIES

Employers have to deduct one day's pay from workers and send the money to the union. Some firms give full details on workers in their plants on forms provided by the unions. For five large firms with 3,615 workers, lists were supplied referring to March 1981, which gave for each worker his/her name, date of entry to the plant, wage, and occupation. In two plants the age of workers was also supplied.

Appendix 2 Information sources on employment

The following provides some background information on the main published and unpublished data for the post-war period on employment cited in the text.

DEMOGRAPHIC CENSUSES

The demographic censuses taken in 1950, 1960, 1970, and 1980 are based on household surveys. They contain a limited amount of occupational information, but the coverage and accuracy are open to doubt. Tables are published on age, marital status, number of children, and hours worked by sex and sector of economic activity. Definitions have changed over time. From 1950 through to 1980 the definition of economically active population has been extended (Ministério do Trabalho 1976: 75), but the censuses have been shown to be particularly unreliable in the measurement of women's economic activity, particularly in agriculture.

INDUSTRIAL CENSUSES

These are available for 1950, 1960, 1970, 1975, and 1980. Being establishment-based they are a more accurate guide to industrial employment than the demographic censuses, particularly in the more developed regions of the country. Unfortunately only one table gives employment by sex, and this only for the twenty-one basic sectors of manufacturing. The work-force categories used in this table also vary from census to census. In 1950 and 1960 the census distinguished between 'workers' and 'supervisors'. In 1970 the census used the categories 'technical staff' and 'workers and supervisors'. In 1975 the categories were switched to 'technical staff and supervisors' and 'workers', while in 1980 all three groups were listed under the single heading 'persons linked to production'. Whenever possible, this last term and the group it delineates is used when reference to census employment figures is made.

RELAÇÃO ANUAL DE INFORMAÇÕES SOCIAIS (RAIS)

Data for the RAIS are collected from registered establishments in all sectors of activity. The information is detailed and the first published results, for 1976, provided unrivalled coverage of labour force composition. Detailed statistics on age, sex, length of employment, wages, turnover, and so on, were made available for the first time. Unfortunately the RAIS has serious shortcomings. After 1976 no more data were published, except for glossy and uninformative brochures in 1982 and 1983. For 1979 onwards the ministry made print-outs available to some research institutions. Even here, however, there are problems. The data on employment by industry, sex, age, and major occupational classification were available only for 1979 and 1983, although direct contact with the Ministry of Labour secured figures for 1981. No sex breakdowns were available for 1980 and 1982. The coverage of the RAIS is also erratic. No checking of replies is carried out, and firms may fill in the forms at head office, rather than at establishment level – hence one of the country's largest steel mills was once transplanted to the commercial district of São Paulo. The industrial classification is not the same as that used in the census, and firms are grouped according to their major activity at the time of their initial registration with the Finance Ministry. The unpublished material occasionally contains serious flaws. However, coverage and reliability have been improving since 1980. For a discussion of the value of the RAIS as an indicator of formal sector employment, see Sabóia and Tolipan (1984).

SENAI WOMEN'S EMPLOYMENT SURVEY

In the late 1970s the National Industrial Apprenticeship Service (SENAI) research department in São Paulo carried out a survey of women's employment in the city of São Paulo. This covered establishments with more than fifty employees in the areas of manufacturing, construction, public utilities, and industrial services. SENAI's research department made some of the results of this survey available, and I am grateful for their co-operation. The survey paid particular attention to women's employment by sector of industry, area of work (production, maintenance, and so on), and skill. It provided detailed figures on skilled occupations and the types of skilled work performed by women. For a discussion of the concepts used by SENAI in their studies, see Faraone (1978). After considerable delay, SENAI published some of the results of the survey in Ida (1985). Without the co-operation of SENAI's São Paulo research department in 1982, the findings of their survey would not have been made available in time for use in this book.

Notes

INTRODUCTION

1 This is merely a hypothesis, and it will be questioned in Chapter 6.
2 Even in the case of so-called 'statistical discrimination', where individuals are judged on the basis of the average characteristics of their class, there is no discrimination against the class as a whole, even though the personal qualities of particular individuals may not be assessed correctly.
3 In Brazil this category includes the metallurgical, mechanical, electrical, and motor industries, which are grouped together for the purposes of union recognition.
4 For more information on the seven firms, access to them, and the types of data collected, see Appendix 1.
5 For some of the results of the joint research, see Hirata and Humphrey (1984; 1985; 1986).

1 INDUSTRIAL DEVELOPMENT AND EMPLOYMENT IN BRAZIL

1 Furtado estimated the decline in Brazil's capacity to import at 35 per cent, comparing 1925–29 with 1930–34 (1970: 41).
2 For an indication of some of the thinking behind industrialization strategies in Latin America at this time, see Prebisch (1969).
3 For consideration of these issues, see Oliveira (1977: 76–92).
4 The industrial census is used here in preference to the demographic census material on occupational structures because it is a more reliable indicator of employment trends. For further discussion of this point, see Appendix 2. The figures refer to workers in 'occupations linked to production' in all establishments, which is a rough indication of the number of manual workers in factory production.

5 The four industries – metallurgical, mechanical, electrical equipment, and transport materials – are grouped together in Brazil for the purposes of union recognition. Henceforth they will be referred to collectively as the metal-working industries.
6 Some of the decline in textiles and the growth in clothing and footwear was the result of changes in their definition between censuses. Unfortunately the censuses are not very forthcoming about such changes and their impact.
7 The 'traditional' industries are defined by Mata and Bacha to include timber, furniture, leather and hides, textiles, clothing and footwear, food products, beverages, tobacco, and printing and publishing (Mata and Bacha 1973: 303).
8 See Appendix 2 for more information on the definition of these terms. The figures from the demographic censuses include manufacturing industry, public utilities, and construction. Manufacturing employment as measured by the industrial census rose by 264 per cent, compared to an increase of 338 per cent in the economically active population in 'industrial activities' in the demographic census over the same period.
9 There has to be some question of the reliability of Saffioti's data for 1872 and 1900, particularly as most of the women registered as employed in the censuses were in agriculture and domestic activities. The latter category is not clearly defined. In one article a reference is made to 'domestic work . . . including seamstresses' (1976: 149), while in the book the term domestic service is used. In both sectors employment figures are notoriously affected by the framing of the census questions and the criteria used to define people as economically active, and it is quite likely that the figures for 1920 were constructed on a rather different basis from those of the earlier censuses. Saffioti's conclusions about the trend of industrial employment in the period are less problematic, although Moura's figures, for example, do not seem to indicate a drastic expulsion of women workers from industry around the turn of the century (1982: 61–8).
10 However, it is worth noting that Kowarick argues that female artisanal employment (as reflected in the number of women in self-employment) grew strongly in the 1950s and that the supplanting of artisanal by factory employment took place in different regions of the country at different times (1981: 154–59).
11 Figures taken from the industrial censuses for Brazil, calculated in the same way as in *Table 1*.
12 For information on the definitions used and the basis of the census data, see Appendix 2.
13 See FIDEPE (1982: 5) for a discussion of this problem, and also a comment on possible biases in the samples used for the advanced tables of the 1980 demographic census. For an exposition of the criteria used to

define the active and non-active populations in the 1950, 1960, and 1970 censuses, see Ministério do Trabalho (1976: 65).

14 For a more detailed analysis of this point, see Humphrey (1984: 236–39).

15 The city of Rio de Janeiro was known as the state of Guanabara from the time Brasília was declared the new capital city up until it was merged with the surrounding state of Rio de Janeiro during the 1970s to form one state called Rio de Janeiro.

16 The figures are taken from the RAIS for 1979, rather than 1976, because the 1976 wage data are presented only in wage groups, not in averages. The industrial census provides no wage data discriminated by sex.

17 See Appendix 2 for details of the sources of these data.

18 It should be noted that demographic census data are being used here, and they include women in artisanal work.

2 GENDER, HIERARCHY, AND SEGREGATION IN INDUSTRY

1 In many cases figures will be presented for hourly-paid workers, as this is the division used in many company statistics. This does not exactly correspond to the manual category, but it is a good approximation to it.

2 See Appendix 2 for details on the coverage of this survey and the categories used in it.

3 It should be stressed at this point that skill definitions are being taken at face value here. A questioning of the concept of skill will be left to later chapters.

4 The figures for employment in the plant include twelve hourly-paid workers (eleven men and one woman) employed in ancillary functions – security and cleaning. The numbers in such occupations depend on the degree to which they are subcontracted and also the appointment of some staff in these areas to salaried posts.

5 The figures refer to June 1982.

6 These calculations for E2 exclude from consideration the significant numbers of men and women recruited in the three months prior to the date on which the data were collected, as this would distort the figures.

7 The proportion of salaried staff is also much higher in these industries.

8 These calculations are based upon the initial wage for each occupation. Wages in all occupations rose according to length of service.

3 WORK AND HOME: DOMESTIC SITUATION AND WAGED EMPLOYMENT

1 For full details of the workers interviewed, sampling, and so on, see Appendix 1. The research in E3 was designed and carried out jointly

with Dr Helena Hirata of the CNRS in Paris. Some results have been published, as can be seen in the bibliography.

2 For the purposes of the analysis, exact quantification of time spent in household work was not necessary, and quantification is in any case problematic.

3 It may mean some of it being transferred to other women, as will be seen below (see p. 62).

4 This group included women with husbands and/or children whose households also contained other adult females, women living with other families, women living in incomplete nuclear households, and women living alone.

5 Approximately half the women production and quality control workers in the plant fell into this category, but they were under-represented in the sample, which was weighted towards the women with a longer period of employment, who tended to be older. This weighting will not be reflected in the calculations made in this chapter.

6 Westwood found a similar pattern among some single women working in a British factory, although she does not provide details (1984: 167).

7 Although by law establishments with more than thirty women workers over the age of 16 are supposed to provide crèche facilities on the premises or within 1 kilometre for women to use during the breast-feeding period (CLT, art. 389, section 4), only one of the seven firms visited appeared to comply with this law. More generally, the women interviewed shared the distrust of nurseries and child-minders mentioned by men. Leite (1982: 107) also finds this attitude expressed in São Paulo. It is not one confined to Brazil; Westwood reports similar attitudes in a British clothing factory (1984: 219).

8 Evidence from the *second* electrical factory showed that many women were forced to abandon work because of problems with childcare: 20 per cent of the women interviewed by the personnel department when leaving the plant stated explicitly that the reason for resigning or being dismissed by the firm was related directly to difficulties with childcare. Some were dismissed for lateness or absenteeism resulting from problems with their children, and others were forced to resign because childcare arrangements had broken down. In the latter case the most common problem was that the people who were looking after the children could no longer do so: an aunt was returning to the north-east, a mother had fallen ill, or a neighbour was not looking after the children properly. In such circumstances continuing to work was just impossible.

9 After 1949 workers in Brazil were paid for a notional eight-hour rest-day. In the case of all the factories studied, the workers worked for forty-eight hours per week, but were paid for fifty-six hours. However, this extra eight hours' pay was forfeit if 'without justifiable motive the worker had not worked through the preceding week, fully observing his

working hours' (Law 605, art. 6, January 1949). In effect, if a worker misses a day's work without an adequate justification, or is late for work by more than a stipulated amount, he or she loses not only the time not worked, but also a further eight hours' pay.

10 The information on male and female labour presented so far matches that provided by Roldan for Mexico (1985: 266–67). However, in the city of São Paulo, at least, outworking seemed to be a relatively limited option for married women; see Sarti (1985: 69).

11 Bilac found a similar set of attitudes in a town in the interior of São Paulo state. The men thought that their homes needed a woman and that male wage-earning and female domestic labour were complementary (1983: 120–26).

12 Some of these may have worked elsewhere before entering the plant.

13 See, for example, Wajcman (1981: 22).

14 In F1 the number of males leaving (eight in two years) was too small for any conclusions to be drawn. The general issue of turnover will be discussed at greater length in Chapter 6.

15 Workers leaving a firm after being employed for more than one year are entitled to compensation of approximately one month's wages for each year worked, if the breaking of the contract is on the employers' initiative and 'without due cause'. Thus workers who wish to leave a firm have a financial incentive to provoke dismissal. Uncooperative behaviour might, in some circumstances, lead to dismissal '*with* due cause' (and loss of compensation), but most employers do not go to the trouble of proving this in the labour courts.

16 The data come from a sample of job application forms, as specified in Appendix 1. In all probability the real figure was higher than this, as it is common for women to conceal their true parental status.

17 Women are legally protected against dismissal 'without due cause' while pregnant, although firms can find ways of forcing them to resign – deliberately transferring them to heavy or dangerous work, for example.

18 The personnel department refused to be drawn on the issue of these exceptions to the rule, referring vaguely to 'social and political factors' preventing their dismissal.

19 Information on the struggle was contained in the leaving interviews registering disapproval of obvious cases of women being sacked for marrying, which was held to be in contravention of official company policy. By 1983 the policy had been changed in practice, and this was confirmed by interviews with women in quality control jobs.

20 Fewer than 10 per cent of over 1,000 female production and quality control workers employed in 1982 had worked in the plant for five years or more.

21 See Guilbert (1966: 200) on the systematic attempts of French metal-working firms to employ widows and single female parents for the same

reasons as seen in Brazil. In the case of A2, no information is available as to whether a policy of employing single parents was actually put into practice.

4 FACTORY HIERARCHY AND GENDER

1 Not only male-female relations are affected in this way, of course. Skill categories, for example, are forms of establishing hierarchies *between* men which have as much to do with power and privilege as with objective work abilities.
2 Rubin is referring to the construction of gender identities in society in general, but the point still holds.
3 Such stereotypes are not confined to modern society, of course. Godelier notes that sexual division of labour among the Baruya in New Guinea is also constructed along the lines of male work requiring greater short-term effort, exposure to the risk of accidents, co-operation, and so on (1982: 37).
4 In Chapter 5 the actual characteristics of male and female work in the factories and workers' attitudes to them will be discussed in some detail.
5 The association of masculinity with strength and femininity with lightness is so strong that in some cases work is considered light precisely because it is done by women, even though in purely physical terms it is no lighter than that performed by men, such as Delphy's observations of work amongst the French peasantry (1984: 48). However, in the case of E3 (although not in all the factories studied) there was a clear and genuine difference in the characteristics of the work performed by the two sexes.
6 Brazilian labour legislation provides 'special protection' for women, limiting working hours and nightwork (albeit with an extensive series of exceptions), prohibiting work in mining and construction and particularly dangerous or unhealthy environments. There are also provisions concerning pregnancy and crèches (Consolidated Labour Laws, Articles 372 to 391).
7 This case is taken up in more detail in Chapter 6.
8 Longer-term migrants to São Paulo tend to acquire the characteristics of the local population in terms of job opportunities, but in the shorter term men tend to go disproportionately into construction, while women migrants are found to a large extent in domestic service.
9 The positions of women and migrant or black workers are different because gender and race differences in society are constructed quite differently. This also means that the position of black men in the labour market relative to white men is rather different from that of black women to white women (Anthias and Yuval-Davies 1983: 69). For this

reason the global concept of 'secondary labour market' is inadequate, describing neither the origins nor the structures of disadvantage. This point will be taken up in Chapter 6.

10 The reverse movement is also ruled out, and this is equally important. An end to the sexual division of labour would involve men doing jobs formerly classified as female, as well as women entering male jobs.

11 The promotion opportunities for women and men in segregated work groups will be discussed in Chapter 6.

12 This is one of the reasons why men have a virtual monopoly of certain servicing functions, such as stores, setting, and maintenance. Such jobs often give status and power to those who perform them.

13 This case was found only late on in the research, and it was not possible to study the circumstances and impact of such female supervision.

14 Promotion was decided by department managers in consultation with supervisors, and within limits prescribed by higher managements.

15 The interview took place at the gates of the plant.

5 GENDER AND THE LABOUR PROCESS

1 See, for example, Clawson (1980), Katherine Stone (1975), and Coriat (1979).

2 The term 'assembly line' is defined here according to the formulation of the 1978 French study: either automatic displacement of the product or the product being passed from one worker to another without any buffer stocks being maintained (Molinié and Volkoff 1981: 51).

3 The reasons for this will be discussed later in this chapter.

4 This information is taken from an unpublished interview made available by Jeroen Peijnenberg of the Transnational Information Exchange in Amsterdam.

5 See, among others, Game and Pringle (1983: 31), Kergoat (1982: 54), Guilbert (1966: 84 and 135), and Lim (1978: 22).

6 See, for example, Purcell (1979: 124–28).

7 This manager was interviewed in 1979 during the fieldwork for Humphrey (1982).

8 This unionist was interviewed at the gate of the factory where the equal pay strike had taken place, and where he had worked at the time. Some of the women who had been involved were also present.

9 Elson and Pearson have challenged the 'naturality' of women's greater dexterity, arguing that it is acquired through training in the home (1981: 93–4). This is confirmed by results from the second electrical factory, where women were generally quicker than men in a test of manual dexterity involving placing coloured washers on pins of

matching colour, but where women who had previously worked in electrical factories were faster than those who had not.

10 This was also true for operations of the type seen in the components department in E3.

6 GENDER HIERARCHIES AND THE STRUCTURE OF INDUSTRIAL LABOUR MARKETS

1 Dual labour market theories divide the labour market into two parts, while segmented labour market theories allow for more than two parts. However, in most analyses the extra divisions are usually subdivisions of the basic dual structure.

2 If the last or 'marginal' worker produces more than the price of his or her labour, then the employer would earn greater profits by hiring more workers and altering the capital–labour ratio until such time as the last worker hired produced the same level of extra output (in price terms) as the wage rate. Likewise, were the productivity of the last worker to be less than the wage rate, the employer would gain by using less labour and more capital.

3 Doeringer and Piore define an internal labour market as any administrative unit where 'the price and allocation of labour is governed by a set of administrative rules and procedures' (1971: 2), but they quickly define internal promotion systems as the dominant example of restrictions on competitive labour markets in the North American economy.

4 The empirical validity of this argument about the impact of modern technology on patterns of skill and training will not be questioned here. However, the reader is referred to the accounts of Gallie (1978) and Coriat (1980), which suggest that even in process industries such as oil-refining and cement, promotion opportunities are somewhat limited.

5 For a discussion of the application of orthodox dual labour market theory to Latin America, see Humphrey (1982: 57–63).

6 One would be more inclined to agree were it be considered that endowments might be acquired as well as natural.

7 Workers in Brazil do sometimes demand that promotion be according to length of service in order to prevent such control and to guarantee promotion to longer-service workers, but such demands are rarely conceded.

8 For examples of even relatively minor features of jobs which can be used to establish differences of classification and payment in the metal-working industry, see Guilbert (1966: 138–39).

9 Actual hourly rates of pay for each occupation vary with increments for merit or length of employment, but there were no piece-rate or bonus systems in the plant.

10 See Lloyd and Niemi (1979: 70–9) on this issue.

11 Ministry of Labour unpublished figures from the 1980 RAIS. The figures cited express the number of employment contracts over the period of a year in relation to the average number of workers employed. A figure of 100 would mean no turnover, while a figure of 200 would indicate an average of two workers for each job, or a turnover rate of 100 per cent.

12 The information is taken from the leaving interviews conducted by the personnel department, details of which can be seen in Appendix 1. The calculations in the following paragraphs have been made after those workers who did not know the cause of their dismissal and workers who said they were dismissed because of cut-backs in employment have been excluded from the calculations.

13 It should be remembered that factory E2 had an exceptionally high proportion of women with children in its labour force.

14 This was particularly evident in the 1970s when labour shortages gave workers good chances of finding alternative employment. Turnover rates for both men and women fell sharply following the onset of recession in 1981.

7 ECONOMIC CRISIS AND THE SEXUAL DIVISION OF LABOUR

1 From 1978 to 1980 the average annual rate of increase of industrial production was 7.2 per cent, Relatório do Banco Central do Brasil, 1982.

2 These figures refer to manufacturing industry in Greater São Paulo. They were collected by the employers' federation, FIESP, collated by the state statistical angency, SEADE, and published in the *Anuário Estatístico de São Paulo*, 1982.

3 The figures are taken from the RAIS for 1979. For further details see Chapter 1 and Appendix 2.

4 *Anuário Estatístico de São Paulo*, 1983.

5 See Appendix 2 for a discussion of the shortcomings of these figures.

6 The figures for E2 and A1 exclude apprentices. The calculation for A1 also excludes supervisors, who were employed as salaried staff in E2 and did not appear in the firm's data.

7 In E3 the possibility of substitution can be ruled out categorically. Management denied that it took place, a high degree of departmental segregation remained in 1982 (see Chapters 2 and 4), and a detailed examination of the company's payroll before and after 1981 revealed no transfers of workers from production to non-production departments.

8 Access to the plant and production management was not obtained, apart from one tour of the shop floor, and this means that detailed study of the impact of the crisis at departmental level was not possible.

8 CONCLUSIONS

1 A survey of job loss among male and female industrial workers in Sao Paulo carried out by the author and Dr Helena Hirata in 1986 showed that married men were much more likely to do either temporary jobs for employment agencies or odd jobs while unemployed than were single men, even though single men were unemployed, on average, for longer periods.

References

Anthias, F. (1980) Women as a Reserve Army of Labour: a Critique of Veronica Beechey. *Capital and Class* 10: 50–63.

Anthias, F. and Yuval-Davies, N. (1983) Contextualising Feminism – Gender, Ethnic and Class Divisions. *Feminist Review* 15: 62–75.

Arizpe, L. (1977) Women in the Informal Sector: the Case of Mexico City. In Wellesley Editorial Committee (eds) *Women and National Development: the Complexities of Change*. Chicago, Ill: University of Chicago Press.

Barrett, M. and McIntosh, M. (1982) *The Anti-Social Family*. London: New Left Books.

Barron, R. D. and Norris, G. M. (1976) Sexual Divisions and the Dual Labour Market. In D. L. Barker and S. Allen (eds) *Dependence and Exploitation in Work and Marriage*. London: Longman.

Beechey, V. (1977) Some Notes on Female Wage Labour in Capitalist Production. *Capital and Class* 3: 45–56.

—— (1978) Women and Production: a Critical Analysis of some Sociological Theories of Women's Work. In A. Kuhn and A.-M. Wolpe (eds) *Feminism and Materialism*. London: Routledge & Kegan Paul.

—— (1983) What's So Special about Women's Employment? A Review of some Recent Studies of Women's Paid Employment. *Feminist Review* 15: 23–45.

—— (1984) *The Changing Experience of Women, Unit 11*. Milton Keynes: Open University Press.

Bilac, E. (1983) *Família e Trabalho Feminino*. Unpublished PhD thesis, University of São Paulo.

Boserup, E. (1970) *Women's Role in Economic Development*. New York: St Martin's Press.

Braverman, H. (1975) *Labor and Monopoly Capital*. New York: Monthly Review.

Bruegel, I. (1979) Women as a Reserve Army of Labour: a Note on Recent British Experience. *Feminist Review* 3: 12–23.

Bruschini, M. C. and Rosemberg, F. (1982) A Mulher e o Trabalho. In M. C. Bruschini and F. Rosemberg (eds) *Trabalhadoras no Brasil*. São Paulo: Hucitec.

Cavendish, R. (1982) *Women on the Line*. London: Routledge & Kegan Paul.

Chabaud-Rychter, D., Fougeyrollas-Schwebel, D., and Sonthonnax, F. (1985) *Espace et Temps du Travail Domestique*. Paris: Librairie des Meridiens.

Chaney, E. and Schmink, M. (1976) Women and Modernization: Access to Tools. In J. Nash and H. Safa (eds) *Sex and Class in Latin America*. New York: Praeger.

Chiplin, B. and Sloane, P. (1980) Sexual Discrimination in the Labour Market. In A. Amsden (ed.) *The Economics of Women and Work*. Harmondsworth: Penguin.

Chodorow, N. (1979) Mothering, Male Dominance and Capitalism. In Z. Eisenstein (ed.) *Capitalist Patriarchy and the Case for Socialist Feminism*. New York: Monthly Review.

Clawson, D. (1980) *Bureaucracy and the Labor Process*. New York: Monthly Review.

Cockburn, C. (1981) The Material of Male Power. *Feminist Review* 9: 41–58.

—— (1983) *Brothers*. London: Pluto.

—— (1985) *Machinery of Dominance*. London: Pluto.

Coriat, B. (1979) *L'Atelier et le Chronomètre*. Paris: Christian Bourgeois.

—— (1980) Ouvriers et Automates: Procès du Travail, Economie du Temps et Théorie de la Segmentation de la Force de Travail. In J.-P. de Gaudemar (ed.) *Usines et Ouvriers*. Paris: Maspero.

—— (1981) Transfert de Techniques, Division du Travail et Politique de la Main d'Oeuvre: une Etude de Cas dans l'Industrie Brésilienne. *Critique de l'Economie Politique* 14: 25–47.

Costa, L. (1982) Mulher e Trabalho: Considerações e Perguntas Suscitadas pela Comparação dos Resultados dos Dois Ultimos Censos. *Informe Demográfico* 7: 265–86.

Cunnison, S. (1983) Participation in Local Union Organisation: School Meals Staff, a Case Study. In E. Garmikow, D. Morgan, J. Purvis, and D. Taylorson (eds) *Gender, Class and Work*. London: Heinemann.

Delphy, C. (1984) *Close to Home*. London: Hutchinson.

Delphy, C. and Kergoat, D. (1982) Les Etudes et Recherches Feministes et sur les Femmes. Paper presented to the Seminar, 'Femmes, Feminisme et Recherches', Toulouse.

Doeringer, P. and Piore, M. (1971) *Internal Labor Markets and Manpower Analysis*. Lexington, Ky: D. C. Heath.

Edwards, R. (1979) *Contested Terrain*. New York: Basic Books.

Elson, D. (1982) The Differentiation of Children's Labour in the Capitalist Labour Market. *Development and Change* 13: 479–97.

Elson, D. and Pearson, R. (1981) 'Nimble Fingers Make Cheap Workers': an Analysis of Women's Employment in Third World Export Manufacturing. *Feminist Review* 7: 87–107.

Faraone, M. L. (1978) Estudos de Mercado de Trabalho no SENAI/SP: Alguns Dados Necessários a Sua Compreensão. SENAI, São Paulo, Documento de Trabalho, no. 1.

FIDEPE (1982) *Informe Têcnico FIDEPE* 1(1). Governo de Pernambuco, Secretaria de Planejamento.

Furtado, C. (1970) *Economic Development of Latin America*. Cambridge: Cambridge University Press.

Gallie, D. (1978) *In Search of the New Working Class*. Cambridge: Cambridge University Press.

Game, A. and Pringle, R. (1983) *Gender at Work*. Sydney: Allen & Unwin.

Godelier, M. (1982) *La Production des Grandes Hommes*. Paris: Fayard.

Guilbert, M. (1966) *Les Fonctions des Femmes dans l'Industrie*. The Hague: Mouton.

Hartmann, H. (1979) Capitalist Patriarchy and Job Segregation by Sex. In Z. R. Eisenstein (ed.) *Capitalist Patriarchy and the Case for Socialist Feminism*. New York: Monthly Review.

—— (1981) The Family as the Focus of Gender, Class and Political Struggle. *Signs* 6(3): 366–94.

Herzog, M. (1980) *From Hand to Mouth*. Harmondsworth: Penguin.

Hirata, H. (1984) Division Internationale du Travail et Taylorisme: Bre̒sil, France et Japon. In M. de Montmollin and O. Pastre (eds) *Le Taylorisme*. Paris: La Decouverte.

Hirata, H. and Humphrey, J. (1984) Crise Economique et Emploi des Femmes. *Sociologie du Travail* 3/84: 278–89.

—— (1985) Economic Crisis and the Sexual Division of Labour: the case of Brazil. *Capital and Class* 24: 45–58.

– (1986) Division Sexuelle du Travail dans l'Industrie Brésilienne. In N. Aubert *et al.* (eds) *Le Sexe du Pouvoir*. Paris: Epi.

Humphrey, J. (1982) *Capitalist Control and Workers Struggle in the Brazilian Auto Industry*. Princeton, NJ: Princeton University Press.

—— (1984) The Growth of Female Employment in Brazilian Manufacturing Industry in the Nineteen Seventies. *Journal of Development Studies* 20(4): 224–47.

—— (1985) Gender, Pay and Skill: Manual Workers in Brazilian Industry. In H. Afshar (ed.) *Women, Work and Ideology in the Third World*. London: Tavistock.

Humphries, J. (1983) The 'Emancipation' of Women in the 1970s and 1980s: from the Latent to the Floating. *Capital and Class* 20: 20–69.

Ida, I. T. (1985) A Mão de Obra Feminina no Município da Capital. São Paulo: Serviço Nacional de Aprendizagem Industrial, Departmento Regional de São Paulo, Divisão de Pesquisas, Estudos e Avaliação.

Joekes, S. (1982) Female-led Industrialisation: Women's Jobs in Third World Export Manufacturing. Brighton: Institute of Development Studies.

Kergoat, D. (1982) *Les Ouvrières*. Paris: Le Sycomore.

Kowarick, L. (1981) *Capitalismo e Marginalidade na América Latina*. Rio de Janeiro: Paz e Terra.

Labourie-Racapé, A., Letablier, M. T., and Vasseur, A.-M. (1977) *L'Activité Feminine: Enquête sur la Discontinuité de la Vie Professionelle*. Paris: Presses Universitaires de France.

Leite, R. de S. C. (1982) *A Operária Metalúrgica*. São Paulo: Semente.

Leme, M. (1978) *A Ideologia dos Industriais Brasileiros (1919–1945)*. Petropólis: Vozes.

Lim, Y. C. (1978) Women Workers in Multinational Corporations in Developing Countries: the Case of the Electronics Industry in Malaysia and Singapore. University of Michigan, Women's Studies Programme, occasional paper no. 9.

Lloyd, C. B. and Niemi, B. T. (1979) *The Economics of Sex Differentials*. New York: Columbia University Press.

Maruani, M. (1985) *Mais Qui a Peur du Travail des Femmes?* Paris: Syros.

Mata, M. da and Bacha, E. (1973) Emprêgo e Salários na Indústria de Transformação, 1949/69. *Pesquisa de Planejamento Econômico* 3(2): 303–40.

Milkman, R. (1976) Women's Work and Economic Crisis. *Review of Radical Political Economy* 8(1): 73–97.

—— (1983) Female Factory Labour and Industrial Structure: Control and Conflict over 'Women's Place' in Auto and Electrical Manufacturing. *Politics and Society* 12(2): 159–203.

Millett, K. (1977) *Sexual Politics*. London: Virago.

Ministério Do Trabalho (1976) *A Formação Profissional da Mulher Trabalhadora no Brasil*. Rio de Janeiro: Convênio Mtb/SENAI/SENAC.

Miranda, G. V. de (1977) Women's Labour Force Participation in a Developing Society: the Case of Brazil. In Wellesley Editorial Committee (eds) *Women and National Development: the Complexities of Change*. Chicago, Ill: Chicago University Press.

Molinié, A.-F. and Volkoff, S. (1981) Les Contraintes de Temps dans le Travail. *Economie et Statistique* 131: 51–8.

Moura, E. de (1982) *Mulheres e Menores no Trabalho Industrial*. Petrópolis: Vozes.

Oakley, A. (1974) *The Sociology of Housework*. New York: Pantheon.

Oliveira, F. de (1977) *A Economia da Dependência Imperfeita*. Rio de Janeiro: Graal.

Paul, J.-J. (1983) Le Système Technologie, Marché du Travail et Gestion de la Main d'Oeuvre: l'Example de l'Industrie Electrique et Electronique au Brésil. Dijon, IREDU, mimeo.

Phillips, A. and Taylor, B. (1980) Sex and Skill: Notes Towards a Feminist Economics. *Feminist Review* 6: 79–88.

Piore, M. (1975) Notes for a Theory of Labour Market Stratification. In R. Edwards, M. Reich, and D. Gordon (eds) *Labor Market Segmentation*. Lexington, Ky: D. C. Heath.

Prebisch, R. (1969) The System and Social Structure of Latin America. In I. L. Horowitz, J. de Castro and J. Gerassi (eds) *Latin American Radicalism*. New York: Vintage.

Purcell, K. (1979) Militancy and Acquiescence amongst Women Workers. In S. Burman (ed.) *Fit Work for Women*. London: Croom Helm.

Reich, M., Gordon, D., and Edwards, R. (1980) A Theory of Labour Market Segmentation. In A. Amsden (ed.) *The Economics of Women and Work*. Harmondsworth: Penguin.

Roldan, M. (1985) Industrial Outworking, Struggles for the Reproduction of Working-Class Families and Gender Subordination. In N. Redclift and E. Mingione (eds) *Beyond Unemployment*. Oxford: Basil Blackwell.

Rubery, J. (1980) Structured Labour Markets, Worker Organization and Low Pay. In A. Amsden (ed.) *The Economics of Women and Work*. Harmondsworth: Penguin.

Rubery, J. and Tarling, R. (1982) Women in Recession. In D. Currie and M. Sawyer (eds) *Socialist Economic Review 1982*. London: Merlin.

Rubin, G. (1975) The Traffic in Women: Notes on the 'Political Economy' of Sex. In R. Reiter (ed.) *Toward an Anthropology of Women*. New York: Monthly Review.

Sabóia, J. and Tolipan, R. (1984) Relação Anual de Informações Sociais (RAIS) e seu Potencial como Fonte de Dados sobre o Mercado Formal de Trabalho no Brasil. Paper presented to the 12th Annual Meeting of the Associação Nacional de Centros de Pós Graduação em Economia (ANPEC), São Paulo, December.

Saffioti, H. (1976) Relationships of Sex and Social Class in Brazil. In J. Nash and H. Safa (eds) *Sex and Class in Latin America*. New York: Praeger.

—— (1978) *Women in a Class Society*. New York: Monthly Review.

—— (1981) *A Exploraçao da Mulher: do Artesanal ao Industrial*. São Paulo: Hucitec.

Sarti, C. (1983) Cotidiano Feminino, Lugar dos Outros. Paper presented to the seventh annual meeting of ANPOCS, October.

—— (1985) E Sina que a Gente Traz: Ser Mulher na Periferia Urbana. Unpublished MA thesis, University of São Paulo.

Sautu, R. (1980) The Female Labour Force in Argentina, Bolivia and Paraguay. *Latin American Research Review* 15(2): 152–61.

Singer, P. (1976) Evolução da Economia Brasileira: 1955–1975, *Estudos CEBRAP* 17: 61–83.

Snell, M. (1979) The Equal Pay and Sex Discrimination Acts: their Impact on the Workplace. *Feminist Review* 1: 37–57.

Stone, Karen (1983) Motherhood and Waged Work: West Indian, Asian and White Mothers Compared. In A. Phizacklea (ed.) *One-Way Ticket: Migration and Female Labour*. London: Routledge & Kegan Paul.

Stone, Katherine (1975) The Origins of Job Structures in the Steel Industry. In R. Edwards, M. Reich, and D. Gordon (eds) *Labor Market Segmentation*. Lexington, Ky: D. C. Heath.

Tavares, M. da C. (1974) Auge e Declínio do Processo de Substituição de Importações no Brasil. In M. da C. Tavares and J. Serra (eds) *Da Substituição de Importações ao Capitalismo Financeiro*. Rio de Janeiro: Zahar.

TIE (Transnational Information Exchange) (1984) *Brazil: the New Militancy* (TIE Report no. 12). Amsterdam: Transnational Information Exchange.

Wajcman, J. (1981) Work and the Family: Who Gets 'The Best of Both Worlds'? In Cambridge Women's Studies Group (ed.) *Women in Society*. London: Virago.

—— (1982) Working Women. *Capital and Class* 18: 135–51.

Walby, S. (1983) Patriarchal Structures: the Case of Unemployment. In E. Gamarnikow *et al.* (eds) *Gender, Class and Work*. London: Heinemann.

Westwood, S. (1984) *All Day Every Day*. London: Pluto.

Whitehead, A. (1978) Some Preliminary Notes on the Subordination of Women. *I.D.S. Bulletin* 10(3): 10–13.

Willis, P. (1977) *Learning to Labour*. Westmead: Saxon House.

—— (1979) Shop Floor Culture, Masculinity and the Wage Form. In J. Clarke, C. Critcher, and R. Johnson (eds) *Working Class Culture*. London: Hutchinson.

Index